Young, Po

The Psycholo

Judith S. Musick

Yale University Press New Haven and London

Library of Congress Cataloging-in-Publication Data
Musick, Judith S.
Young, poor, and pregnant : the psychology of teenage motherhood / Judith S. Musick.
p.   cm.
Includes bibliographical references and index.
ISBN 0-300-05353-3 (cloth)
0-300-06195-1 (pbk.)
1. Teenage mothers—United States.   I Title.
HQ759.4.M87   1993
306.7'0835—dc20   92-34612
CIP

A catalogue record for this book is available from the British Library.

The paper in this book meets the guidelines for permanence and durability of the Committee on Production Guidelines for Book Longevity of the Council on Library Resources.

for Stuart and for Fran

Contents

A c k n o w l e d g m e n t s

Irving B. Harris made it possible for me to study the adolescents and children whose lives are described in this book. His caring is deep, and his contributions to the welfare of children and their families, immeasurable.

Bernice Weissbourd introduced me to the world of family support programs. I have learned so much from the example of her work and her life.

I could never have written this book were it not for the efforts and insights of the five truly exceptional program developers who were with me at The Ounce of Prevention Fund: Katherine Kamiya, Portia Kennel, Vicki Magee, Candice Percansky, and Saundra Lightfoot. They made it all happen.

The ideas of Robert Halpern have been very meaningful to me throughout this project. Additionally, his concept of "domains of silence" has been useful to my thinking about the problems of lay workers in programs for disadvantaged families and children.

Toby Herr's innovative work on the journey out of welfare has contributed to my ideas about the desire and capacity for change. Her comments on draft chapters helped clarify these ideas and move them forward. Toby is a treasured friend as well as colleague.

Carol Bryant of the University of South Florida offered me her wonderful data on disadvantaged mothers across the southeastern region of the country. These data proved invaluable in developing the concepts found throughout the book. Jeannie Gutierrez shared her rich material on Hispanic adolescent females and her clinical insights about them as parents and partners. Many thanks to these fine and generous colleagues.

Many others shared thoughts as well as works-in-progress that were essential to the development of the concepts in this book. Special appreciation goes to Phillip Bowman, Linda Burton, Lindsay Chase-Landsdale, Byron Egeland, Martha Erickson, Shirley Feldman, Frank Furstenburg, Joan McLane, Dolores Norton, Anne Petersen, Denise Polit, Janet Quint, and William Julius Wilson. Special thanks as well to Ruby Takanishi at the Carnegie Council on Adolescent Development for the many times she directed me to the right person for information on a particular issue.

The early part of the work for this book was done while I was a visiting scholar at Northwestern University. My thanks to David Wiley and Roxie Smith for encouraging me to come to Northwestern and for making it a pleasure to be there. Thanks as well to Margaret T. Gordon for her interest in the work and her support when she was at Northwestern's Center for Urban Affairs.

Grants from the Woods Charitable Fund and the Spencer Foundation made it possible for me to obtain additional, exceptionally rich material on former adolescent mothers (Woods) and parents raising competent children under extremely difficult circumstances (Spencer). I thank Jean Rudd of the Woods Trust and Marian Faldet and Linda Fitzgerald of Spencer for their support. Much appreciation is owed to my colleagues Holly Ruch-Ross on the Woods Fund project and Sydney Hans and Robert Jagers on the Spencer Foundation study. The wise and practical assistance of Eliza Childs, production editor at Yale University Press, and Maija May, librarian at the Erikson Institute, is greatly appreciated.

Staff at the Ounce of Prevention Fund and its programs have gone out of their way to help me. Special thanks go to Jan Stanton for her assistance with Heart-to-Heart material and to project directors Gloria Zurinaga at Youth Service Project and Velma Brown at Roseland. The direction and dedication of Executive Director Harriet Meyer has given the Fund a broader role in the field of prevention programs and research. She values the work and it shows.

My deepest gratitude goes to those who encouraged and enabled me to pursue this work: Tom Cook and Joy Dryfoos gave me the initial push; Harold Richman listened and offered helpful advice (which I took). A generous grant from the Rockefeller Foundation made it possible for me to step away from my administrative duties at the Fund and devote myself to the task of analyzing the data and organizing my thoughts. James Gibson (now of the Urban Institute) and Phoebe Cottingham at Rockefeller believed in me and the work. Their support and guidance made all the difference in the world. Ruth Belzer of the Harris Foundation believed in the work and let me know it. Barbara Ruhman was always there. Lucky me to have such a wonderful friend. Lucky me, as well, to have an editor like Gladys Topkis.

Frances Stott was my collaborator in studying and writing about lay workers and spent weeks observing and thinking about the Heart-to-Heart program. Fran read the manuscript in every draft, commenting, discussing, and bringing her own exceptional perspective to bear. She helped me to go where I wanted to go, kept me from going off track, and was with me from start to finish. This book is dedicated to her and to Stuart Musick who, more than anyone, has encouraged and enabled me in my life and my work. They are my mentors and models.

Young, Poor, and Pregnant

Introduction

T h i s book emerged from two separate but related sources. The first is an enduring professional interest in the developmental and psychological origins of change. This interest goes beyond the professional to the personal themes that have inspired me for as long as I can remember. My favorite books—whether biography or fiction—are those in which the protagonist reconstructs his or her life after a miserable childhood or "wasted" youth. My favorite movies and plays are those in which a young person surmounts bad beginnings or undoes past mistakes and moves on to make a new and better life. These tales of transformation have always fascinated me, along with the events and relationships that act as catalysts for change and the people who care, counsel, or model a different way.

At another level, the book emerges from my experiences working with, studying, and developing programs to help adolescent mothers reconstruct their lives. It is the outcome of the challenges I faced in designing effective interventions for adolescents off to an inauspicious start. The themes I find most compelling—risk and resilience, self-loss and self-recovery—manifest themselves repeatedly in such work, and I feel fortunate to have been engaged in it.

The Ounce of Prevention Fund

In 1981, Irving Harris, a philanthropist in the field of child development, and Gregory Coler, director of the Illinois Department of Children and Family Services, joined forces to create a public-private partnership called the Ounce of Prevention Fund. Their idea was to implement a statewide system of community-based family-support programs following the Family Focus model developed by Bernice Weissbourd in the 1970s (Kagan et al. 1987; Halpern and Weiss 1988; Weissbourd 1987). Although the first six programs were aimed at preventing child abuse, most of the participants were or had been teenage mothers. In its second year, when twenty new teen-parent programs were added, the Ounce of Prevention Fund became an adolescent parent initiative.[1]

Since it was created in 1981 the Ounce of Prevention Fund has grown to be a statewide system of research, training, and technical assistance working with community-based organizations to develop programs that address in an integrated fashion high-risk adolescents' needs, their responsibilities as parents, and their future as potentially productive adults. In doing this it has sought to apply state-of-the-art knowledge while at the same time testing the validity of this knowledge against practice under difficult community conditions. The Fund has critically examined its intervention strategies in action, seeking to understand why particular local programs, components, and ways of

1. Additionally, Governor James Thompson allocated all of the Federal Emergency Jobs Bill funds to a statewide teen-parent initiative called Parents Too Soon. The Ounce of Prevention Fund received and still receives substantial funding from this source.

delivering service were or were not working. This recurring cycle of program development, field testing, refinement, and assessment provides important lessons on the challenges of improving the well-being and life chances of disadvantaged young women and their children.

The services offered by the Fund today range from parenting education and support for teens who are already parents to school- and agency-based prevention programs for those who are not. The Fund runs three adolescent health clinics in inner-city high schools, more than forty community-based family support and education programs for adolescent parents, and demonstration projects, such as the Center for Successful Child Development (known informally as the Bee-thoven Project), a comprehensive early-intervention program in the nation's largest housing development. There are numerous home-visiting programs in isolated, underserved rural areas; teen and family drop-in centers; Head Start and infant-care programs; and junior high school projects aimed at building literacy and other skills in youth at risk. There are also a variety of programs-within-programs targeted to special populations and special needs.

As the first director of the Ounce of Prevention Fund, I was responsible for developing and implementing its programs. Having spent the previous four years directing a research and intervention program for psychiatrically ill mothers and their children,[2] I was eager to move from a treatment to a prevention approach and to work with a younger, less troubled group.

For the first several years I spent almost half my time in the field working directly with the programs, observing and talking to staff and participants, trying to assess which strategies were effective and which were not. It soon became obvious that for these young mothers, change was not simply a matter of providing new opportunities, teaching new skills, or helping them to feel better about themselves. It was not simply a matter of prevention.

These adolescents were bringing their histories with them to our programs—bitter legacies not easily discarded. Indeed, they lived the past every day in their homes and communities and "remembered" it

2. The Thresholds' Mothers' Project (Musick et al. 1987).

in their behavior as parents and partners, in school and at work. It was in them as well as around them. Overcoming such histories would be a much more difficult and complicated enterprise than the prevention rhetoric suggests. I began keeping a clinical journal on this issue and several years later had compiled a vast and varied body of data on the developmental and psychological dimensions of teenage childbearing.

How do the recipients of services perceive the Fund's purposes? What does it mean to them in the context of the other forces impinging on their lives? What are the mechanisms underlying and facilitating positive changes in their lives, and what mechanisms account for lack of personal and programmatic success? From the beginning, I have learned as much—and sometimes more—from what did not work as from what did; from our missteps and setbacks as well as those of the girls.

Plan of the Book

This book focuses primarily on the psychology of adolescent motherhood, but it also emphasizes the social and economic roots of that problem. Poverty, female development, and change are what teenage childbearing is about in America today—being poor, being female, and lacking the desire or ability to do things differently from, and better than, many of the people around you. Although middle-class teenagers certainly do get pregnant, it is mostly poor teens who have babies but do not go on to finish school, get married, or get good jobs. Further, they often turn their back on opportunities, deliberately sabotaging their prospects for success. Many of these young women show the effects of developmentally damaging childhoods in how they respond to the challenges and changes of their adolescent years. Although the members of this group are as varied as a field of wildflowers, they share two common qualities: poverty and a tendency to define themselves through motherhood. To make sense of why they have babies and why they resist change, I have looked at the intimate histories, as well as the broader social factors, that shape the development of disadvantaged girls within the context of interventions designed to help them find better lives.

Chapter 2 describes the rationale, sources of data, and the sample on which the book's ideas are based, raising certain questions that have not been adequately addressed by program developers, scholars, and policy makers. It puts forward the interventionist perspective on adolescent childbearing that underlies and connects the separate chapters.

Chapter 3 looks at the family and community problems that accompany poverty in light of their influence on the development and socialization of preadolescent and adolescent girls. It raises the question of how girls negotiate the universal developmental tasks of the preadolescent and adolescent years in the context of poverty.

Chapter 4 analyzes family and environmental influences on the gender and sexual socialization of disadvantaged females, with special emphasis on how this affects their relations with males, their contraceptive behavior, and their desire to achieve in school or work. It pays particular attention to the role of fathers and father figures and to the sexual victimization and exploitation of preadolescent girls.

Chapter 5 is concerned with the complex motivations underlying adolescent childbearing. It looks at the social, cultural, and economic factors that make early motherhood seem like the best (or only) option for many girls. Strong emphasis is placed on the role played by mother-daughter relationships as these mesh with the developmental and psychological functions served by premature parenthood.

Chapter 6 focuses on adolescents as parents, on how they interact with, feel about, and raise their children. It considers both the role of motherhood and the functions of mothering. The chapter also looks at factors that place the children of adolescents at greater risk than the children of adults.

Chapter 7 explores the issue of personal transformation. It describes the developmental, psychological, and environmental circumstances that promote or thwart positive change for adolescent mothers. It considers the various domains in which change takes place, the markers signifying that it has occurred, and the personal and programmatic mechanisms that facilitate it. This is the chapter most directly concerned with the role of intervention programs in fostering change: it portrays their inadequacies as well as their strengths. It addresses the challenge of creating the climate for change—a climate that enables adolescents to act wisely on their own behalf and move beyond their mistakes, whatever these are. Given the significance of psychological factors, how must our current programs and policies be altered to meet this challenge?

In the pages that follow, I have attempted to present adolescent mothers in a somewhat different light, the light in which I came to see them. Although I was sometimes frustrated or annoyed by what they did, I often admired them for their struggles to be good mothers; their caring for each other; their humor, resilience, and courage—for their wisdom beyond their years. I have never seen adolescent mothers as problems but rather as people with problems as difficult and complicated as their lives.

Although this book is written from an interventionist's perspective, it is not a "how to" book for creating a teen-parent program, and although it is not a review of current interventions for adolescents at risk, it does imply a criticism of many of these efforts. Also, the book is not a promotion of Ounce of Prevention Fund-type programs or an uncritical call for more programs of this kind. Its purpose, rather, is to raise certain issues and reframe others, so that adolescent motherhood—and what is being done about it—are seen in a new light. Few would question the need for intervention or that programs succeed in making teen mothers feel better. But they must do better as well, and in ways that make a genuine difference. The current solutions have proved to be largely ineffective in bringing about positive change because they are seldom connected to the motivational roots of the problem. Without a better understanding of the people for whom interventions are designed—a developmental and psychological understanding of them as people—there can be no useful understanding of the problems and no basis for solving them.

An Interventionist's Perspective on Adolescent Motherhood

T e e n a g e motherhood is not a new phenomenon, nor is it the critical issue. The issue is being a mother at 15 or 16 or 17 in this time, in this place. When an adolescent girl "does motherhood" in the ways young mothers do it today, it generally means that she is not doing other things, things that must be done in order to survive and succeed and to insure the adequate development of her children. It means that she and her children are more likely to be—and to stay—very poor.

Since the last great wave of interest in the poor, in the late 1950s and early 1960s, important social forces have altered both the terrain and the subject of public debate. When social scientists began focusing on disadvantaged families, positing an identifiable set of adaptive but pathological behaviors that perpetuated poverty from one generation to the next, they were discussing more or less intact families living in communities that, although miserably poor, contained a variety of elements that buffered some of poverty's worst effects. In the early 1980s, they were looking at a problem that had seemingly become intractable and a population that was both smaller and more sharply defined. The social indicator that appeared to define this change was the growing association between poverty and births to unmarried mothers. A significant proportion of these mothers begin childbearing during their adolescent years.

The circumstances surrounding teenage motherhood have changed dramatically over the past two decades. Formerly, most adolescent mothers were married—if not by the time of their child's birth, then soon after. Today most teenage mothers are and will remain single.[1] And whereas it is difficult for all families with young children to lift themselves out of poverty once they are drawn into it (Masnick 1986), it has become almost impossible for single-parent families to do so. Teenage mothers today face even more obstacles than those faced by their counterparts during the 1950s and 1960s. They live in neighborhoods that are more dangerous, have access to fewer basic services, and have fewer opportunities for employment. They are more likely to lack both a family to instill high expectations and a community environment to provide a vision of a productive future, two time-honored pathways for getting up and out of poverty. Moreover, they usually face these obstacles without the marital and other supports available to many young mothers in the past. In terms of practical childrearing assistance—as well as financial, material, and emotional support—contemporary adolescent mothers are on their own to a far greater extent than were their mothers and grandmothers. Sources of support, even when they are available, may not be sufficient to insure the

1. For example, in 1988, 54 percent of births to white and Hispanic girls under age 20 and 91.5 percent of births to black girls under 20 were out of wedlock (Guttmacher Institute 1991/92). Although black teens still have a higher rate of unmarried births, the percentage of births to unmarried white teens has increased substantially (Garcia Coll, Hoffman, and Oh 1987). When teen mothers marry, their marriages tend to be unstable and brief. Marriage disruption is twice as likely among couples who marry before age 20 than among those who marry later (Teachman 1983).

optimal child-rearing environment (Wasserman, Brunelli, and Rauh 1990), and some apparent sources of support may ultimately prove harmful to the young mother and her child. These realities make teenage motherhood more problematic today than it was in the past.

There is currently a call for early social interventions[2] to prevent or ameliorate a cluster of interlocking problems that include educational and subsequent vocational failure, child maltreatment, family and other forms of violence, economic dependence, and repeated cycles of social pathology. Many, if not all, of these problems are closely associated with adolescent childbearing. Thus, the strategies aimed at preventing or solving the problems of teenage motherhood are part of broader social and economic policies for the poor.

The work of Furstenberg (1987, 1990), Schorr (1988), Ellwood (1988), Wilson (1987, 1989), and others has stimulated public interest in issues of poverty and its transmission from generation to generation. For that interest to go beyond rhetoric and good intentions, closer attention must be paid to what it takes to bring about personal change profound enough to improve the lives of poor women and the children they bear when they are scarcely out of childhood themselves. Very little is known about the motivations and mechanics of such change, but it is certain that for the disadvantaged young woman, personal change will not come about simply in response to greater social, educational, or vocational opportunities. The inner realities that govern her response to these opportunities must be altered as well. This book is about those inner realities, how they develop, and how and why they change or remain the same.

A Clinical-Developmental View

A counselor speaks:

> Just as Carrie was on the brink of making some positive changes
> in her personal and educational life, she seemed to *deliberately*

2. The term *intervention* as it is used in this book refers to a range of enabling experiences and relations, not just to formal social service, health, or educational programs.

stop herself from succeeding by getting pregnant *again*. I'd have to say that Maria accomplished much the same thing by dropping out of her teen-parent support group—right after we told her that she had been accepted to a really good job-training program. Lisa just happened to "forget" to register for the junior college program she had been planning to attend for months, and Ginny took her twin sons out of the day care program that was enabling her to finish high school. And after going round and round with us about how bad he was for her, Dina went back to the boyfriend who tyrannizes her and practically keeps her a prisoner in the house.

What is the matter with these young women? Don't they want these opportunities? Don't they welcome a change for the better? Did they intentionally sabotage themselves? These are questions we ask each time we are confronted with a failure at the moment of potential growth. Such failures are not the exception in programs for adolescent mothers; they are common occurrences and sources of frustration and bitter disappointment for teachers and guidance counselors, nurses and social workers, "big sisters," home visitors, ministers, and others involved with adolescent mothers. On the threshold of what appear to be clear changes for the better, many an adolescent mother, even one who is bright and promising, will find a way to avoid moving forward, at least for the moment. My experience with teenage mothers has led me to see such failures as occurring where personal history and contemporary pressures interact negatively with what is offered by those outside the young mother's family and peer networks—especially if taking up the offer means changing in some way.

Adolescent childbearing is a developmental and psychological problem, as well as a societal one. Thus, the educational, vocational, and social setbacks described above are not solely or even predominately socioeconomic in origin. Predicting the direction, degree, and timing of forward movement on the young mother's part, will require a more useful understanding of these developmental and psychological sources, for just as they are implicated in her current troubles, they are implicated in her responses to efforts to overcome them. Oppor-

tunities that appear to interventionists to be objectively available may
well be subjectively unavailable to the adolescent mothers they serve.
When an opportunity is psychologically unavailable to her, a girl may
not see it, let alone be able to take advantage of it. She fails at a moment
of potential growth because she senses that for her change may entail
losses that will outweigh its still debatable or dubious benefits. Isn't
Maria pleased to have been accepted for that wonderful training program? Isn't she thrilled about what it's going to mean for her future?
Not necessarily. She may be ambivalent, because the gains are still
abstract, unknowable; but the risks and the potential losses—these she
knows. She knows, if only on an unconscious level, that she will be
different from her mother, her sisters, her friends—the emotionally
significant women in her life. And, if they think that she thinks she is
better than they are, she will be alone. For all people, but especially for
adolescent females, the threat of such self-generated separation is a
frightening one.

Rena, a 17-year-old mother, complains about her difficulties at
home, telling anyone willing to listen that she and her new baby
must get out, absolutely *must* get a place of their own! Only then,
she says, will she be able to move ahead with her life. Aware that
her family is troubled and chaotic, staff at the program she
attends help Rena to find an apartment and move out on her
own. Unfortunately, the physical separation from her family is
psychologically premature, for she still yearns to be close to her
mother, yearns for the loving, secure relationship they never
had. Out she goes before she is developmentally or psychologically ready. Loneliness, emotional pain, and panic follow.
How can she acknowledge such weakness, such babyishness, to
her family, her program mentors, her friends, herself? It would
be too humiliating. At the same time, she must find a way to go
back, to finish her unfinished business or simply to get a little
older and more mature. One way to accomplish this is to get in
trouble again. For some teens this means drugs, running away,
or dangerous relationships. But for the adolescent who is already
a mother, the best kind of trouble is very often another preg-

nancy. Rena finds herself pregnant again and has to go back to her mother's house. Moving out may have seemed to be the right thing to program staff. Sadly, it was imprudent and untimely for this girl.

Much has been written about the role of social and historical forces in the etiology of problems such as early childbearing. Yet macro-level social and economic factors do not explain why some young people can be helped and others cannot, why some are able to internalize new attitudes and skills and others are not. They do not explain why girls like Rena have another child so soon after their first, or why some strategies are helpful whereas others have the opposite effect or no effect at all. Ellwood (1988) has remarked that the effects of macro-level forces such as the economy are more complex and lagged. This is the case, I submit, because such forces are mediated by psychological and, for adolescents, developmental factors. This dynamic interplay between internal and external reality—between self and world—is what makes the problems of adolescent childbearing so robust, so strongly resistant to change.

To date, little attention has been given to the role of these factors in early childbearing and less to their role in influencing the capacity for change. Yet self-sufficiency for adolescent mothers is intimately linked to their mental health; their internalized expectations; and their ability to manage the care and nurturance aspects of family life, to seek and make use of help from people and institutions beyond the home, and to handle the emotional stress of change—often to radically different modes of thinking and behaving. Practitioners and researchers often remark that greater insecurity and lower self-esteem seem to characterize many of the girls drawn to early parenthood. Rarely, however, do they seek to understand the etiology and functional significance of such psychological vulnerabilities or how, once created, they combine with and magnify social and environmental risk factors and act as barriers to the adolescent's personal growth in school, work, and reproductive and parenting behavior. Self-esteem is more than a matter of how the young woman feels or thinks about herself—or says she feels and thinks about herself. Like other self-constructs, it is a mirror of who she really is.

One of the major tenets of this book is that in order to avoid teenage motherhood, girls growing up in poverty need to possess not just average but above-average psychological resources and strengths, self-concepts, and competencies. Considering the many forces drawing poor females toward early unprotected sex and early parenthood, the scarcity of viable alternatives steering them toward school and work, and the responses of family and peers, which validate pregnancies once they have occurred, it is remarkable that rates of adolescent childbearing are not even higher. As it is, these ever-present forces interact with developmental need and psychological vulnerability to draw many poor young women—even those with considerable promise—into early parenthood.

The broader debate about how best to address persistent poverty in families and to renew healthy social life in the communities where these families live has tended to gloss over the developmental and psychological factors associated with phenomena such as adolescent childbearing. Although the notion that psychological difficulties can lead to lower social and work-related functioning and downward mobility among middle-class people is generally accepted, there is resistance to this notion in regard to poor people. Perhaps such a notion carries an unwelcome message about the complexity and deep-rooted nature of these problems; perhaps it outwardly resembles the now discredited "culture of poverty" perspective. For many people, attention to psychological issues implies a blame-the-victim viewpoint, calling for psychotherapeutic approaches to people simply because they are poor. Or perhaps the reluctance to look at personal issues stems from a common reluctance to look inward for fear of stirring up repressed feelings and vulnerabilities. Developmental and psychological issues are, after all, universal human phenomena. Touching these issues in others, we risk touching them in ourselves. Better to substitute a litany of social and economic horrors; better to keep telling the same sensational stories of crime and drugs and family violence and teen pregnancy and educational and economic disaster.

Whatever the reasons, there is little exploration at a deeper, more analytic level of inquiry that considers how underlying processes at work within individuals mesh with interventions directed to altering their life course. Thus we lack essential knowledge about the relation between the nature of the problems and the strategies designed to solve them. This lack is in no small way responsible for the inadequacy of most interventions to date.

There has been a proliferation of programs for adolescent mothers in communities across the country in the past ten years or so (Dryfoos 1990). As the need for such programs has become more widely recognized, they have gained greater acceptance by policy makers, community leaders, and especially the young women for whom they have been created. But most of these efforts have shown minimal success in interrupting cycles of teenage childbearing (Polit 1986, Polit and White 1988) or improving the quality of care provided for the children of teens (Musick and Stott 1990). They have certainly not improved adolescents' caregiving sufficiently to improve their children's development meaningfully, especially beyond the early childhood years (Furstenberg, Levine, and Brooks-Gunn 1990; Chase-Landsdale, Brooks-Gunn, and Paikoff 1991). Although there have been some positive long-term effects for both mothers and children, these have been found principally in comprehensive demonstration programs such as Project Redirection (Polit, Quint, and Riccio 1988; Polit and White 1988; Polit, Kisker, and Cohen 1989), not in the far more numerous and typical programs for teen parents in disadvantaged communities.

Although social and economic conditions have clearly worsened over the past few decades (Wilson 1989; Sum and Fogg, 1991), structural variables alone cannot be blamed for the failure to solve the problems associated with adolescent childbearing. The interventions devised to address these problems have also failed. Clearly, the failure is due in large part to faulty implementation of programs, poorly trained or selected service providers—often with problems or limitations of their own (Halpern 1990; Musick and Stott 1990)—high staff turnover, disorganized and inconsistent programming, and inappropriate facilities (Musick and Halpern 1989). Still, equal blame must be placed on ill-conceived intervention strategies based on shallow or inadequate understanding of the problems. Young mothers are initially attracted to these programs because they sense the promises they hold. Sadly, many of these promises will remain unrealized. Program developers seem to know very well how to attract the attention of teens, but they often do not know what to do with it once they have it. When a program participant turns back at a moment of potential growth, it is more than a personal deficiency, it is a programmatic one as well.

The best way to understand the meaning of risk and resiliency for an adolescent mother is to observe the transactions that take place between her personal strengths and vulnerabilities, the pulls of the context, especially the relational context, in which she lives her life and the opportunities and interventions available to her. The best place to observe such transactions is from the vantage point of an intervener, a potential agent of change. Phenomena such as failures at moments of potential growth are revealed and understood through intimate, ongoing contact with adolescents whom one is trying to help, with whom one has developed a relationship. This special kind of relationship makes practitioners acutely aware of the significance of developmental and psychological phenomena. When adolescent mothers tell us what matters to them, developmental themes are prominent. When they tell us their own stories, in their own words, psychological themes predominate. In the reasons they give, the questions they raise, in issues of self and other, of changing and staying the same, the themes are those of the heart.

> Now to my mother. I hate her so much. She has never been a mother to me. . . . I hate her to my heart. . . . I have so many problems with my boyfriend. I just want to leave him alone and find someone else but I just can't. . . . My mother used to treat me like shit, that's why I had a baby. So I can show the best possible love always towards my baby than anyone has ever given me.
>
> My life is hurting so bad. All my life has been hurt. My stepdad started it. I went through so much mental abuse. I feel so lonely. Why . . . does life have to be cruel? Why are people so egotistical

and self-centered? Why do I bitch (excuse me) so much? Why am I who I am? Why do I live like this? I guess I am learning life the hard way.

When it comes to people I love, it is like I have no right and should give them all of myself without ever expecting a return on this. I would really like help in changing this. Cause I don't know how. . . . Missy [the counselor] is trying to force me into decisions that I am not ready to make. I know she is worried about me being around Alex cause he has beat me up. But I am hoping that him having the responsibilities of a child will change him. Maybe I am only dreaming, I don't know. I feel that I don't make good choices for friendships.

I think I might be pregnant again . . . 18 and three children—I don't know if I can handle it. If I'm pregnant again, what should I do? Keep it? Adopt it out? How did I get caught in this mess? Am I ever going to be loved by a real man? Will I be a great mother? . . . Why is Mom such a witch toward me? Why doesn't Dad treat me like a daughter? He never buys me gifts or cards on any occasion. Does being 18 mean anything? DO I MEAN ANYTHING TO ANYONE? . . . I will prove everyone wrong. I won't be like my mom! My mom had three kids by different fathers. Me, I will have two kids by Kevin, and he is going to adopt Hilary.

Source Material

The rules of social science are very constraining when it comes to the psychological complexities of adolescent sexual and reproductive behavior. Although rigorous, large-scale studies are important for getting a sense of the breadth of this phenomenon, they provide only one perspective, limited in depth and in attention to the psychological meanings of key social processes—what the adolescent makes of what she experiences. Thus they exclude some of the most potent, personally significant forces in her life, forces that interact to organize her attitudes and behavior and provide the emotional fuel for her openness or resistance to change.

In order to make sense of what I encounter in programs, I draw on and integrate both clinical and research-based knowledge from diverse fields and disciplines and a variety of data derived from programs I have developed or implemented. The use of multiple sources is a necessary safeguard against the biases and limitations of only one or two perspectives. Interventionists can ill afford such narrow-sightedness. In developing the ideas in this book, my vantage point is that of a practitioner-scholar,[3] and the sources chosen reflect this perspective. Although I draw on data from large-scale research studies, many of the concepts discussed in the following chapters are based on smaller and, for me, richer qualitative sources. In the "study of lives" tradition, much of the evidence is presented in the words of adolescents as they reflect on their lives and the people and institutions that have meaning for them. These are their own stories, told to people they trust.

In her book on the women of India, Elisabeth Bumiller (1990) remarked that she interviewed hundreds of women but learned the most from the handful she counted as friends. I, too, seek to find "the larger truths that came from the exploration of individual lives" (3). Therefore, the insights and hypotheses put forward in this book are based on my observations as a developmental psychologist, clinician, and clinical researcher. My objective is to direct the reader's attention to processes and mechanisms key to understanding the problems of adolescent childbearing, to look deeply rather than broadly, and to generate questions and hypotheses for others to test. The sources used for this purpose are described below.

The Data
Ounce of Prevention Fund Programs

Ounce of Prevention Fund programs provided most of the basic material used in this book. This consists of the following data sets.

3. My approach is also a form of psychological ethnography, an approach that Miller and Sperry (1987) describe as seeking and validating patterns through the use of various sources of evidence. They comment that "each type of data raises questions about the interpretation of the others" (6).

1. Follow-up interviews with twenty-five adolescent mothers eighteen months after their participation in programs at four urban sites. This was a qualitative component of a larger quantitative study, funded by the Woods Charitable Trust. The research was concerned with how aspects of program participation were (or were not) related to changes in teen mothers' relationships with their parents, their children, and with males, especially as these affect reproductive behavior and forward movement in terms of school, work, and personal goals.

2. Data from a study on the attitudes of adolescents and service providers about adoption[4] (Musick, Handler, and Waddill 1984), based on group interviews with forty-six pregnant and parenting teens and providers at six program sites. These interviews covered issues of sexuality; attitudes and feelings about motherhood; and influences of family, friends, boyfriends, and providers.

3. Qualitative data, clinical case material, videotapes and observations of adolescent mothers, children, and staff in the Developmental Program, an innovative training and intervention module incorporated into some Ounce of Prevention Fund teen-parent programs (Musick and Stott 1990). This program-within-a-program focuses on the adolescent in her parenting role. The material covers parent-child relationships and childrearing practices; attitudes and behaviors of lay and professional service providers; and changes in teens, staff, and children in these domains.

4. Data from the Peer Power Project, a junior high school-based prevention program (Handler 1987, 1990). These surveys and interviews with several hundred preadolescent and early adolescent girls portray the developmental and psychological effects of growing up and living in high-risk environments.

5. Findings from a study of the prevalence of coercive sexual experience during childhood and adolescence among 445 pregnant and parenting teens (Gershenson et al. 1989). This was the first study to look

4. This is an understudied topic because today so few unwed adolescent mothers—only about 5 percent—place their children for adoption. Adoption was far more prevalent in the not-so-distant past. The reasons why so few young women today choose adoption are not yet clear (Kalmuss, Namerow, and Cushman 1991, 17).

at possible connections between a history of sexual victimization and adolescent childbearing. It has been replicated by other researchers in different regions of the country.

6. Systematically collected clinical and interview material on the causes and correlates of closely spaced subsequent childbearing among teens in Ounce of Prevention Fund programs (Ruch-Ross and Mosena 1991). These data encompass environmental factors, developmental-psychological factors, and the interactions between and among them.

7. Interviews with community-based service providers, most of them former adolescent mothers. The focus is on adolescents as parents and as sexual decision makers, particularly as this relates to subsequent childbearing.

8. Transcripts of conversations with seventy-five parents raising their children under conditions of extreme urban poverty. These data come from a study of the relation of family functioning to early cognitive and social competencies in disadvantaged preschool and kindergarten children.[5] The main focus of the research was on the small subgroup of parents raising very competent children, those who enter public kindergarten emotionally and academically well prepared to take advantage of school (Hans, Musick, and Jagers n.d.; Musick, Hans, and Jagers 1992).

9. Diaries and journals of adolescent mothers.[6] In response to the disclosures of sexual abuse from many mothers at Fund sites, reinforced by the results of a sexual-abuse-prevalence survey (see chapter 4), Heart-to-Heart was developed as an Ounce of Prevention Fund program-within-a-program. Its primary goal is to prevent sexual abuse by strengthening the abilities of adolescent mothers—especially current or former victims of abuse—to protect their children from this as well as from other forms of victimization. In a specially designed

5. Funded by the Spencer Foundation, this study was designed to develop measures of childrearing attitudes and practices that could be used in assessing outcomes for parents in the Beethoven Project. Although many of the parents were young, few were teenagers (the children in the study were already of preschool or kindergarten age). Some fathers were also included in this study.

6. For the purposes of this book, the terms *diary* and *journal* are used somewhat loosely (and interchangeably). Letters addressed to the girls' children, boyfriends, parents, and other significant people are sometimes included in these documents.

twelve-week curriculum, group members learn about and discuss children's social-emotional and sexual development, sexual victimization and its prevention, and indicators and treatment of sexual abuse. Discussions of the young mothers' own sexual socialization and their past and current relations with males are core features of this program. Heart-to-Heart groups are led by facilitators from the community who have undergone extensive training. Most of these women were themselves adolescent mothers, and many are adult survivors of childhood sexual abuse. Group leaders are supervised by professional clinicians connected to area child welfare and social-service agencies.

Celie, the protagonist of Alice Walker's *The Color Purple*, begins her lifelong correspondence at the age of 14 when she writes asking God to help her understand and survive the unrelenting cruelties of her home.

> Dear God,
> I am fourteen years old. I~~am~~ I have always been a good girl.
> Maybe you can give me a sign letting me know what is happening to me.

As a writer herself, Walker recognized the adaptive benefits of writing for the lonely and unloved Celie. As interventionists, Vicki Magee and I recognized the power and possibilities of the written word for the troubled young women with whom we worked and incorporated journal writing into the program. Encouraging adolescent mothers, especially those known (or suspected) to have been sexually abused, to reflect on their own sexual histories and present and past interpersonal relationships seemed to be an important strategy for preventing sexual exploitation. Realizing that some girls would find it too uncomfortable to engage in such self-reflection within the group-discussion format, we decided to make journal writing an integral part of the project. "Mom's Diary" soon became the centerpiece of Heart-to-Heart.

Although I have made extensive use of clinical interviews, observations, and case material from this program in developing the ideas in this book, the diaries have yielded the richest, most useful insights. Journal writing fulfills developmental and psychological functions for all adolescents who choose to write (Litowitz and Gundlach 1987), but some of its functions seem to be specific to the distinctive realities and needs of disadvantaged adolescents (Musick, 1992). Studying the diaries of adolescent mothers has given me a different perspective on these realities and needs.

We were so impressed by the success of writing in the Heart-to-Heart program that we created another project, called Dear Diary, devoted exclusively to journal writing. Both programs use a mixture of private writing and "journal dialogues," in which the journal contains not only private thoughts but also written interaction between the writer and someone else. In Heart-to-Heart there were "letters from Vicki"; in Dear Diary, "letters from Judee." Vicki and I were not the only people who read the journals, but we were the only ones who wrote back to the individual girls.[7]

As I read the journals, I began to appreciate the diverse psychological functions they served and to see how well suited personal writing could be to the central issues of these adolescents' lives. In the pages of their journals the young mothers expressed thoughts and emotions they were unable to tell others directly, laying out their personal histories as they perceived them. Such an enterprise seemed to be more than merely self-expressive; it was self-enhancing as well, promoting a sense of mastery over life experiences that were often confusing, to say nothing of cruel.

No matter who the adolescent is or how she lives, personal writing can provide an authentic means of self-expression, a new and different route to self-awareness.[8] For an adolescent at risk, it can also provide a certain distance between feeling and doing, a way to help her think before she acts. As an intervention, journal writing may be modest, but it is honest. It may not be right for every adolescent, and it is

7. Now others carry on this function for Heart-to-Heart, which has been expanded to more sites within the Ounce of Prevention Fund network, to other programs across the country, and, most recently, programs in Third World countries such as Brazil. Dear Diary was a pilot program that ran for only three months.

8. See "Middle Adolescence: The Diary of Anne Frank" in Dalsimer, *Female Adolescence*. Dalsimer analyzes the adolescent psychological functions served by dairy writing, especially the relationship to the diary as an "imagined presence," a friend who, unlike everyone else, does not misinterpret the writer's intentions. In particular, she underscores the functions of Anne's diary writing for the normal developmental tasks of adolescence, which she faced along with the problems caused by her special circumstances.

clearly only one part of a total intervention package. Still, because it is so psychologically authentic, it helps.

At the same time that personal writing serves the teen, it serves the researcher or practitioner. In examining the journals of young people, we gain access to their world and a unique perspective on the social forces and psychological themes that motivate and guide their behavior. The journal offers a unique view of an adolescent's inner life, a glimpse of her working sense of self. As an adolescent writer creates her own distinctive narrative, her interpretive framework rises to the surface, revealing how she perceives and comprehends herself and the world. In her written words, she tells us what she must cope with and how she copes. And though some adolescent mothers may initially tell only the "good" stories, as they continue to write, the real stories surface, allowing us to see sexual and other significant relationships through the eyes of the adolescent and of the little girl she so recently was. With an adolescent mother the view is often not a pretty one. For her, the lessons of self and others may have been hard and harmful, teaching her ways of thinking and relating that will be very difficult to change, even when there is opportunity and encouragement to do so. Through internalization these lessons have become the psychological themes that structure and guide her life.

I kept a diary when I was little. It was like my best friend. I called it Cassie. Cassie is one of my nicknames. My father called me Cassie.

Dear Diary, It has been a really long day for me. The baby is sick and I can't give him anything for it. I have been really down all day, school was really pitiful. When I came home the baby wanted to go to sleep as usual, and believe me so did I. It is hard to be a teenage mother . . . it hurts just to think about it. . . . Maybe one day I will get what I want and when I do you will be the first to know, and you are the best person to talk to because you can't talk back.

Dear Diary, . . . things that had happened, that even though they happened a long time ago, they had left profound scars in me. I had never been able to have enough courage to tell that to anybody. Nobody but my dear diary.

I like writing in my journal because it helps me get things off my mind and sometimes I can write about things I can't talk about in person. Writing in my journal has helped me understand things more clearly and better.

If I had time to write I could write about my whole life.

Project Match

Although they were not technically a part of the basic data set, I have gleaned valuable insights from the findings of Project Match, an award-winning welfare-to-work demonstration program developed by Toby Herr at Northwestern University's Center for Urban Affairs and Policy Research (Herr and Halpern 1991). This program's unique tracking system and clinical observations provide information about the motivations, abilities, and conditions necessary for disadvantaged young people to use opportunities beyond their family and peer networks. Housed in the same community-based health service agency as an Ounce of Prevention Fund teen-parent program, Project Match serves some of the same participants.

Bryant's Research on the Determinants of Breastfeeding

I have made extensive use of selected material from thirty-five group interviews with economically disadvantaged women in six southeastern states, part of a study of "BEST START: Breastfeeding for Healthy Mothers and Healthy Babies Campaign." Carol Bryant, director of this study, and her colleagues (1989) document a variety of factors influencing a mother's choice of feeding method. These data are equally pertinent to a range of other issues, including motivation for childbearing, pregnancy resolution choices, and feelings about motherhood; family planning and preventive health care; childrearing practices; attitudes toward marriage; relations with family, partners, and peers; and responses to preventive programs such as Best Start and the Special Supplemental Food Program for Women, Infants, and Children (WIC).

Bryant's subjects are identified by age (including a division between younger and older adolescent mothers), ethnicity (mostly black or white with only a few Hispanics), residence (rural or urban), method of feeding (breast or bottle), and parity (pregnant, primiparous, or multiparous). I have used only the responses of the adolescent subjects in this study.

The Sample

Most research on adolescent childbearing has focused on the prototypic teenage mother—black, urban, poor, and unmarried—making it difficult to generalize to other groups. The adolescents whose words you will read throughout this book represent a wider, more diverse sample. They are white and Hispanic[9] as well as black. They reside in small towns and rural communities as well as cities, in the Southeast as well as the Midwest. They come from families that are working poor and working class as well as welfare dependent, and some—not many, but some—are married. Most are between 15 and 17 years of age, but there are many 14 and 18 year olds and a few 12 to 13 and 19 to 20 year olds as well.[10]

Ethnicity

The relationship between adolescent parenthood and ethnicity is complicated since both are intertwined with social class and economics. Further, there are questions of ethnic or cultural group definition that strongly affect what we look at and thus what we find. For example, what is meant by the term *Hispanic*? Surely there are as many differences among Cubans in Miami, Dominicans and Puerto Ricans in New York, and Mexicans in Illinois or Texas or California as there are between these families and other ethnic groups. How long has a family

9. The Hispanic adolescents in the sample are either Mexican or Puerto Rican. They represent different levels of acculturation: a few, who are new immigrants, speak only Spanish, but most are bilingual or English-speaking only. Many were born or have lived in the United States for most of their lives.
10. Twenty-year-olds were included in this sample because they gave birth in their teens.

been in this country? How acculturated are its members to mainstream American social values and ways of life? What is the economic situation, level of education, and occupation of its principal wage earner? What role do religious beliefs play in the way the family raises its children? Such questions must always be considered when interpreting findings of ethnic differences among various populations. Poverty appears to be far more influential in teenage childbearing than any ethnic factor. Adolescents from all socioeconomic groups get pregnant, but it is overwhelmingly those from lower economic groups who elect to have and keep the children they conceive. In addition, culture is so intertwined with psychology that it is not possible to say where the influence of one ends and the other begins.

Alicia Rivera came to the United States from Mexico with her mother when she was just an infant. When she was eight, her divorced mother sent her back to Mexico to live with her maternal grandmother, a common practice among new immigrant families.[11] For the next seven years she rarely saw her mother but became very much attached to her grandmother and seemed happy with her. She was a good student and by all accounts a good girl. When she was 15 her mother sent for her. On her return to the United States she found a stepfather and a new brother, both complete surprises to her. She began to do poorly in school, although she was very bright and fluent in English. She started to act out with boys and before long she was pregnant. After an abortion she decided to enter therapy and has remained in treatment with the same therapist from that time until the present. Now in her early twenties, Alicia is beginning to put her life together.[12]

11. Mexican families frequently emigrate to this country in shifts. The father may come first, followed by the mother and some of the children, and later the rest of the children and perhaps the grandparents. In this case the divorced mother arrived first. There is also a good deal of moving back and forth between the new and the old country because of vagaries of work and economic life.

12. This example is based on material presented by Dr. Jeannie Gutierrez in her discussion of my paper at the Erikson Institute conference on applications of Erik Erikson's work (May 1991).

Was Alicia's pregnancy an indirect result of the cultural group custom of sending children to live with relatives in another country? Was it the psychological consequence of her two abrupt separations from primary attachment figures and her attempts to cope with the emotional loss these engendered? What part did the developmental tasks and needs of adolescence play in her school failure and sexual acting out? Surely developmental and psychological issues played equal if not greater roles than cultural group membership in leading to Alicia's pregnancy and other problems.

All this having been said, it must still be acknowledged that ethnicity often does make a difference in the age at which a girl first has sexual intercourse (Bingham, Miller, and Adams 1990), in her subsequent sexual activity and fertility behaviors (Zelnick and Kantner 1980; Hogan and Kitagawa 1985; Jones et al. 1986; Furstenberg et al. 1987; Gibson and Kempf 1990), and in the adolescent's (and her family's) responses to and decisions about her pregnancy (Darabi, Dryfoos, and Schwartz 1986; Furstenberg et al. 1987). The evidence is fairly clear that poor African-American girls experience greater pressures to engage in early sex than do their white and Hispanic counterparts, and that both African-Americans and Hispanics experience greater pressure to have and keep their children once they become pregnant.

Ethnicity appears also to make a difference in adolescent mothers' patterns of prenatal care and pregnancy outcome (Smith 1986); in their coping behaviors during pregnancy and new motherhood (Codega, Pasley, and Kreutzer 1990); in how they relate to and rear their children (De Cubas and Field 1984; Field et al. 1990; Miller and Sperry 1987; and in the social context in which early childbearing and childrearing take place (Garcia Coll, Hoffman, and Oh 1987; Garcia Coll et al. 1987)—that is, in the amount and kind of support the young mother has in raising her child and moving ahead (Burton 1990; Garcia Coll 1988, 1990; Wasserman et al. 1990; and Mayfield-Brown 1989).

If it wasn't for my mother helping me out and stuff, I don't know what I would have done cause I was still young and it's just like my baby is hers, cause she treats it like hers.

versus

> Before I had her, everybody said they'd take care of her, but afterward . . .

Although in the chapters to follow, ethnic differences will be discussed where they are especially prominent or meaningful, caution is called for in this regard. Many clinicians and researchers familiar with adolescent mothers from different ethnic or cultural groups would agree with Codega, Pasley, and Kreutzer (1990) that "there may be more similarity between groups of pregnant and parenting adolescent females than between these adolescents and adolescents in general" (46).[13] Thus, whereas in some ways adolescent mothers are a very diverse group, in other ways they are fundamentally similar to one another.

Psychological Diversity

Longitudinal studies have found that there is substantial variation in educational competence and motivation within any population of adolescent mothers. This accounts for substantial variability in life course (Furstenberg, Brooks-Gunn, and Morgan 1987) within ethnically, geographically, and economically narrow populations (for example, urban, poor, black). In Ounce of Prevention Fund programs participants are good students as well as high school dropouts, conscientious family planners as well as mothers of baby after baby, interpersonally skilled as well as difficult to relate to, and hard workers as well as "laid back." Many are actively trying to move themselves and their children up and out of poverty; others are not.

Any teen-parent initiative includes some girls with serious psychosocial deficits as well as some with exceptional abilities or potential. Both of these groups are relatively small, however; most teenage mothers fall somewhere in the middle. In their skills and motivations,

---

13. For example, these investigators found that although Mexican-Americans used more avoidant-passive (versus active-direct) coping behaviors than Anglos, the use of unprescribed drugs was the most frequent coping behavior for both groups of adolescent mothers.

psychological strengths, and capacities for change, most young mothers need help to get and stay on track. Some will be able to use the help whereas others will not—at least not as help is currently conceived in all but a handful of interventions. These "girls in the middle" represent the major population and the major challenge for strategies aimed at preventing or remediating the problems of adolescent childbearing. "The challenge is not to arrange handholds and direct routes into the mainstream for the one or two in a dozen with exceptional talent, exceptional intelligence. The challenge is to arrange routes into the mainstream for six or seven more of that dozen" (Lynn 1990).

Adolescent Dreams

The story of adolescent motherhood is in some ways the story of all of us, especially those of us who are female. An adolescent mother is what we might well choose to be, given the psychological meanings and emotional risks of being something else. Young women who make this choice have many of the same dreams as their more socially or economically or emotionally fortunate sisters. They just go about realizing them in ways that are ultimately self-defeating and fruitless. In order to construct their identities, all adolescents need to have dreams and to weave fantasies about their futures. They need to experiment with—and eventually discard—a number of roles. Unhappily, when the role they try on is that of motherhood, reality often makes short work of those dreams.

> Today I had a lot of time to think! About me, my life and what I have been trying to do with it. . . . I always tell my boyfriend to please get me a home of my own because I *hate* living with people, I can't raise my kids the way I want to. Sometimes when I am not thinking about this dream I sit and cry because I feel I am never going to get out. Now I am going to have another baby and I really can't take it anymore. I feel like taking all my things and just leaving. I want my own apartment so bad. . . . My baby can't do what she wants to, I always have to be yelling at her. Sometimes I feel like sending her to my mother in West Virginia.

And here is the poem by Sarah Jane:

A Dream Come True
grass so green
with flowers in bloom
grass so green
growing in my room

house so white
watch them stare
with a white picket fence
and a porch swinging chair

every day
people passing by
wishing their family
as happy as mine
not a care in the world
not a frown in sight
I would watch them play
by day, by night

beautiful and happy
my husband would be
their shining like the sun
eyes sparkling like the sea

my fantasy of the future
Is the same as you
people wishing for happiness
a dream come true

Thank you for reading this
whoever you may be
goodluck with your dreams
Look and you may see

That is her dream, but then there is her reality. Eighteen and pregnant with her third child, Sarah Jane has an extremely volatile relationship with her boyfriend, the father of two of her children. They have no money and chronic housing problems. Steven moves out and moves back in. He drinks and they fight. Sometimes he hits her. Their parenting difficulties are periodically serious enough to require the intervention of child protective services. The children already have some developmental problems. Still, Sarah Jane writes:

> I love Steven so much . . . every day, all I can do is think of him and our future together. Hoping someday I'll have that little white house with a white picket fence. A beautiful array of flowers growing in the garden. A swing set in the backyard with beautiful little boys and girls playing happily . . . a dream yet to come true.

She dreams, but she also despairs. She sometimes feels hopeful but more often feels lost.

To have a meaningful impact on the factors that lead to early motherhood, interventions must in some way alter young women's identities, their inner representations of themselves. No intervention, no social or economic or educational opportunity will change them, no "better option" will be chosen, unless it is grounded in their psychology and their dreams.

Adolescent Development in Social Context

The German ethologists introduced the word "*Umwelt*" to denote
not merely an environment which surrounds you, but which is also
in you. And indeed, from the point of view of development,
"former" environments are forever in us.
—Erik Erikson, *Identity, Youth and Crisis*

A d o l e s c e n c e is a period of life when there are many
changes, both within the person and within the social environment.
The personal resources needed to cope effectively in adolescence are
likely to be useful in responding to challenges throughout life (Petersen
1988).

Although each culture or subculture evolves its own ideas and
values about the meaning and means of making this universally experi-

enced transition to maturity (Mead 1958), all societies acknowledge its psychosocial as well as its biophysical aspects. The mature adult is expected to be able to form and maintain caring and gratifying relationships with others (including, but not limited to, mates and children); to gain the skills, motives, and interests needed to share in and enjoy work and leisure; and to acquire the values and concerns to enable her to contribute to the well-being of the community (Steinberg 1991). All cultures acknowledge, at least implicitly, that an individual who has failed to negotiate the developmental tasks of adolescence will be ill-suited for productive adult functioning within the society. For instance, if young people relate to their parents in the same way at age 18 as at age 9, they will be poorly equipped to enter into the networks of same- and opposite-sex relations that characterize the normative adult life of the society.

In the process of trying to cope with the challenges of adolescence, some girls will become mothers while they are still very young. Girls reared in poverty, who must attempt to resolve normal developmental issues in contexts where normal options and models are scarce and pressures to engage in risky behaviors are plentiful, are those most likely to bear children. Overwhelmingly, it is poor girls who become mothers in their teens.

This chapter is not a review of the literature on adolescent development,[1] but an examination of the developmental issues most pertinent to adolescent childbearing. Its objective is to describe how the social context of disadvantage influences adolescent development and how negotiating the developmental tasks of adolescence within that context leads to premature parenthood and wasted potential for many girls.

My purposes in raising these issues are, first, to set the stage for a discussion of early childbearing and the attendant problems in the domains of school, work, and interpersonal relationships and, second, to provide a developmental framework for considering how current strategies for preventing or ameliorating problems such as adolescent

1. An excellent book on adolescent development is S. Feldman and G. Elliott, eds., *At the Threshold: The Developing Adolescent* (Cambridge: Harvard University Press, 1990). See also Muus, *Theories of Adolescence* and L. Steinberg, *Adolescence*, 2d ed. (New York: Knopf, 1989).

childbearing mesh with the underlying psychological dynamics—that is, how well our externally constructed solutions match the internal realities of the problems.

Choices and Risks

I'm tired of seeing people like Steven and Patty end up with crumbs, and of hearing people like this man give the facile reasons why. They explain the crumbs as the result of unwise choices; they fail to realize how often unwise choices are the result of a crummy life.

—Garret Keizer, *No Place but Here*

Many of the choices[2] made by disadvantaged girls have serious negative consequences for their lives and later for the lives of their children. Nevertheless, for the adolescent these actions make psychological sense at the moment. They feel right because they promise to spare her greater turmoil and disequilibrium. These self-destructive or self-defeating behaviors, which may appear puzzling to outsiders, seem logical to the adolescent since they are the natural outcomes of her personal history and sense of self as these interact with the day-to-day realities of her life.

To understand why an adolescent girl does what she does, we must go beyond simple notions of peer pressure, limited options, negative role models, or low self-esteem to analyze the meaning of these phe-

2. There is clearly some question about the use of the word *choice* in referring to behaviors that relate to dependency, especially adolescent reproductive behavior. Ellwood (1987), for example, argues that rational choice models have only limited utility in explaining family structure patterns such as out-of-wedlock adolescent childbearing. He finds cultural and expectancy frameworks more helpful in accounting for this phenomenon and comments, "There seems to be ample evidence to support almost any model of teenage behavior except a model of pure rational choice" (16). I use "choice" largely to refer to behavior itself rather than to the presumed causes which may underlie it. That is, when referring to a teen's engaging in unprotected sexual relations, as an unwise choice, I do not mean that she has rationally chosen this course of behavior. Rather, I see her behavior as stemming from a combination of compelling social (external) and psychological (internal) forces which promote unprotected sexual activity and premature childbearing and would agree with Ellwood that rational choice has very little to with such actions.

nomena for the girl as she forms and begins to consolidate her various identities as daughter, friend, girlfriend, student, potential worker, and, frequently, parent. In looking at how she deals with her changing role within her family, seeks autonomy without sacrificing attachment, struggles to find and establish a new identity, and continues to work on the various unfinished agendas of her childhood, one begins to uncover the adolescent's internal working models of herself and others. Through development, her experiences and information about self and world are incorporated into mental representations of who she is and what she can do. These self-representations are used to construct and to guide her life.

Sometimes a young woman is aware of how she is actively using what she knows and feels to guide her actions; sometimes she is aware of the role her thoughts and emotions play in influencing her relationships with others. Frequently, however, she is without this awareness and thus is not so much controlling these aspects of her self as being controlled by them. This is not worrisome in itself but becomes worrisome in relation to the risks involved in the actions the girl undertakes and the particular decisions she makes or fails to make.

Some of these behaviors have received special attention from those concerned with the problems of disadvantaged adolescent females: doing poorly in school and dropping out; engaging in early, unprotected sexual activity; having a child while still a teen, and then having another, and another; failing to get and keep a job to support herself and her children; failing to provide a nurturant, protective home environment for her children; and, most significant, being unable or unwilling to make and maintain positive changes even when opportunities are provided (see Hayes 1987; Furstenberg et al. 1987; Ellwood 1988).

Social programs and policies, public and private rhetoric, and the media have continued to focus on these troubling attitudes and behaviors with little recognition of the role of developmental factors in their origins. But adolescent childbearing and many of its most disturbing sequelae are developmental as well as social and economic problems. They are failures of adolescence, not merely failures of adolescents. The psychological complexity of these problems, and their considerable resistance to change, are the result of developmental histories that have poorly prepared youth for the trials and transformations of adolescence.

Poverty and Adolescent Development

I grew up with two alcoholic parents—that's a bad start. . . .
One of my babysitters made me sleep with her son. I had my
first boyfriend at 11; he was 22. I guess I needed a father figure.
Well, I didn't stop there, I always had older boyfriends. . . . I
never knew how to say "no." . . . Somehow I managed to get in
and out of relationships never going all the way. Meanwhile my
mom'd get drunk every weekend and my dad was messing up
too. My brothers left one by one. . . . I stayed home and took
care of my mom. When my parents got a divorce Mom got worse
if that's possible. I got crazy. I got into a gang when I was 12. I
got drunk with friends, tried a joint, and came home at 1 A.M..
At 13 I was getting bad grades. Going into seventh grade Mom
quit drinking, I quit messing up. Well, I graduated a honor
student and got into Brooks [a good public high school that
requires an entrance examination]. At this time I knew everything about guys and how not to get myself into trouble by
looking to fall in love. My Freshy year I got bad again cause I
cared more about having fun. Soph year I met Bob, the father of
my son. I fell in love and wasted my virginity on him. I got
pregnant and was lost alone and confused. Lucky I
found God. I have my son now and I have a new life.

—Louisa, age 16.

Too-early childbearing and the problems that surround it are the
products of poverty's multiple and noxious effects on developing
young people, effects that reduce the capacities of families to provide
average, expectable, or "good enough" childrearing environments.[3] In

3. The concept of the good enough childrearing environment is derived from
D. W. Winnicott's notion of the good enough mother. In *A Good Enough Parent*
(1987), Bruno Bettelheim extended this concept to include two parents. The concept suggests that it is possible for parents to raise their child well even though they
themselves are far from perfect. Mistakes in rearing one's child are, in this frame-

so doing, they poison the lives of its youngest, most vulnerable members, thwarting their development, blocking their paths to success in school and work, and diminishing their capacities for healthy, self-enhancing interpersonal relationships.

A developmentally poor start, in turn, prepares the ground for early motherhood by encumbering young females with psychological burdens that, in the context of disadvantage, lead to self-limiting choices and self-defeating behaviors during the adolescent years. Many of these same burdens will be implicated in yet another cycle of dependency and family pathology if they reduce the adolescent mother's capacity for providing growth-facilitating care for her own child. Unlike their mainstream sisters, when poor girls make bad choices and engage in risky behaviors they are likely to close doors that can never be reopened. Those who come of age in poverty are given very little margin for error in negotiating the tasks of adolescence.

What are the central developmental tasks of the early, middle, and late adolescent years? In what ways are these tasks related to becoming a reasonably well-adjusted and competent adult member of society? How does growing up in an environment of risk affect the negotiation of these tasks? What developmental compromises are made in adapting to aspects of home and street life that mitigate against a sense of oneself as a person of worth, someone who counts? And how do the adolescent girl's sense of self and developing identity affect her capacity for learning, working, and relating to others in responsible and healthy ways? Most important, how do they influence her capacity for positive growth and change during the transitional period between childhood and adulthood?

---

work, more than compensated by the many instances of competent childrearing. I would extend the notion to include the total ecology of childrearing as conceptualized by Bronfenbrenner (1979, 1986) and Garbarino (1982). In this case, threats to development arising from one sector of the environment—e.g., the family—may be mitigated by compensatory factors in the other people and institutions to which the young person is exposed. Conversely, the effects of noxious or highly stressful community conditions may be buffered by exceptionally strong and nurturing family life. Of course, such notions assume an intact organism. If this is not the case, greater compensatory mechanisms will be called for. See, e.g., the transactional model of Sameroff and Chandler (1975).

Such questions are at the heart of the puzzle of adolescent child-bearing and its relationship to repeated cycles of poverty and psychosocial dysfunction. In order to answer them we need to keep in mind, first, that the various domains of experience that affect a person's capacities for learning, working, and relating to others are intimately connected with one another, since each has originated within an interpersonal context (Bruner 1975; Vygotsky 1978; Stern 1985). Second, these connections may be stronger during the adolescent years and are likely to be especially powerful for females because of their deeper involvement with interpersonal concerns (Gilligan 1982, 1990; Belenky et al. 1986). In addition, there is evidence that the behavior of minority females is even more strongly motivated by social and interpersonal concerns than is that of their white counterparts (Fu et al. 1984; McAdoo 1989). Thus an adolescent girl's problems around interpersonal issues related to autonomy and self-efficacy, for example, could easily spill over into other spheres, compromising her desire and her ability to succeed as a student or worker, as well as her capacity to act wisely in her relationships with boys.

Developmental-Environmental Roots of Motivation

The psychological consequences of growing up in potentially growth-thwarting milieus are not the same for all adolescents, of course: some youngsters are naturally stronger and more resilient than others.[4] Nevertheless, in an environment of risk, relatively minor developmental damage can create vulnerabilities that diminish the ability to sense and actively avoid dangerous or risky situations and behavior—and in such environments danger and risk are the order of the day. Indeed, developmental damage incurred during childhood and early adolescence is most likely to interfere with later capacity for competent

4. The work of Norman Garmazy (Garmazy 1981, 1983, 1987; Garmazy and Masten 1986), Michael Rutter (1985, 1987a, 1987b), and Emmy Werner (1977, 1982, 1989, 1990) gives striking evidence of the remarkable coping and adaptational abilities of many children raised in environments of risk. See also the review by Luthar and Zigler (1991). Even for the most resilient young people, however, there are often serious, albeit subtle, costs.

functioning in mainstream society when it is compounded or exacerbated by ongoing exposure to certain attitudes, ideas, or values prevalent in the community. Rampant drug and alcohol abuse, lack of identification with mainstream culture, acceptance of welfare dependency, defeatism about job prospects, tolerance for interpersonal violence, and comfort with sexual or other misbehavior—these can steer even a very healthy and resilient girl toward trouble, keep her from realizing her potential, and block her interest in and capacity for making use of help to change.

The attitudes and values a family holds and the support, protection, and guidance it provides help to determine how children will experience adolescence. At this critical developmental juncture, the family has special significance, particularly in an environment fraught with risks. Whereas certain adolescent difficulties arise in response to serious family dysfunction, others emanate primarily from the attitudes, values, and ideas held by the girl's family, peers, and community. Not surprisingly, the most serious and intractable difficulties are the result of interactions among these motivational systems.

Let us say, for example, that a disadvantaged girl has been raised in a loving and supportive home, but one in which a high school diploma is viewed as an end in itself rather than as a launching pad for further achievements. This girl may lack direction or be unlikely to seek and work toward college or career goals, but once presented with previously unthought-of possibilities, and given adequate time, guidance, and support to make them realities, she may well embrace new goals and seek the knowledge and experiences required to reach them. This young woman is open to opportunity; she is, or can be, motivated to change.

On the other hand, what if the adolescent's lack of direction stems not only from her family's notion that high school is an end in itself but also from their mistreatment and neglect of her emotional needs or from their disparagement of any accomplishments that threaten to make her different or better than they are? Such an upbringing is unlikely to engender the considerable willpower, perseverance, and sense of purpose it takes to stick with and master new knowledge and ways of interacting with people and institutions, especially in a community environment that offers so few supports to its youth. In this instance, there is a different and more complex set of motivations at work, deeply rooted and thus more resistant to change. The adolescent with this kind of personal history must do more than merely take on new attitudes about education and work; she must also acquire new ways of thinking and feeling about herself and others and of interacting with people and institutions. Unfortunately, the adolescent from such a home is often without the critical underlying motivations for change, since such an upbringing makes change a subjectively risky endeavor.

Motivations underlying the ability to envision a future; to make reasonable, self-enhancing choices about moving toward it; and to see and seize opportunities do not automatically unfold within the human psyche. Rather, they are acquired only under certain conditions and are predicated on the existence of essential familial and societal lessons and supports. Optimally, these are available when the child, and later the adolescent, is most ready for them. At present, we do not know whether or under what circumstances an adolescent can learn (or be taught) motivations or psychological skills that should have been acquired as a child. Unfortunately, the personal histories of many disadvantaged adolescents are made up of conditions under which these lessons and supports are least likely to be provided.

The adolescent females who are sliding (or actively propelling themselves) toward futures of disorganization, dysfunction, and dependency are therefore coming of age without the preparatory experiences essential for success in our rapidly changing society, which increasingly requires its members to be literate, able to acquire and deploy new skills, and, above all, interpersonally deft. Those who seek to interrupt the self-defeating behavior patterns of disadvantaged adolescents are frequently puzzled by their apparently stubborn resistance to mainstream ideas and values, by their continuing to take risks and make ruinous personal choices, and, worst of all, by their refusal to take advantage of chances to acquire new knowledge and skills. This behavior is not so puzzling when its antecedents are understood.

To begin to solve these puzzles, potential agents of change must get psychologically closer to those whom they wish to change. They must try to understand them as people. This can best be accomplished by observing how these girls negotiate the developmental tasks of the years immediately preceding adolescence. Unfortunately, very little is known about the transition from childhood to adolescence among non-white and non-middle-class youth (Brooks-Gunn and Reiter 1990; Montemayor, and Flannery 1990). In spite of growing acceptance of the notion that the years immediately preceding adolescence set the course for later success or failure in adolescence and adulthood, there is relatively little information about how cognitive abilities and social-interpersonal competencies develop during this period, especially among poor and minority youth. Although most people recognize that the onset of adolescence demands a totally new set of behaviors and coping skills (B. Hamburg 1980; D. Hamburg 1986; Petersen and Crockett 1985), there is little knowledge about how such behaviors and skills develop and, equally important, about the circumstances under which they do not.

At the Edge of Adolescence
Psychological Aspects of Puberty

The effects of puberty may be positive or negative and tend to be felt differently by males and females (Tobin-Richards, Boxer, and Petersen 1983; Petersen 1988). For example, puberty seems to be most stressful when it puts early adolescents in a deviant status vis-à-vis their peers or when the physical changes it involves are not perceived to be advantageous or desirable (Simmons et al. 1983, 1988). Thus, for boys, early maturation leads to social benefits such as increased strength and athletic ability, whereas early-maturing girls (and those unprepared for menarche) are more likely to have negative feelings about themselves (Ruble and Brooks-Gunn 1982, Brooks-Gunn and Reiter 1990). For at least some girls, pubertal changes such as weight gain may conflict with desired goals such as thinness (Attie and Brooks-Gunn 1987; Attie and Brooks-Gunn 1989). Pubertal changes that are noticeable to others, such as increased height and weight, are also more likely to influence psychological functioning than are more hidden changes, such as pubic hair growth (Brooks-Gunn and Warren 1988).[5]

These findings indicate that pubertal status and pubertal timing play important roles in the psychological functioning of early adolescents. Most of the observed effects, however, appear to be mediated by the social and psychological responses of the young person and the emotionally significant people in her social environment (Conger and Petersen 1984). Although the support of peers is surely important in helping the young person accommodate to bodily changes, the family environment plays a significant role. Indeed, it is probable that the relative influence of peers is at least partially dependent on how well or poorly the parents fulfill their roles. A family's attitudes and values concerning sexuality and physical maturation and the direction and counsel they provide for coping with these issues help to determine how their daughter will experience puberty. In an environment of risk, their guidance and counsel take on far greater significance, as does their ability to protect her from psychological harm at this critical developmental juncture.

The Social Context of Development

The psychological histories of many disadvantaged girls are likely to have included at least some of the following conditions: frequent separations from primary attachment figures in early life, which leave residues of vulnerability to threats of abandonment; the absence of appropriately protective fathers or father surrogates, which creates

5. There are no doubt ethnic and social-class differences in these pubertal-psychological interactions, probably related to the meaning of particular aspects of puberty such as early or late maturation. For example, Conger and Petersen (1984) note that for middle-class girls in one study, early maturation was related to greater self-confidence, whereas for working-class girls there was a negative relation between these variables. They speculate that higher-status parents may be better able to help their daughters handle early maturation and shield them from the pressures of older peers to engage in premature sexual activities. On the other hand, since extreme preoccupation with thinness appears to be largely a phenomenon of middle-class girls, one would think that they would react more negatively to the weight increase that accompanies maturation. It is difficult to answer questions about the effects of class and ethnicity since most research on adolescent development has been done with middle-class, generally white, samples.

later vulnerability to exploitation by males, particularly older males; and family disorganization or exposure to family violence such as physical and sexual abuse. Finally, there may be little consistent, useful guidance from significant adults and few positive alternative role models, particularly when there is parental absence or failure.

In both the popular and scientific literature there is mounting evidence of the developmentally toxic influences of disadvantage during early childhood. Infants and young children born and reared in poverty are far more likely to die young, are sicker, and fare worse in virtually every aspect of life—from cradle to frequently early grave (see Schorr 1988). Much of this research on younger children has a strong developmental flavor and reflects an awareness of the interaction of environment with the development of competence and individual potential. Why is such awareness all but invisible in regard to the late school years, the period between childhood and adolescence?

Although we may have data on such biosocial phenomena as response to puberty, we still lack some fairly basic knowledge on the relation between the social context and other aspects of development during that period—that is, how the environment shapes the central developmental tasks confronting youth at this time and how these will in turn affect development and psychological functioning later, during adolescence proper. For example, what do we know about continuities in family relations between childhood and adolescence (Steinberg 1988)? Is the history of a girl's relationship to her mother prior to adolescence relevant to their relationship during adolescence? At the same time, early adolescence brings about certain discontinuities with the past because of the shift in role status from child to adolescent. Because these major social changes are superimposed on the profound biological transformations of puberty, their stressful impact is bound to be high (Hamburg 1974; Petersen and Taylor 1980), especially within an environment of risk.

According to Erikson (1968), the principal developmental task of the years before adolescence, especially the latter part of that era, from age 9 or 10 to approximately age 14, is to establish a sense of *industry*. During this period the young person's energy is supposed to be devoted to learning and mastering the basic skills needed to function in society, acquiring fundamental knowledge, coming to take pride in and wanting to do well in the world of work. In our society, for preadolescents the world of work is that of school. In addition to school, the preadolescent world of work usually includes such extracurricular activities as sports, hobbies, and a host of other avocational interests including the arts. These experiences provide the preteen with a sense that she is a person who gets things done and does them well, a person successfully growing up and into the wider world. Such inner resources will be called on shortly to keep her on course and moving forward through the changes of the teen years to follow. They provide the cognitive and emotional anchors to steady her as she makes the transition from child to adolescent and, later, from adolescent to adult. Her sense of industry is her psychological insurance against a sense of inadequacy, hopelessness, inferiority—the sense that she will never amount to much. It is her insurance against identity confusion during adolescence itself.

Whereas a middle-class 10- to 13-year-old's world of work is focused on school and sports and lessons and trips and hobbies, that of her disadvantaged sister is generally quite different. While the former is, in a sense, cared for by her environment, the latter is struggling to take care of herself and frequently of others as well, such as younger siblings or older family members lost to drink or drugs. She is often being raised by a very young mother with her own poorly resolved developmental issues or a mother who, having started childbearing very young, is now too depressed or hard pressed coping with her own survival to respond sensitively to the needs of her children.

> You know I was a mother when I was younger. I used to take care of my brother. I was 9 going on 10 when he was born. By the time I was 11 or 12 I would take him everywhere. I never had a childhood. I was a mother to my brother and then a mother to my children. Another reason was my mother. I didn't have a father figure, he left when I was 10. After that my mother was never home. She had her own social life. I guess she was trying to gain back the freedom she lost when she was with my father. She neglected us kids. . . . I grew up in the streets with my

friends. That's where I learned about sex. If my mother had been there, I don't think I would have started exploring so soon. My friends were my family. . . . If you don't have any love at home you find it in a man or in the streets.

Having to compete with too many siblings for her mother's limited time and attention or being compelled to assume adult responsibilities prematurely and inappropriately requires psychological adaptations that may be at the cost of the preteen's personal development. Coping strategies that were initially useful or even beneficial under these circumstances may become maladaptive if she uses them indiscriminantly during adolescence (Hauser and Bowlds 1990).

In addition to taking care of immature parents and younger siblings, at the very first sign of budding sexual maturity—and often well before—many preadolescent girls become prey for predatory older males in their homes, families, and communities:[6]

> I had a sexual experience with my mother's boyfriend. He made me suck on his penis and he made me kiss him. I was 12 years old.

> I am a 17-year-old with two babies. . . . My son's father is 28 and has been my boyfriend on and off since I was 11.

Without the presence of protective fathers or father figures, young girls in disadvantaged communities are far more vulnerable to sexual

6. As Steinberg (1991) notes, "One of the effects of the salience of physical changes associated with puberty is the tendency (and, at times, the danger) of extrapolating from the physical to the psychological" (21). Clinical and anecdotal data clearly indicate that this is what happens with many early maturing preadolescent girls: males assume they are "ready for sex" because of their physical appearance. On the other hand, some men prefer having sex with prepubescent girls.

Carol Gilligan (personal communication) has a thought-provoking interpretation of the motivation for this behavior. She believes that men who sexually abuse preadolescent girls are responding not so much to emerging female sexuality, but rather to the spirit and feistiness that characterizes girls at this age. According to Gilligan, sexual exploitation is a negative response to female assertiveness; a male's way of putting a woman (albeit a young one) in her place and asserting his power over her. Considering that the men who victimize these girls are often marginal and powerless themselves, this is a plausible explanation. It may also be that they abuse preadolescent girls because they can get away with it more easily than with older, and less naive, adolescent women.

exploitation. In our research on the prevalence of a history of sexual abuse among pregnant and parenting teens (Gershenson et al. 1989; Ruch-Ross, Stucki, and Musick 1990), my colleagues and I found that the average age of first abuse was 11.6 years. The youngest abusers tended to be in their late teens, but most were older. Could one possibly call the pairings of 11-year-old girls and 25-year-old men "dates"?

How does an 11- or 12-year-old girl handle her changing body and her emerging sexuality in a home where she is nightly faced with her young mother's active sexual life? How does she make sense of these psychological and physical changes within the context of her sexual exploitation at the hands of her mother's temporary lovers or older males in her family environment? Does she conclude that she has no right to or control over her own body, that she and her body are somehow tainted and not worth protecting?

> Girls, I think they don't give a care if they are alive because they get sexually abused and they will go around just jumping into any other guy's bed. . . . After it happens they feel so cheap and fleezy and they don't care about their life anymore. "They are hurting me so why shouldn't I hurt myself? . . . *They* don't care. Why should I care?" So they will go out and, you know, ruin their life more.

What messages does she get about what it means to be female when her mother fails to protect her from such victimization?

> When we got up our nerve to tell my mom what he was doing [she and her sister were abused for years by their mother's boyfriend] she didn't believe us. . . . I even thought it was a dream since she didn't believe us and he was still in her life . . . and my mom had a baby from him.

Do such experiences tell the girl that her well-being is less important to her mother than having a man; that females are powerless when it comes to males?

> Mothers should be real careful about the people they date or people they plan to get married with . . . and don't ever choose a man over your own flesh and blood.

Where will the 12- or 13-year-old girl in these circumstances find the psychic energy to invest in school, considering what she is trying to cope with in her relationships? How do such emotional burdens interact with the educational limitations conferred by her home life and the less-than-adequate schools of her community? What compensatory psychological benefits can she derive from doing well in school, and what are the chances of her finding other arenas for developing a sense of industry or other adults to act as mentors and models of alternative life-styles? Unless she has some striking gift or talent, the chances are pretty slim.

Consider another sphere in which the interaction of development and social context can lead to difficulties for early adolescent girls. The early adolescent sense of self tends to be highly dependent on the attitudes, real or perceived, of others. This helps to explain the power of the peer group over the individual, particularly during the early teen years. Although the relationship between child and parent undergoes a variety of transformations, the girl's parents are still vitally important influences on her life (Blos 1979; Grotevant and Cooper 1983, 1986; Youniss and Smollar 1985; Steinberg 1988, 1989). During these years, girls from more nurturing family environments are in the process of transforming their earlier dependent relationships with their parents while continuing to feel a need for their guidance and support. What happens to the girl who must distance herself emotionally in order to survive? What added power might that girl's peer group or boyfriends have when she needs them to fulfill the roles and functions her parents are unable or unwilling to carry out?[7] As one of these young women said, they will be the ones she turns to; they will become her family.

The preadolescent girl cannot have it all. If the social context of her life forces her to divert her energies from the developmental tasks that confer a sense of industry, personal efficacy, and pride in self, the price will be high, and she may well spend the rest of her life paying it.

7. In general, girls are more likely than boys to be swayed by the actual or presumed sexual behavior of their peers, especially their best friends and their boyfriends (Billy and Udry 1983; Cvetkovich and Grote 1980). However, white girls are more susceptible to peer influences than their African-American counterparts.

I was 13 when I had sex for the first time. I was scared, I really didn't want to, but in a way I thought I was ready and now when I look back I wasn't ready. And the guy I was with wasn't the person I wanted to be with. I wish now that I would have been with somebody I really loved and cared about. It would have been a lot better. I just wish I would have waited till I was older. In my opinion no girls at 13 should be having sex. They should be doing other things.

I feel so sick for the way I grew up. There are so many things I've been through that I never should have. I always feel like going back to the age of 12 and doing it all over again. . . . I hate the fact of having sex so young. I would like to forget that part of my life. Too bad I can't. I should have stayed in school and went to college and went on to be somebody.

The experiences of preadolescence shape the girl's self-image and concepts about who she is and what she can do. If these experiences teach her that she exists merely to be used by or to do for others, her desire and ability to achieve will be diminished. Instead of an inner assurance that she can make things happen, she will be convinced that she cannot. In place of competence, she will feel defeat before she begins. A girl who enters adolescence with these feelings has nothing better to do with her future than to have children. Having resolved the industry versus inferiority crisis (Erikson 1968) in favor of inferiority, she lacks the portfolio of motives and skills that are the best protection against pregnancy and thus is much more likely to drift—or drive herself—into unprotected sex and premature motherhood.

Problems of the Self

Clinicians and researchers alike have pointed to a cluster of self-related problems as predisposing factors for adolescent motherhood: girls who are insecure, who have low self-esteem, and who rely heavily on others for approbation are thought to be at high risk for too-early childbearing. But knowledge of what underlies such ostensibly self-defeating or self-destructive behavior is sorely lacking. What are the antecedents and the functional significance of these problems during pre- and early adolescence? How are such developmentally induced or mediated problems created, and how do they magnify or potentiate other risk factors? What particular self-concepts make early adolescent girls especially vulnerable and unprepared to cope with the socially imposed tasks of the middle and later adolescent years? By what paths and processes do these concepts reduce the motivation and capacity for change?

The phrase "low self-esteem" has often been used in explaining such phenomena as adolescent pregnancy. But what does low self-esteem denote in operational terms, and how does it actually influence behavior? Preadolescent and early adolescent girls typically feel insecure from time to time, and most experience fluctuations in self-esteem. Indeed, some researchers have noted a normative drop in self-esteem during early adolescence (Simmons et al. 1979; Petersen and Taylor 1980; Rosenberg 1986). Also, as Brooks-Gunn and Reiter (1990) note, early adolescence may be a time of heightened vulnerability to psychological distress, especially depression, for girls. Rare is the adolescent girl who does not turn to the outside world, especially to males, for self-validation and mirroring. These personal vicissitudes are part of adolescence, part of what makes this a time of anxiety and disequilibrium for many young people. How do such feelings come to exert power over the lives of poor adolescent girls—drawing them toward early, unprotected sex and away from other means of self-enhancement? Many middle-class girls grow up in unhappy, even dysfunctional families, in homes marked by turmoil or neglect. But most of these young women will eventually move into productive adult life, albeit not without pain or problems. Why are dysfunctional families so lethal for poor youth? Why do only the exceptional escape and, even then, only with a good deal of help and at great personal cost to themselves or their children?

To answer such questions we need to look at the girl's subjective sense of self in relation to the stresses and constraints of her life. Subjective concepts such as self-worth, self-esteem, and self-image are gradually constructed over the course of development through transactions between changing cognitive capacities, changing personal relationships, and changing socialization experiences. The early adolescent years are a key transitional period for the developing self. As new intellectual abilities emerge and physical transformations occur, the girl's expectations of others and their behavior toward her will change as well. In concert, these shifts act to alter the adolescent's sense of who she is and what she can and cannot do. Building on earlier selfconcepts, they help to shape and reshape key facets of her self.

When the girl's past and current life experiences combine to lead to a distorted or defeated sense of who she is and what she can do, the meanings she ascribes to the events of her life and the actions she takes or fails to take will reflect that distortion or defeat. The meanings are not simply attitudes she holds; the actions are not merely spur-of-the-moment behaviors. Neither are wholly reactions to the pressures and lack of options in her environment. They have a deeper and more complex history in the development of her self and its adaptations to her environment.

A 14-year-old runs away from home and, in spite of involvement in various youth service programs, repeatedly finds herself in self-destructive relationships. These eventually lead to far more serious troubles.

A 16-year-old mother drops out of school and then abandons her counseling and general equivalent degree (GED) programs. Later she appears to lose job after job and have baby after baby, "deliberately."

When such personal failures take place, it is not simply that the environment has offered few realistic or appropriate alternatives for these adolescents, although this is probably the case. It is not just that the institutions in the community are insensitive or unresponsive to their needs, although most likely they are. Certainly, there are real obstacles in the way; but there are sometimes opportunities as well—people who want to help, chances to start again. These go unheeded or unused.

Many such teens do not trust people to be sources of help. For others, the psychological burdens of their histories lead them to put their trust in the wrong people, those who will hold them back or betray them again and again. Such people fit easily into these girls' working models of themselves. They fulfill familiar roles and serve functions similar to those of people the girls have come to know all too well in the years before adolescence.

> When I was 5 years old I had to go and stay with an aunt. She was very bad with me, and then I had to go to another aunt and she was even worse. . . . One day my mother appeared and picked us up. It's not fair that you have to be going from place to place even if it's with your family, and it's bad when somebody from your family doesn't have pity on you, like you didn't have the same blood, but that happened to me. They did not have pity on me. They did not care for me. They did not defend me. I was so small I could not defend myself against adults. . . . I always ask myself how come God gave me this punishment. What had I done to deserve all this suffering?

> When I was small I got so many disappointments with friends and family that it is hard to trust someone again. . . . When I was small I don't know why but I was scared of big people. . . . Today I feel afraid like if someone is chasing me or something is going to happen to me. I usually have this awful feeling. . . . I hope I can make it disappear someday.

> It is hard to trust anyone because I am still feeling like people are trying to sexual abuse me and I think that about other people.

The sense of self a girl brings to adolescence has developed and will continue to develop within an interpersonal matrix, but it affects far more than her interpersonal relationships. Weaknesses or vulnerabilities in overall self-esteem and the various aspects of the self may interfere with the emergence and resolution of normal identity issues during middle and later adolescence. Without mastery of these issues, a core task of adolescence—the formation of a new identity to bring to adulthood—is left unfulfilled. Without a sense of self-acceptance and worth as a person, the girl is poorly prepared to meet, let alone master, the premier challenge of adolescence.

Adolescence
The Meaning and Importance of Adolescence

A 16-year-old may or may not be a mother, but she is an adolescent, very much a product of her personal developmental history as it has unfolded within the matrix of her particular family, social networks, peer relationships, and community institutions. Poised between the worlds of childhood and adulthood, she is engaged in the reorganization and restructuring of the personality that are the hallmarks of this developmental era (Muus 1988).

No matter where she grows up, a girl is faced with certain developmental tasks during adolescence. As she adjusts to physical changes that may initially make her feel awkward, she must also achieve appropriate independence from her family, develop new social roles with her peers, prepare herself for the world of work, and forge an identity to carry her forward to adulthood.

The maturational changes experienced at adolescence bring about cognitive as well as social transformations (Petersen 1988; Keating 1990). Qualitative shifts in typical adolescent thinking bring with them a new capacity: the ability to look to the future. This, in turn, gives the adolescent the intellectual tools to envision her place in that future and to prepare herself mentally to assume the new roles this will entail.

Building on the maturational accomplishments of puberty and early adolescence, the years of adolescence proper see further changes in body size, shape, and function. These bring about and are accompanied by further changes in the young person's sense of herself and of her relationships to the most significant people in her life (Petersen and Taylor 1980; Tobin-Richards et al. 1983). She feels and acts differently toward them, and they feel and act differently toward her. Her attitudes begin to shift; their expectations have begun to do so as well.

During the years when the adolescent is striving to establish a mature identity her potential for future accomplishment is at a peak. Because of the transformational nature of the adolescent process, the door is open for positive change—given an average, expectable developmental progression within an average, expectable environment. What are the developmental tasks for a girl when such a situation does not exist? How are developmental issues around self and identity resolved in the risk-filled context of poverty? At present, we lack the data to answer such questions with any certainty or specificity.

Perspectives on Adolescence

There is a rich and substantial body of knowledge concerned with how adolescents form their sense of identity, how they feel about and relate to their peers, how they negotiate their changing relationships with parents and other authorities, and how they come to grips with their changing minds and bodies. Most significantly, this literature illustrates the varied ways in which the individual adolescent experiences and consolidates various selves, as knower, doer, observer, and as one who is known and observed (Douvan and Adelson 1966; Erikson 1968; Blos 1979; Elkind 1967, 1974; Conger and Petersen 1984; Youniss and Smollar 1985; Harter 1990; Steinberg 1991). Overwhelmingly, this literature has focused on the development and behavior of adolescents from white, middle-class families and, until recently, on adolescent males.[8] A group of researchers, under the sponsorship of the Mac-Arthur Foundation, is currently conducting a series of longitudinal studies on the successful development of disadvantaged minority youth, but findings from these investigations will not be available for several years (Tom Cook, personal communication). Lastly, college students are frequently overrepresented in the samples of research on adolescence. How relevant are insights derived from studying these more privileged adolescents and young adults to an understanding of what motivates poor youth?

8. There is evidence that most major developmental theories reflect a gender bias (Muus 1988). The work of Carol Gilligan (1982) has provided an impetus for rethinking developmental theory and considering the role of gender differences in our conceptualizations. In looking at the development of moral reasoning, Gilligan challenges Freud and Kohlberg in insisting that the differences between males and females in moral development do not mean that one is either better or worse than the other. Insights from Gilligan's work, as well as those of other feminist scholars on the qualities that have traditionally characterized female modes of feeling and thinking, have much to offer in explaining the vulnerability to male exploitation shown by a broad range of disadvantaged adolescent girls.

Serious scholarship on the lives of poor and minority youth has largely been concerned with problem behaviors such as delinquency (Elliot and Ageton 1980) and substance abuse (Dryfoos 1990; McCord 1990). In considering these problems, scholars tend to focus on their social correlates, giving only cursory attention to their developmental wellsprings. In addition, although some females do engage in criminal activity or substance abuse, antisocial and deviant behaviors are far more common among males, and males have therefore been studied far more often than females.

In studies of disadvantaged females, the major focus has been on sexual and reproductive behaviors, particularly teenage pregnancy and childbearing, and with such correlates as school dropout and later welfare dependency. A somewhat separate line of research, focused on deviance or problem behaviors, points to the ways in which early or excessive involvement in adult behaviors such as drinking or drug use can lead to precocious sexual activity and thus to earlier pregnancy. Clearly, for some troubled adolescents, sexual activity may be part of a more general problem-behavior syndrome that includes illicit drug use and drinking, as well as general antisocial behavior (Jessor and Jessor 1977)[9] and academic underachievement (Dryfoos 1990).

Problems surrounding educational limitations or failures have been of interest in relation to risk for teenage childbearing. Indeed, the literacy skills of many adolescent mothers are pitifully meager, lending support to the theory that there is an association between doing poorly in school and such problem behaviors as early sexual activity and too early childbearing, as well as delinquency and substance abuse (Dryfoos 1990). Recent analyses of national survey data from the National

---

9. In a factor-analytic study, Donovan and Jessor (1985) found that excessive drinking, marijuana use, antisocial behaviors, and sexual intercourse loaded as a common factor for both adolescents and young adults. In an excellent overview of theory and research on problem behaviors during adolescence, McCord (1990) notes that some researchers believe that behaviors such as drinking, smoking, illicit drug use, delinquency, and sexual activity should be considered elements of a deviant lifestyle—that is, different manifestations of a single underlying tendency. Others, according to McCord, consider different sets of deviant behaviors to represent diverse underlying difficulties (414). How this issue relates to the design of prevention and intervention will be discussed in chap. 7.

Longitudinal Survey of Youth indicate that adolescent females in the bottom quintile in basic reading and math skills were five times more likely to become mothers over a two-year period than those in the top quintile (29 versus 6 percent) (Pittman and Govan 1986). And, confirming the interrelations between basic skills, poverty, and teen childbearing, girls with low basic skills from poverty families were five to seven times more likely to become mothers in their teens than girls with average or better skills and not from poverty families (Pittman 1986, as cited in Dryfoos 1990).

> hi my name is Betsy Smith and I have two kids. one are Bobby he 3 years old the other Jimmy he one year. . . . Im begin to learn something from this program.

> I like been a teen mother Because i like kids a lot because when my older sisters had there kids i watch my sister kids for them . . . so thats why i went a baby for because i love kids a hole lot so that why i have two kids for but i am not having anymore kids because my baby dads did not stay with me when i had the baby he said that it was not he [he said the baby was not his].

Poor literacy skills compound social isolation, adding yet another strand to the web in which these girls are trapped. Here again, however, few scholars (or practitioners) have gone below the surface level of description to the underlying developmental dynamics. Nor have they examined the role of developmental problems in lowering academic expectations and skills and limiting the capacity to make use of educational opportunities for positive change.

There is thus a pressing need to know more about how girls' self-concepts emerge and evolve in the various social contexts of risk, more about the developmental origins of their precocious sexual activity[10]

10. Petersen and Crockett (1992) comment that at least two processes may be implicated in the relation between precocious sexual activity and other problem behaviors. First (as suggested by Jessor and Jessor 1977), becoming involved in problem behaviors may be an indication of a teen's psychological readiness to engage in adult behaviors or her "transition- proneness." Second, engaging in one type of problem behavior may bring her into contact with peer groups or activities where other problem behaviors are modeled and encouraged. In either case, these authors have found with their rural sample that substance abuse or deviance at one

and problems with school and (later) work. A reluctance to raise (indeed, even to recognize) underlying psychological or process issues and too heavy emphasis on "outcomes" such as pregnancy, school failure, and deviant behaviors combine to create a problem-focused, nondevelopmental view of poor and minority female adolescents. Such a view contributes few useful insights about the role their adolescence plays in shaping the adults they become.

Many of the earlier ideas about what was typical of adolescence grew out of work with clinical populations. Over the past twenty-five years, scholars have begun to express doubts about the wisdom of basing our notions of adolescent development on the behavior and attitudes of troubled youth (Douvan and Adelson 1966; Offer 1969; Offer, Ostrow, and Howard 1981; Kandel and Lesser 1972; Petersen 1988). The popular view of adolescence as a time of inevitable personal strife and emotional distancing between teenagers and their parents was strongly influenced by the writings of therapist-scholars. The insights and theories of Anna Freud (1958), for example, were based on her experiences in treating emotionally troubled young people. These perspectives have since been modulated by the gathering of data on nonclinical populations. More recent images portray the teenage years as characterized by psychological individuation (Blos 1979), new identifications with agemates and leader figures outside the family (Waterman 1985), and realignments in family relations more than by abrupt or profound ruptures or emotional detachment from parents (Grotevant and Cooper 1985, 1986; Hill and Holmbeck 1986). These newer formulations, however, are based almost exclusively on empirical studies of mainstream rather than disadvantaged or minority adolescents. Again, we will need to see if they generalize to nonwhite and non-middle-class adolescent populations (Collins 1990; Montemayor and Flannery 1990).

Part of the interest in the adolescent issues of mainstream youth rests on the assumption that psychological difficulties, particularly

---

point in time will predict the initiation of sexual activity in the near future. It seems plausible, however, that different processes may be at work in different ethnic or racial groups and environments—that is, that initiation of sexual activity has some different (as well as some similar) precursors across cultures and contexts.

those arising during adolescence, can lead to lower personal, educational, or job-related functioning and eventual downward mobility. It is recognized that such difficulties among middle-class youth are frequently the result of interference with some critical adolescent developmental task(s), most commonly emanating from problems within the family. Why is there resistance to these same notions in regard to the most disadvantaged segment of our adolescent population?

Sixteen in the Mainstream: Struggles and Supports
When I was fifteen, I felt it coming; now I was sixteen, and it hit. My feet had imperceptibly been set on a new path, a fast path into a long tunnel. . . . I wandered witlessly forward and found myself going down. . . . There wasn't a whole lot I could do about it, or about anything. I was going to hell in a handcart, that was all, and I knew it and everyone around me knew it, and there it was. I was growing and thinning, as if pulled. I was getting angry, as if pushed. . . . My feelings deepened and lingered. The swift moods of early childhood—each formed by and suited to its occasion— vanished. Now feelings lasted so long they left stains. They arose from nowhere, like winds or waves, and battered at me or engulfed me.
—Annie Dillard, *An American Childhood*

This is how the Pulitzer Prize-winning writer Annie Dillard describes her emotionally stormy adolescence. Raised in the 1940s by a strong, loving (and well-to-do) two-parent family rooted in the past and current life of their community, Dillard made mistakes and took risks, but the foolishness of her adolescence could be weathered and its experiences successfully integrated as part of her developing self, without pulling her down forever.[11] But there are other, vastly different American childhoods, ones that have more serious and lasting effects both on the young woman's sense of identity and on the kind of life she may well be forced to lead for many years to come. Because of

11. For another revealing picture of a turbulent but fruitful adolescence, see Simon 1986.

the pressures and constraints of adolescence in a risk-packed environ-ment, the mistakes of her youth may be her companions for life.

Most adults in society's mainstream recognize that adolescence is a major crossroads, a time of life when a young person's future life-course begins to be set in earnest. As Steinberg (1991) points out, "adolescence is a period of preparation, defined less by its own essence than what it is followed by—maturity." The process of achieving maturity has its own particular challenges in current U.S. society, but it is a process that most adolescents undergo with reasonable success. For most mainstream girls, entry into the period of adolescence takes place against a backdrop of psychic strength and integrity, gained from the successful execution of the basic developmental tasks of childhood. As identity is being re-tested and re-formed during adolescence and relational skills and practical competencies are being built, there is normally a core of emotional and intellectual wholeness. In addition, parents and numerous other social supports are likely to be available to help the adolescent overcome her problems and to be activated if there is too much adolescent turbulence or too little achievement. Parents and teachers are generally concerned, for example, when a formerly motivated girl suddenly seems to lose interest or fails in school. The significant adults in such a girl's life recognize that for some reason she is not able to handle the various pressures of adoles-cence and to balance its often conflicting internal and external pulls.

Adults will be concerned, if not alarmed, if a girl begins to act out sexually in response to such problems as the loss of a father or to family discord, which leave her without the emotional support and guidance she needs to cope with her unfolding sexuality. Adults (and often peers) worry about the girl who seeks to resolve identity conflicts by involving herself in a series of destructive relationships. Such behavior is felt to portend future problems with men.

When parents are not able or willing to help, a good-quality school, with caring, involved teachers and guidance counselors, can be lifesav-ing, literally as well as figuratively, for an adolescent who is troubled or in crisis. As an external support system, the school can serve as a model, encouraging and reinforcing an adolescent's coping efforts and demonstrating positive values (Rutter 1979). Those who have studied stress resistance in adolescence find that resilient adolescents usually have extensive contacts outside their immediate families, with concerned and caring teachers, ministers, and older friends (Hauser et al. 1985; Werner and Smith 1982).

A mainstream girl whose sexual acting out results in a pregnancy will probably have an abortion. If this is not possible or acceptable to her, she will be far more likely to relinquish her child for adoption than will her disadvantaged counterpart (Musick et al. 1984; Hayes 1987; Kalmuss, Namerow and Cushman 1991). In those comparatively rare cases where a girl from a working-class or middle-class background does elect to keep and raise her baby, she has a greater chance to marry than her disadvantaged counterpart, greater material resources, and, even if she is a high school dropout, greater likelihood of eventually getting a job.

As difficult and potentially damaging as adolescent developmental tribulations can be, they are far less likely to have lasting negative effects if the girl has social and economic advantages. The more privileged adolescent's parents may provide her with therapy, find her a tutor, or even send her to a private school when the going gets too rough. Should her parents be unwilling or unable to do this, the schools in her more affluent community will almost certainly offer counseling or a special program designed for youth experiencing educational and emotional difficulties.

Thus, for the middle-class girl, temporary psychological vulnerability need not inevitably result in permanent disability. For the travails of a troubled youth, there are the cushions and buffers of middle-class life. Where there is social and economic advantage, a "wasted youth" does not automatically lead to a wasted life.

Sixteen, Female, and Poor: A Different Experience, a Different Identity

For adolescent girls raised in severe poverty, reality is different in every dimension. These girls frequently have grown up in damaged and damaging family situations where the basic developmental foundation has been poorly laid or is lacking altogether. In addition, the environment in which they live—at home, in school, and in the community—

is often highly threatening. Surely more of these teens, when compared with their more advantaged counterparts, are highly stressed if not deeply troubled. At the same time, their external supports and their opportunities to find alternative models of coping are fewer and far less adequate.

What happens to one of these teenage girls when confronted with the challenges of adolescence? If she engages in sexual acting-out, finds and involves herself with males who exploit or abuse her, or fails in school, she is more often than not drawn into a vortex from which there is little chance of escape.

The difficulties that regularly face such a young woman can range from overt threats of random and unpredictable violence to subtle but ubiquitous pressure to engage in risky sexual behavior. All these work against any effort of hers to make something of herself or to work toward a better life. Beyond that, there is frequently a deeper problem. These girls handle the transformations in relations with family, peers, and the community that accompany adolescence quite differently than their mainstream counterparts. Even if, in the short term, the ways they handle these transformations are adaptive, in the long term they may be quite damaging.

For example, typical mainstream adolescent girls are struggling to come to grips with such questions as: Who am I? What are these feelings I'm feeling? Do my parents understand me? Are they listening to me? What do they know? I'm old enough, why won't they let me do what I want? What should I do about my sexual attractiveness to boys? How do I feel about sex? How do I balance my social and school lives? And, especially in the middle to later adolescent years, will I go to college? If so, where? What will I do with my life—will I have a career, or marry and raise children, or both?[12]

On the other hand, many girls who come of age in underclass communities—especially those in single-parent, father-absent

12. Some of the best sources of information on normal adolescent development can be found in Feldman and Elliott 1990. I thank Shirley Feldman, of Stanford University, for generously providing me with copies of chapters in progress; they were invaluable for this work. I also thank Dr. Ruby Takanishi of the Carnegie Council on Adolescent Development for directing me to this work and to Professor Feldman.

families—are struggling with different questions. They, too, are asking "Who am I?" but from a psychological perspective that belongs to an earlier period of development. For these girls, the issues of identity often are not predominantly those of redefining and renegotiating family relationships, searching for a sense of where one is headed in the future, and envisioning the place one will take in the broader society. Rather, identity-related issues may still be grounded in the questions of early childhood: Who cares about me? Whom can I trust? Whom can I depend on? Where and how can I find security and safety?

The self's voice in these young women may remain fixed on one basic set of questions: What do I need to do, and who do I need to be, to find someone who will stay close to me and care for me as I wish my mother had done? What do I need to do, and who do I need to be, to find a man who won't abandon me, as the men in my life and my mother's life have done?

If an adolescent's psychological energies are too strongly focused on defensive and security measures, much of her time and effort will be focused on trying to resolve her unmet dependency needs, searching for and trying to maintain attachments. When this occurs, her attention and energies are diverted from the critical developmental tasks that undergird adolescent and, later, adult competence in our society. Girls for whom basic acceptance and love are the primary motivating forces have little interest or emotional energy to invest in school or work-related activities unless they are exceptionally bright or talented. Even then, the pull of unmet affiliative or dependency needs may be more powerful than anything the worlds of school or work have to offer, particularly when these offerings are as inadequate and inconsistent as those typically found in poverty communities.

Fighting the Odds

The adolescent girls most likely to be struggling with the developmental tasks of childhood are those who have been forced to adapt to family and other environments that provide too little care and protection for children and youth. In searching for the acceptance and love they crave, these girls will take many risks and few precautions. The capacity for self-care is, after all, predicated on a history of being cared for and protected by others. While growth-thwarting personal histories are by no means exclusive to impoverished communities, they are more predominant there for a variety of reasons, and their effects are far more lethal.[13]

Noxious early childhood and preadolescent life experiences not only foster bad attitudes and actions; they act to shape an inadequate sense of self, an identity that prohibits forward movement in positive, self-enhancing ways. Such experiences leave girls developmentally unprepared for the rapid and extensive physical and psychosocial changes of adolescence. There are too few "stakes in the ground" to help these girls withstand the strong winds of adolescence. The internal and external pressures of the teen years find them psychologically unprepared and overwhelm their psyches.

Certain experiences, especially within the family, take a heavy toll on development, affecting intellectual as well as social emotional functions: "I had a terrible young life. So many things I made sure they were not in my mind. I would black them out. When he hit her he would hit me. I lost a lot of my memory."

Most important, traumatic experiences leave a residue of emotional discontinuities—breaks between present and past, between thought and feeling, between actions and intentions. Mental health professionals generally refer to such discontinuities as forms of dissociation, psychological defenses used to retain a sense of self under traumatic or brutalizing conditions. When this happens, the girl is functionally the prisoner of the disavowed and unacknowledged pain of her past (Miller 1983; 1986). She is caught between the security-seeking behavior that experience has taught her to engage in and want, on the one hand, and the security-threatening results of that behavior, on the other. She cannot easily learn from these repeated "mistakes" because the feelings and perceptions are not related to each other. For psychic self-protection,

---

13. The work of Robert Halpern (1990a, 1990b), William Julius Wilson (1987, 1989), and David Ellwood (1988) provides a sense of the cumulative effects of poverty on the family. Halpern deals more with family functioning—specifically parenting—whereas Wilson and Ellwood are more concerned with structural issues such as family formation.

she has developed a pattern of compartmentalizing, so that what appears to her to be functional (even rational) survival-oriented behavior is not psychically related to its invariably negative outcomes. She has learned to perceive her participation in self-injurious interactions that cannot be avoided as, in effect, a positive skill and thus has come to insulate her emotions from the normally associated pain.

Emotional discontinuities between what she does and what she intended to do are likely to be intensified by the normal adolescent tendency to be somewhat oblivious to the internal reasons for one's actions. Thus the stage has been set for a series of personal crises that the girl has instigated, either actively or passively, but about which she appears to be bewildered. "How did this happen to me?" " How did I get pregnant?" "How did I get kicked out of school?" "How did I lose the job? I didn't do anything wrong." "How did I get involved with a (another) guy who takes advantage of me, who beats me up and abuses my kids?" "Why did the state take my kids away?"

For those who question why a disadvantaged adolescent, even one in an intervention program, continues to seek and find more trouble, it is well to remember that defensive patterns of behavior are usually grounded in necessary, perhaps even life-saving, adaptations to terrible life circumstances. Because such adaptations initially (and repeatedly) "worked" they are deeply entrenched in self and identity and strongly resistant to change. Few of the young women who participate in intervention programs could be said to be mentally ill or to have serious personality or character pathology. Indeed, many have remarkable strengths and resilience. Still, seriously and continuously depriving experiences are rarely without psychological consequences, which interfere with the ability to negotiate the critical tasks of this transitional period and create additional vulnerabilities that magnify the effects of risk factors in the environment. When this happens, the adolescent is left without the personal resources and coping skills she most needs to withstand the multiple pressures of her daily life or to thrust herself up and out of poverty. It is fate's cruel trick that in order to move beyond a life of poverty, today's disadvantaged adolescent needs to possess not just good psychosocial resources and skills but extraordinarily good ones; not just an adequate self-concept but one that is invincible.

Adolescent Identity and the Process of Change

The precise developmental tasks of the early, middle, and later adolescent years vary considerably over time (Kett 1971, 1977), culture (Mead 1953, 1958; Whiting 1963) and gender (Gilligan 1982, 1990). They also vary according to the individual's psychological characteristics and general mental health. The nature of the girl's relationship with her parents before adolescence; the structure of her family; the expectations they hold about what it means to be an adolescent; and the expectations held by the girl, her peers, and the community at large—all are likely to affect how she makes the transition from child to adolescent, and from adolescent to young adult.

Within this variety, there are central themes or invariants. During adolescence these themes revolve around the construction of personal identity and the establishment of a meaningful self concept in which past, present, and future are integrated to form a unified whole (Muus 1988). Processes of identity are psychological invariants, common human qualities. No matter where an adolescent lives or what her social class or ethnic group, she shares with all other humans the need to know who she is in relation to the world of others, to feel a progressive continuity between what she was, what she is, and what she perceives others to see in her and expect of her (Erikson 1968).

For many years scholars representing a broad range of perspectives have discussed and debated the development of self (for example, James 1892; Sullivan 1947, 1953; Montemayor and Eisen 1977; Lewis and Brooks-Gunn 1979; Kohut 1971, 1977, 1983; Rosenberg 1979, 1986; Stern 1985; and Harter 1988, 1990) and identity processes (for example, Erikson 1959, 1968; A. Freud 1965; Marcia 1966, 1980, 1988; Marcia and Friedman 1970; Gilligan 1982, 1990; Hauser and Follensbee 1984; Waterman 1985; and Harter 1988, 1990). Despite considerable diversity in their methods and their conclusions, all acknowledge the significance of self and identity in directing an individual's life course, and most are concerned with the period of adolescence in this regard.

Well Diary, I'm scared. A scared little girl on the inside, and an immature adult on the outside. I don't want to grow up. Gees, I never thought—17 years old and two kinds of lives. A mother in one life and a teenager in the other and put it together and you got a Teen Mom. As a little girl I was deprived of a father—as Courtney is now. I never did want that for my child—any child. A single mother is hard. *Very Hard.* It is hard finding yourself. Who am I, Diary? Really, I don't know.

Nina

Nina's question is about identity. Such questions are at the heart of adolescent childbearing; they are its developmental wellsprings. Identity issues explain why so many girls, even those with considerable promise, become mothers while still in their teens. They also explain why some are able to move up, creating a better life for themselves and their children, whereas others so clearly are not. Identity processes inform us about the causes of teenage childbearing, as well as the conditions necessary for positive change to occur. Although identity formation is a continuous process throughout the life cycle, it has its crisis during the adolescent years. Shaped by what went before and shaping what comes after, identity is the primary motivational force of adolescence. Because of this, it is the primary motivational force of adolescent childbearing.

Erikson first called attention to the central role of identity formation in adolescence, and his ideas continue to guide some of the most fruitful work in this field. He characterizes adolescence as the period in the life cycle when the individual must establish a sense of personal identity and avoid the dangers of what he terms *role diffusion* and *identity confusion*. For Erikson, identity is not something given to the individual by society, nor is it a maturational product that appears when the time has come. Rather, it is something that is acquired through sustained personal effort. For this to transpire, adolescents require a moratorium—a period of time in which they are provided with and take advantage of—opportunities to widen their experience, to increase the breadth of their exposure to diverse aspects of life, to explore alternatives, and to experiment with various roles. The adolescent selects, sorts through, tries on, discards, reshapes, and eventually fashions a unique sense of self by integrating the values, beliefs, and goals that feel most personally expressive and appropriate—the ones that feel right for him or her.

This is what is supposed to happen—the ideal situation—but several decades of research based on Erikson's work reveal that in reality things may be quite different. Many adolescents commit to a role without exploring alternatives, either because there are not many (or even any) alternatives, because their family and social environment in some way pressures them to assume a particular role, or because of some combination of both sets of determinants. The premature assumption of a particular role during adolescence is referred to as *identity foreclosure*.

Whereas foreclosure adolescents take on their roles too early, other adolescents simply fail to engage in any meaningful identity activity. This happens not only because their environment has failed to provide them with the time and opportunities to explore other roles, but also because it has failed to provide them with the basic psychological tools essential for identity achievement. This psychological fluidity, or *identity diffusion*, is a developmentally normal state during the early adolescent years. It becomes problematic only when it persists into late adolescence and adulthood.

Erikson conceives of identity formation as "a process located in the core of the individual and yet also in the core of his communal culture" (22).[14] This attention to the interaction between adolescents and the worlds in which they live makes Erikson's ideas relevant for an examination of adolescent childbearing. Adolescents are very finely tuned to their culture: they breathe it in psychologically. For Erikson, it surrounds them and it is in them as well. Interpreted in this light, an adolescent becomes a mother because this fits with her internal sense of who she is and what she can do, her externally derived awareness of what else is available to her, and because the ceaseless interweaving

14. Erikson generally uses masculine pronouns when discussing developmental issues that are not gender specific.

of these inner and outer forces tells her that the emotional costs of doing—or trying to do—otherwise are going to be too high. An adolescent fails to make use of options other than motherhood not only because fewer are actually available but also because even those that are may threaten to estrange her from all or most of the emotionally significant people in her life, the people who confer and validate her sense of identity. Thus even when opportunities and alternatives to early childbearing are objectively available, for some adolescent females, they are not subjectively available.

The self processes and structures that underlie and organize adolescent identity are rooted in the young person's psyche. Rarely are they in her awareness. These internal processes and structures determine how her life is lived through their continuing interactions with external reality. Indeed, they strongly influence how she perceives external reality: what she sees as a threat and what she sees as an opportunity, what she recognizes or fails to recognize as a risk, and what she decides to do about it. In some way her identity affects virtually everything she does, from what she believes she can learn and accomplish to what she chooses or merely leaves to chance. By organizing her emotions and thoughts about herself, it motivates her actions and becomes a powerful determinant of whether she is resistant or open to change. Identification of factors that influence self and identity concepts during the adolescent years could thus provide explanatory models of the capacity for growth and competence across a variety of domains. Such models would hold considerable promise for prevention and intervention because they are developmentally appropriate models for change.

In order for a program or policy to have an impact on the factors that lead an adolescent to become a mother, it must in some way alter her identity, her internal representation of herself. Whenever an intervention is effective with a particular teen; whenever it helps her to feel and be more competent, to better understand what motivates her actions, to think before she does something; whenever it effects a shift in her values or behaviors, it is at least partially the result of the intervention's "fit" with her developmental needs and psychological makeup.

If we seek to facilitate positive change in adolescents, particularly when such change requires thinking and acting in ways radically different from those of the most significant people in their lives, the supposed benefits of such change will have to be both developmentally appropriate and powerfully motivating on an individual psychological level. If they are not, they stand little chance of altering downward trajectories. To be so motivating, interventions must reach and touch the girl at the level of the self, the deepest and most strongly felt sense of who she is.

Although one hears from policy makers and others concerned with the association between adolescent childbearing and poverty a good deal of rhetoric about the complexity of the problems and the need for more comprehensive interventions for at-risk youth, few have been willing to grapple with the psychological and developmental aspects of that complexity. They fail to understand that key developmental purposes of adolescence are being served by engagement in early sexual activity and parenthood. It is precisely the fact that it addresses such fundamental needs—however unsuccessfully—that causes too-early parenthood to occur in spite of all argument and apparent reason. If these needs could be met in more functional, self-enhancing ways, they would be. That is the psychological meaning of having few options.

Those concerned with youth at risk and with programs to help them seldom take account of what comprehensive intervention strategies might actually entail in terms of the interactive relationship between adolescent development and interventions,[15] especially as these influence and are influenced by other significant relationships in the girl's life. For the average disadvantaged adolescent girl, to choose actively not to have a child is symbolically to "do it better" than all the emotionally significant people in her life—with virtually no material, educational, vocational, or emotional supports for doing so.

Consider what that takes. If a parent does not (or cannot) actively enable her child to go beyond where she herself has gone, does not

15. The phrase "interactive relationship between adolescent development and intervention" came from a conversation several years ago with Robert Selman of Harvard University's Judge Baker Clinic. It nicely captures what should be happening in community-based programs for youth and adolescents but so seldom does.

consistently tell the child that she wants and expects to see her succeed, and does not show her how, the child can rarely do so. Poor adolescents who succeed generally have more than skills and strengths; they usually have extraordinary families who act as buffers and enablers (Clark 1983; Comer 1988; Hans, Musick, and Jagers 1992). Sadly, sometimes these families cannot keep their daughters from early parenthood.

That some very bright and promising girls from loving families have children too early is powerful testimony to the strength of the forces promoting and surrounding premature motherhood. When these forces interact with the teen's developmentally normal desire to fill adultlike roles, to be a woman, and with aspects of her social milieu that encourage or at least do not condemn teenage parenthood (Dash 1989), it is no wonder, that many girls want a baby. Who wouldn't?

The desire for motherhood grows out of and is intimately connected to the adolescent's sense of herself and where she fits into the world. At the developmental crossroads of adolescence, when everything in her life seems up in the air, in an environment that offers no chance to explore other options, no other models or avenues out, motherhood promises a path to personhood, a path to her own place in the world. Having a baby means the adolescent no longer need wonder who she is: she knows—she is a mother.

This new identity may indeed work—for some girls forever; for others, only a while. Then, like Nina, they will once again wonder, "Who am I?" and maybe, like Nina, they will answer, "I don't really know."

Four

Relating to Men

I don't understand how I got from one bad circumstance to another.
I could have prevented the second one. I was working, going to
school, doing fine, and then I was careless. . . . I didn't take birth
control that weekend I got pregnant. There was no reason for this, I
had the information in my hand, I thought it's not going to happen
to me, I'm not going to have sex. I was trying to deny the fact that
it was me, my ignorance.

I learned about sex from my dad. I never had a chance for my first
time with my boyfriend. Who knows, maybe I [would have] wanted
to wait until I got married. But no, I never got to have that chance.
I don't even remember the first time. . . . I feel it ruined my life.

I learned about sex by being molested by friends and a couple of family members. . . . I sometimes think I have a sex drive cause I was molested so many times as a child.

I felt when my grandfather was abusing me like the world was on top of me. When I finally got away from him I was so relieved. I finally got a chance to start over with my life and my used body. I didn't want to look at [my body]. When I met the father of my child I was so scared that he was just going to use me like my grandfather did.

It started at the age of 13. I had sex with a boy named Will and I didn't even know what we were doing because my mom never told me about sex. . . . That's when it went downhill. I had a wild teenage period. I should be dead three or four times already. Will was the first to turn me on to drugs. I guess doing the drugs and having sex went together cuz that's the only thing Will wanted me for. So I developed the idea that guys wanted sex, and I owed it to them.

A Broader View

As a girl learns about sex, she learns other lessons as well—about giving and getting affection, about what she means and is worth to others. A girl learns about truth and trust from the ways in which she first comes upon the mysteries of sex and from the ways in which she is and is not protected from exploitation. If she is unlucky, she will also learn shame and fear and guilt—and how to keep herself from knowing and feeling what is simply too painful to bear. When these lessons shape her sexuality in developmentally inappropriate ways, they are destined to have far-reaching negative implications for how she perceives the world and lives her life. The how, who, and when of her sexual socialization, the social and interpersonal context in which it occurs, will affect much more than her sexual behavior. Because it shapes her deepest sense of who she is and what she can do, it will affect her capacity to care for and do for herself and her children, to conceptualize and control her own destiny.

For a disadvantaged girl, inappropriate sexual socialization is often the last straw in a mounting accumulation of risk factors. When its effects interact with those of fatherlessness and other interpersonal deprivations, she becomes extremely vulnerable to males. Social isolation that results from a lack of sustained contact and exposure to other people and institutions then administers the psychological coup de grace, fixing interpersonally dysfunctional ways of relating and weakening the boundary between the personal and other aspects of her life. Together, psychological vulnerability and social isolation ensure that the lives of many poor young women will be ruled by their relations to men—not just in bed or on the street, but in the classroom, factory, or office; not just as women, but as students, workers, and parents as well.

Studies of adolescent sexual behavior fail to capture either its psychological complexity or its relationship to coping and adaptation in the broader sense. Whereas research may identify and describe factors associated with early versus later sexual initiation or with variations in sexual practices or contraceptive use, it does not tell us about the meanings and functions of sexuality in the lives of teens, particularly disadvantaged teens. In the absence of such understandings there is very little that can be done to change the attitudes and actions that lead girls toward early unprotected sexual activity and, perhaps more significant, away from success in almost every sphere of their existence.

It has been said that the best way to understand something is to try to change it. In this chapter insights from practice are used to illuminate the special circumstances that characterize the sexual and gender socialization of disadvantaged girls. Using data collected as part of the intervention process, it examines the roles played by family members and by social-environmental factors in creating vulnerability to self-destructive or exploitive relationships and early, unprotected sexual activity. The adolescent female's sense of self in relation to males is the internal representation of her past experiences with men and—perhaps equally important—of her mother's roles and relationships to these and other men. The particulars of her sexual socialization create the form and substance of her images of self. This chapter concerns not adolescent sexual behavior per se but the interpersonal roots and branches of sexual behavior. The central topics are the motivations and psychological meanings underlying the adolescent girl's relationships with males.

Good Reasons and Real Reasons

In trying to understand and change the self-destructive behavior of the girls in our programs, particularly their sexual behavior and relationships with males, I found little that was useful in the scholarly literature. Indeed, as Brooks-Gunn and Furstenberg (1989) note, "What sexuality means to adolescents, how it relates to other aspects of teenage life, and what strategies teens use to manage or incorporate it into their lives have not been studied in any detail" (249). In the absence of such data, they say, "program development occurs in what seems to be a social science vacuum. Often untested assumptions have driven program initiatives, some of which have turned out to be good bets and others unfortunate guesses" (256).

There are two reasons a person does anything: a good reason and a real reason. When efforts to prevent or ameliorate problems of teenage childbearing fail, it is, I believe, largely because they have addressed themselves to the good rather than the real reasons for these problems. Successful interventions are those that have, either thoughtfully or through educated guesses, reached and touched on the real reasons. Both successes and failures offer opportunities to bring to light the forces that motivate various behaviors and make some so strongly resistant to change. They hold up a mirror to the self-other concepts underlying interpersonal relationships and sexual behavior. In considering the circumstances under which an adolescent experiences personal growth, we can see the interpretive framework she has been using to make sense of her life. Let us look briefly at an example of how this process works.

In a parent support group focused on prevention of sexual exploitation, a young woman breaks the silence about her own victimization by an abusive but beloved father-figure. In so doing she begins to break his psychological hold over her, to loosen the grip of the unacknowledged pain of her past on her current thoughts and actions. Shortly thereafter, for the first time, she begins to connect feelings about her earlier experiences with her current behavior and troubles. She sees how these feelings repeatedly draw her to men who initially fascinate but eventually abuse her, and who have also abused her daughters. Having made these connections on an emotional as well as an intellectual level, she is ready to consider the possibility that she can do something to change this pattern. Equally significant, she comes to recognize how very difficult this is going to be for her. In the ensuing months we observe her ambivalence about taking charge of her life, doing it differently than the other women in her family, and being with men she finds less exciting (and less dangerous to herself and her children). She struggles to stay on the new path she has chosen while living among those with whom she has always lived, impinged upon by the same forces she has always felt: "Still I'm constantly around these people. At times I feel like running away."

In this light, the causes and correlates of her sexual behavior take on more subtle shadings, indicating that intervention strategies will miss the mark if they rely on unidimensional approaches to what are clearly multidimensional issues. Sexual behavior is not like a vocation for which one can be trained or retrained. Rather, it is embedded in an interpersonal relationship and therefore is bound up with one's personal and developmental history.

A young woman's sexual behavior is a reflection of how she has acquired her sense of identity as a female and how she has learned to relate to men. It is also a reflection of how these psychological factors have prepared her to cope with the realities of adolescence in her milieu. The struggles of disadvantaged girls with these realities and the words they speak to those who try to show them a better way give striking evidence of just how dangerously inadequate this preparation has been. Their struggles and their words reveal the real reasons for their actions and choices.

The practice-based material woven throughout this chapter provides a window into the interpersonal lives of disadvantaged females. Since these girls are black, white, and Hispanic, working class, working poor, and impoverished, urban, rural, and small town in background, there are variations, and these are very interesting. But there are also common themes, and these are illuminating.

Lessons of Sex and Self
Family Conditions and Psychological Themes

> Probably more than one girl has had her boyfriend's baby as a
> preferable alternative to having her father's.
>
> —Garret Keizer, *No Place but Here*

Appearances can be deceiving. More than one observer of adolescent sexual behavior has commented that girls seem to initiate sex as often as their boyfriends, that they are not luckless victims of force or exploitation but rather are willing (even eager) participants, expressing and exploring their own sexuality and pressuring their friends into early sexual activity. That certainly is what it might look like, and indeed might be, for some girls. But it is probably not the case for many girls who become mothers in their teens, and it is surely not the case for those who become pregnant in their very early teens. Whereas Dash (1989) is correct in his observation that most adolescent mothers want to have babies, the wish for a child is not the entire or the primary motive for their sexual behavior, although this motive may come into play in their acting (or failing to act) to prevent a pregnancy, or electing to terminate a pregnancy rather than bear the child, or choosing to raise the child rather than relinquish it for adoption. The motives governing early childbearing and those that govern sexual behavior are not the same although they arise from overlapping social and psychological systems.

From my clinical journals and field notes and from the diaries and letters of the Heart-to-Heart and Dear Diary participants, certain psychological themes regarding relationships to males began to emerge. These were clarified and extended by insights drawn from my and others' observations, from survey and interview data, and from theory and research in a variety of disciplines. The themes describe the psychological vulnerabilities conferred by unmet dependency and affiliative needs—problems of trust, guilt, humiliation, and low or distorted self-concepts in regard to control, efficacy, and personal worth. Underneath the various themes run the subtexts of adolescent development and female gender schema. These themes and subtexts also illuminate the psychological processes and environmental contingencies necessary for positive change.

The feelings, thoughts, and actions of these adolescent girls can be understood as logical outcomes of their attempts to cope with father absence and the often harsh realities of life with a young, sexually active mother and her partners. They are also the results of psychological adaptations to family disorganization and its sequelae of premature, distorted sexual socialization, especially sexual exploitation. These feelings, thoughts, and actions are reflected most dramatically in the girls' own words—words about life with father and life without him, words about emotional abuse and sexual abuse, and words about family and upbringing. These words reveal the sexual ambience in the homes and communities of poor females.

I was molested by my father from the age of 6–12 years old. . . . I would like to know why people are so sick in the head & do these things to little kids and make their life a living hell.

I was not even 1 year old so I don't remember yet but I was 7 years old and remember somewhat I was 16 and afraid to talk to someone again 18 was afraid of boys and to talk and associate with boys. Now I am 21 and really don't know how to cope with men. [Men] only want one thing. [A]nd theres (some)thing I would like to understand. My foster mother would get money from men to touch me. Please help.

I was sexually abused at 7 years old. It bothers me to talk about it. My father was hooked on acid and heroin. My mother never had any time for me. I grew up really fast. I never had a childhood. . . . My father broke a promise to me. He'd be a good father and get a job and never leave me. But he did leave me and now my family split up. Dad's in [prison] for sexually abusing my stepsister and stepbrother. I went and seen him one time and cryed. My father is a very sick man. . . . My mother's in Iowa. My father's in jail. My brother in Iowa too. So my family is split up because my father didn't keep a promise. Thats why I never believe when someone promises me something.

My sister was asked to have sex with my mother's boyfriend. I made her tell my mother the same night it happened (he was living with us) my mother said she was lieing and blocked it out. He was drunk and told her to come play with his penis for 5 dollar and if she told he was going to get her.

Dear Diary, Do you think it was right for me—they pay me to have sex with them? They got me broken in for this person I was going with.

Then when they divorced my mother worked nights and my older brother didn't have a girlfriend so I guess that's why he thought he had to get it from me. This carried on for a long time. I tried to tell my mother but he was very spoiled so she wouldn't believe me.

I didn't know it was wrong. I thought that we were playing and that was how older people played.

My father would lay against me and push and groan. Sometime he grabbed me and wouldn't let me breathe until I stopped trying to get away.

I came out of the shower and my 8-year-old brother and Dad were looking at dirty books. I wanted to get dressed but my Dad took my towel away and made me look at the books.

I was so scared that I used to sleep in my clothes every night. Sometimes I still do since I'm used to it.

There is no feeling in the world like it. It takes away your pride and I don't want my child to feel they are a bad person because of the things another person did to them.

Still today I have problems with this terrible thing which has happen to me. . . . I was abused when I was 5 and believe me I'm 17 years old today and I still carry the memory, hurt, and guilt with me.

When I was about 10 or 11 he used to sleep with me and my brother because he said it was too cold in his room and I felt someone touch my butt. Then I woke up crying and told my other brother and mom and they said it was probably my imagination. That's when it started happening. And my Mom just broke up with him in '84 or '85 and now she believes me but all this time she didn't. They had been going together for 8 years. When I was pregnant my stomach was hurting and he started rubbing it. I didn't want him to but was scared to tell him to stop.

These quotes suggest some of the injurious effects of sexual exploitation by older males within the family on the social-emotional development of young females. The absence of appropriate male figures in fathering (or grandfathering) roles along with its other growth-thwarting effects appears to foster and fix a kind of learned helplessness in relationships with males. This can have serious and wide-reaching consequences for the girl's choice of partners, her sexual behavior, and her later capacity to protect her own children from similar experiences. Such vulnerability to males frequently extends beyond the purely interpersonal domain, affecting attitudes and actions in school and work.

Fathers Present and Absent

Long ago I realized that love is all that is required of fatherhood, that love will spark the action that it takes to mold a child. I have grown strong and whole from the blessings of my many fathers. Everything they gave me—roughness, gruffness, awkward gentleness, the contrast to my female world, their love—is as much a part of me as my bones, my blood. I was given a rich and privileged childhood, an American childhood, a solid foundation on which to stand and, yes, even go forward. I was guided by good men, powerful men. I was raised right.

—Bebe Moore Campbell, *Sweet Summer*

The reason I fell in love with my husband is because he showed me he cared about me. He was the first man that ever cared. I have always loved my dad, but he was my stepfather and I didn't think he cared. . . . When my baby was about 6 months my stepdad told me he loved me. I think if he would of told me sooner I wouldn't of looked for it somewhere else.

—Olivia, an adolescent mother

It is not so much the structural component of being without a father—that is, being fatherless per se—that is most harmful to the developing child; rather, it is the functional component of lacking consistent experience with older males in loving, protective, and other roles, both instrumental and expressive.[1] To have a father means ideally to have a caring figure of the opposite sex, a significant love object, a mirror for one's femininity. Indeed, the father-daughter relationship gives a young girl her earliest and some say most important sense of her acceptability as a female person. Through it she acquires her attitudes about men and, most important, about herself in relation to them. In spite of increasing interest in the father-child relationship, much of it motivated by a concern with changes in sex roles—specifically, shared childrearing functions between mothers and fathers—and the effects of these changes, the role of the father, especially in relation to adolescent girls, is frequently overlooked in the developmental literature (Maccoby and Martin 1983; Lamb, Owen, and Chase-Landsdale 1979). The limited available evidence does suggest, however, that fathers, both by their presence and by their absence, play key roles in contributing to the psychological adjustment of their daughters. If others (females as well as males) are available and willing to fill these roles, the negative effects of fatherlessness may be greatly ameliorated.

A father's influence does not end in childhood. In one of the few studies of father-adolescent daughter relationships, Sarigiani and Petersen (1988) found that depressive and anxious moods, poor general adjustment, and negative body image were all associated with early adolescent girls' perceived lack of closeness to their fathers. In adolescence and in adulthood, females' relationships with males are more powerfully influenced by their relations with their fathers than by their relations with their mothers (Parke 1981). Nor is the influence of fathers limited to the affective domain (Radin 1981). Retrospective

1. For example, in discussing the importance of the function that a father (or other males living in the family) serves in the life of a poor inner-city girl, Elijah Anderson (1989) comments, "In those domestic situations in which there is but one adult—say, a woman and her three teenage daughters with no male presence—the dwelling may be viewed by young boys . . . as essentially an unprotected nest. . . . In such settings, a man, the figure the boys are prepared to respect, is not there to keep them in line" (68).

studies, biographies, and memoirs of such prominent women as Indira Gandhi and Margaret Mead give eloquent testimony to the importance of fathers as enablers and facilitators of their daughters' motivation to achieve in the spheres of education and work.

Gandhi and Mead were daughters of privilege, as were the adolescent girls in the Sarigiani and Petersen study. What roles do fathers serve in the development of low-income girls? Consider for a minute Sarigiani and Petersen's suggestion that a good relationship with her father may help a young adolescent girl adjust to the physical changes of puberty. Commenting on Maine's (1985) finding that anorexic girls feel emotionally disengaged from their fathers, they corroborate these links between body image and father-daughter closeness with their own nonclinical sample, noting, "Perhaps those adolescent girls with poor father-daughter relationships are less capable of dealing with society's pressures for thinness (e.g., they lack a protective masculine aspect of self-image—they are too 'feminine'), and they internalize negative feelings about their bodies" (28).

Being without a father is in some ways similar but in other ways very different for disadvantaged girls than for more privileged girls. What is the psychological equivalent of eating disorders for poor girls: substance abuse? sexual acting-out? adolescent childbearing? involvement in self-destructive relationships? overdependence on the approval of males? Is a father's role in his daughter's adjustment less potent when he has never been an active part of her life, when he continuously moves in and out or lives separately from the start? What effects does his absence per se have on his daughter's emotional health when he has always lived apart?

When a father leaves or dies, his daughter will suffer whether she is rich or poor; whether she is 3, 12, or 17 years of age. The manner of her suffering will vary depending on her current developmental stage, the nature of her attachment to her father, and the nature and compensatory qualities of her other relationships. It will also depend on her family's robustness and general circumstances and her mother's adjustment and lifestyle. It is these factors that have made father absence so pernicious an influence in recent years.

Many researchers have remarked that fatherlessness is characteristic of girls who become mothers while still in their teens (Hayes et al. 1987; Ellwood 1988). Most of these girls are poor, and many are from minority populations; yet the research on father absence has largely been conducted with white middle- or upper-middle-class samples (see, for example, Hetherington 1989; Hetherington et al. 1989; Wallerstein, Corbin, and Lewis 1988). A further limitation of this line of research comes from its focus on father absence as a result of divorce, a form of family disruption more characteristic of advantaged than of poverty samples.[2]

Studies of troubled youth such as delinquents or drug abusers, most of them male, are the other major source of data on father absence.[3] Though there are many valuable insights to be gained from these studies, as from those on divorce, neither line of research describes the experience of father absence in the day-to-day lives of poor girls, especially those whose mothers are still young and sexually active. Without such specifics, we cannot understand the ultimately self-injurious adaptations to fatherlessness and its correlates or the developmental compromises (for example, the strong need or compulsion to please or placate males) that are among the psychological antecedents of such problem behaviors as adolescent childbearing. On the other hand, there is a growing body of ethnographic and journalistic material that portrays the everyday stream of experience for disadvantaged children and youth (for example, Williams and Kornblum 1985; Lefkowitz 1987; Dash 1989) and a plentitude of clinical case material from social service, child welfare, and educational institutions. Although such sources do not yield the kind of data behavioral scientists prefer, they do provide descriptions of the realities of daily existence for the fatherless daughters of poverty. None of these sources, however, provides descriptions of the inner meanings of these realities— the psychological sense these girls have made of being without their fathers.

2. There is a relatively small but important body of knowledge on loss as a result of death. Father loss is included in this body of work, much of which is clinical in nature. See Bowlby 1980 for an example of this work.

3. Retrospective studies of the backgrounds of young males who engage in antisocial and violent behavior generally find a lack of consistent, appropriate father figures (Jessor and Jessor 1977; Lamb 1986; McCord 1990).

I don't want my son to go through what I did. He doesn't have a
father. I did not have [a father]. . . . I didn't know him, only in a
photograph. I would have liked to know him in person. I know
one feels bad not to have a father.

A great many disadvantaged girls have never known a father. This
is often the case when a girl's mother was a teenage parent. It is quite
common for a young mother to end her relationship with the father
before or soon after the birth of the baby, generally with strong encouragement from the maternal grandmother, who reminds the girl that
the father—that worthless guy who got her pregnant—is not even
buying food and diapers for his child. Who needs him! When a father
is unable or unwilling to provide minimal support, the mother disen-
gages, removing herself and her child from the orbit of the father and
his family. Even without discord, adolescent mothers are still adolescents and thus are likely to fall out of love with last year's romantic
interest.

In many instances, the father loses interest in the mother and, by
association, in the child, visiting them only rarely, if at all (Anderson
1989). This seems to be equally true for older as for adolescent fathers.
Indeed, older men who seek adolescent girls as sexual partners may be
motivated by the need to exploit or control a younger, more passive
female (see, for example, Furstenberg, Brooks-Gunn, and Morgan
1987; Gershenson, et al. 1989).[4] After she becomes a mother, she may
be angrier or less pliable. As she sees his weaknesses as a father (and
thus as a man), she begins to deidealize him. Suddenly she seems older
and less appealing to him. Finally, the low-income adolescent is far
more likely than her middle-income sister to come from a home characterized by disorganization and unpredictability, family disruption and
separations from both parents, little opportunity to relate to the same
father figure for long periods of time, and exposure to males as threatening and violent rather than protective and nurturant.

Whatever her circumstances, the poor girl is likely to be more

4. These studies found that many of the sexual partners of adolescent mothers
are considerably older than the teenage fathers discussed in the literature on adolescent childbearing and thus represent significantly different causal dynamics.

isolated from her father (psychologically, if not physically). And, unlike past generations (even the fairly recent past), she has very few stable older males available to take on at least part of the fathering role when a father is absent, abusive, or emotionally unavailable. Whereas a middle-class child may lose her father to death or divorce, a poor child is far more likely to have lost her father at or soon after her birth. If, as is commonly the case, her mother has a series of relationships or moves in and out of her own family home until she "gets back on her feet," the daughter may be faced with a number of different men who temporarily fill fatherlike roles. If she becomes emotionally attached to any of these father figures, their loss or her mistreatment at their hands further increases her vulnerability in relation to males.

> Mom was married to [a man] who I accepted as my father since my real father wasn't around. He was very strict, mentally abusive, and sometimes physically. I was a freshman and not allowed to participate in school activities. I even tried to have a boyfriend but "Dad" scared him away. One day he got so out of control he shoved me against a wall. I thought my arm was broken. Then he started choking Mom with cigarettes. I ran out the door and called the police. I told Mom it was either him or me! I won. Then, I think this is where my life turned. . . . I got freedom, and got pregnant.

> Grandpa doesn't even care about us now. He hasn't ever seen Jonathan [her son]. I miss him so much. I wish he never left. . . . I cared about him a lot. He was kind of like my dad. . . . Some day we'll find him.

Even advantaged girls need strong family and other external supports to help them master the psychological stresses of father absence and attend to the developmental tasks of adolescence. The absence of a father in early life, for whatever reason, creates a vulnerability so serious that it may prevent the girl from fulfilling the expectable, ordinary tasks of her development. The emotional cost of coping with fatherlessness will be a lowered capacity to care for herself adequately, particularly in relation to men. If the pressures and experiences with males that characterize daily life for many girls in underclass communities are added to this vulnerability, there is cause for the gravest concern. It is not only the absence of a father that puts such girls at risk, but also the lack of appropriate, protective surrogate fathers and the lack of positive images of males who are competent, respected, and do not exploit females. It is not only the absence of a father that harms a child, but the presence of a stream of men who move in and out of the life of her mother, behaving toward her with disdain or cruelty and mistreating her and her children.

Today more than ever before, a girl who becomes a mother in her teens is likely to be from a single-parent, female-headed household. Her often quite young and unmarried mother rightfully wishes to have a normal social life, to be fussed over, loved, and cared for. She also wants her male partners to be committed to her and (in theory, at least) to her children. Because of this she may encourage the current man in her life to "play daddy," hoping he will like the role and that her children will make it easy for him to like it. If he doesn't he might leave. But allowing someone to play daddy under these conditions in effect gives him carte blanche—the child is his to do with as he sees fit. All too many males will see fit to threaten, force, coerce, or seduce the woman's daughters into sexual activity. This aspect of the family-life experience of a fatherless girl poses a serious risk to her psychological development, embodying as it does a failure of the normal protective function of parenting combined with repeated exposure to parent surrogates who have, at best, only a transient interest in her well-being.

Such a family situation is an accident waiting to happen. Whereas most research on sexual abuse indicates that father absence is a risk factor, numerous studies (for example, Gruber and Jones 1983; Finkelhor 1984; Russell 1986) have found that the presence of a stepfather augments risk. The records of child welfare and protective service agencies are filled with cases of child maltreatment, both physical and sexual, in which the perpetrator is the stepfather or current partner of a single mother. Add to this the probability that a mother who repeatedly fails to protect her children has serious self-worth deficits, which she communicates to the child directly by her behavior toward her and indirectly by her failure to prevent harm at the hands of her partners or other males. Simultaneously, the mother's own diminished sense of self-worth is communicated (and perhaps passed on) to her daughter by the behavior she models in her relationships with the significant men in her life.

> Sometimes you have to be weary [wary] . . . especially about stepfathers. Some of them are very tricky, you should never trust a stepfather that is not good to you, I can say this because I had it happen, he lived with my mother. Even though they lived with my mother doesn't mean that I have to love them as my father, because even sometimes we cannot even trust our own fathers. I never met my father so I don't know what it is to have a father, but I know about stepfathers because I have had them. . . . To tell you the truth I hated him. . . . Some of them take advantage of you. They resemble animals that don't even respect their own family.

Of all the forms of maltreatment a girl may suffer at the hands of those who are supposed to be closest to her, the most developmentally and psychologically toxic may well be sexual victimization.

Sexual Exploitation

Research demonstrates that sexual abuse in childhood and early adolescence is far more prevalent than had been previously believed (Finkelhor 1984; Russell 1986; Wyatt 1985; Peters, Wyatt, and Finkelhor 1986) and that it often goes unreported, even in high-risk samples (Polit, White, and Morton 1987, 1990). I first became concerned with the issue of sexual abuse when project directors began to tell me about the increasing numbers of adolescent mothers in their programs who were disclosing sexual victimization, both current and past. As the girls became more comfortable and secure in their relationships with staff and with each other, many felt the need to relieve themselves of the burden of these secrets. At around the same time, the director of Peer Power, a citywide, school-based prevention initiative for sixth-through eighth-grade girls (Handler 1987), observed that when she encouraged girls in Peer Power groups to raise any questions they had about sex, they overwhelmingly asked about incest and other forms of sexual abuse. Although the curriculum of Peer Power had initially been designed to cover a broad range of family-life and skill-building topics, a new priority became, in the words of one guidance counselor, to "teach these girls that they have a *right* to their own bodies."

The preteen girls asked whether it was right to have sex with their fathers, stepfathers, or their mothers' boyfriends. The older girls in the parenting programs spoke of having been forced or tricked into sexual relations with fathers, uncles, brothers, older cousins, and grandfathers. Most of these actual and potential adolescent mothers had fathers who were at best intermittently and infrequently involved in their lives. Those whose father was present often found themselves his victim rather than his beloved and protected child. Paternal absence or dysfunction had left these girls in a position to be easily exploited by older males.

Despite public concern and an increasing body of research on adolescent sexuality, very little attention has been given to the specific circumstances under which disadvantaged young women become aware of or are introduced to sexual activity. Thus, we know little about the sexual histories of girls who become teenage mothers or about the possible connections between adolescent childbearing and childhood sexual experiences. Studies of adolescent sexual behavior do not examine the social and psychological milieus in which early sexual experiences occur, nor do they question adolescents about unwanted sexual encounters, both present and past (Hogan and Kitagawa 1985; Smith and Udry 1985; Zelnik, Kantner, and Ford 1981).[5] When the sexual socialization literature discusses the differences between females and males, it tends to emphasize the female's stronger desire for love and affiliation and the male's greater concern with genital arousal (Chilman 1983). Rarely has this literature been concerned with the nature or extent of coercive behavior on the part of males or with girls' perceptions that they should comply with others' wishes whether they want to or not (Handler and Gershenson 1985).

5. On the basis of nationally representative data, Moore, Nord, and Peterson (1989) estimate that 7 percent of Americans aged 18 to 22 have experienced at least one episode of nonvoluntary sexual intercourse. Almost half of these incidents occurred before the age of 14. Unfortunately, as these investigators note, the National Survey of Children did not seek to determine the identity of sexual partners, the frequency or duration of the abuse, or if contraceptives were used.

Recent investigators have commented on the frequency of sexual abuse in the life histories of girls who become pregnant in their teens (Dash 1989; Gershenson et al. 1989; Moore, Nord, and Peterson 1989; Butler and Burton 1990; Dryfoos 1990; Boyer and Fine 1992). Moore, Nord, and Peterson (1989), for example, note: "If the prevention of pregnancy and disease is difficult for adults, the obstacles to rational prophylactic behavior among children and adolescents exposed to nonvoluntary sex seem almost insurmountable" (110). Indeed, even when compared with adolescent women who become pregnant but had not been sexually abused, victimized teenagers began intercourse a year earlier and were less likely to practice contraception (Boyer and Fine 1992)

Is there a relation between a history of premature and exploitive sexual experiences with kin and near-kin and premature pregnancy and parenthood? Are girls who have been sexually abused in childhood and early adolescence more often drawn to exploitive males or less able to resist coercion? No clear etiological patterns have yet been established. Nevertheless, clinical and research data do indicate that a significant number of adolescent girls are impregnated by males who are at least five years older (see, for example, Furstenberg, Brooks-Gunn, and Morgan 1987; Musick 1987; Gershenson et al. 1989). Are these pregnancies the result of sexual exploitation or merely of inappropriate dating relationships? Contextual, especially cultural, issues clearly need to be considered in all such instances.

Although those who work in the separate fields of sexual abuse and adolescent pregnancy tend to overlook the potential areas of overlap between the two domains, integrative work could contribute to the development of theory, resulting in a new generation of cross-disciplinary research and program development. In particular, recent studies of the effects of childhood sexual abuse, suggesting altered psychosocial and sexual adjustment on the part of the victims, shed light on the developmental, psychological, and behavioral outcomes of early victimization (see Finkelhor 1984, 1985, 1986; Fromuth 1986; Briere and Runtz 1987; Steele 1986; Conte and Schuerman 1987). These studies offer potentially useful insights into the early sexual environment and social-emotional experiences of females who bear children while still in their teens.

The Ounce of Prevention Fund Research

In considering the clinical evidence on sexual victimization, I reasoned that young women who had experienced abuse would not be in a good position to protect their own young children from becoming victims without considerable supportive and educational, perhaps even therapeutic, intervention. To gain a better sense of the nature and extent of sexual victimization among our population, the Ounce of Prevention Fund staff developed a survey, which was then given to a sample of 445 black, white, and Hispanic pregnant and parenting teens in its programs in Illinois (see Gershenson et al. 1989; Ruch-Ross, Stucki, and Musick 1991).

Sixty-one percent of the sample reported having been sexually abused, and 65 percent of these victims reported abuse by more than one perpetrator. For many of the victims, the abuse was an ongoing situation: although one-quarter of the victims stated that the abuser had committed the act only once, 50 percent reported having been abused between two and ten times, and the remaining 25 percent reported being abused more than ten times. Thirteen respondents (5 percent of the victims) said that they were currently in a sexually abusive situation. Although many girls had been abused early in life, abuse was most common during puberty and early adolescence. The average age of first occurrence was 11.5 years of age.[6]

The findings of this study reveal a pattern whereby girls are sexu-

6. Analyzing data from the second National Incidence Study of Child Abuse and Neglect (NIS-2), Jones and McCurdy (1992) found that sexual abuse occurred at even younger ages. This may be partly the result of the type of samples involved; the Fund's participants are not clients recruited from mental health or social service agencies, but rather voluntary participants in community-based programs, open to all young mothers in a community. Additionally, Jones and McCurdy note that, "surveys based on recollections may inflate the average age because the individual may not be able to remember exactly when the abuse began. Because the NIS-2 includes nonreported cases seen by professionals in addition to those reported to CPS, it may reflect a more accurate picture of the age of the victims of sexual abuse than previous data sources" (212).

ally socialized into passive victim roles by a range of male kin and near kin. This sexual exploitation is facilitated when young girls are left unprotected by their mothers, who are often quite young and may also be in victimizing relationships.[7] In some cases the perpetrator served as the girl's sitter while her mother worked; in other cases he was regularly left alone with her during her pubertal and early adolescent years.

> We had just moved to [a new town]. . . . My mother worked at night. Her boyfriend stayed home. Two weeks after we got there I noticed he was changing. That nice guy that my mother brought home to meet grandma was changing. . . . One night my mother went to work and . . . we were watching TV. . . . Don't you want to sit on the bed instead of that hard floor? I said O.K. Suddenly he began to kiss my face. He tried to put his tongue in my mouth but I ran in the other room. . . . From that night on I slept in [my] clothes. The next day I called my oldest sister back home and told her. She told my mother. When my mother brought it back to me it came out as "You brought it on yourself." At that moment I knew I had to leave. I ran away. . . . I have never forgotten it.

The difference between the ages of victim and perpetrator is a significant marker of an abusive experience. We found that only 18 percent of the abusers were two or fewer years older than the victims, another 18 percent were three to five years older, and 17 percent were six to ten years older. The remaining 46 percent were more than ten years older than their victims. Very large age differences were especially common among victims abused before the age of 14 years.

What is the psychological meaning of the age differences between adolescent girls and their boyfriends? Are there important differences between girls who consistently go with much older men and those who

7. About 23 percent of the victims—but only 8 percent of the nonabused girls— knew that their mothers had suffered abuse when they were younger. However, 56 percent of the abused girls did not know whether their mothers had ever been abused. This suggests that the prevalence of abuse among victims' mothers could be considerably higher.

don't? Are the former more likely to have been sexually exploited by older males when they were younger? What about the characteristics of males who are attracted to much younger females? Are they simply less mature: "My boyfriend is 14 years older than me but he doesn't act it or look it." Or are they exploitive, disturbed, or sexually deviant? If so, what does this tell us about the kinds of relationships these girls are repeatedly drawn to, and how might these men function as revictimizers? Conte (personal communication) comments that sexual offenders seem to have special antennae that pick up signals of vulnerability in the girls they select as victims. These girls tend to be needier and more passive, dependent, depressed, and unhappy. They may be more conspicuous to adults interested in molesting them (Finkelhor 1986). Could a less severe form of this dynamic be at work when older males prefer to date adolescents, particularly younger adolescents?

There were substantial ethnic differences in type of abuse (intercourse versus nonintercourse); perpetrator (father-figure versus other family versus nonfamily); frequency (one time versus multiple experiences); and age of first abuse (younger versus over 9 years of age).[8] For example, white adolescents reported a higher incidence of actual incest than did their black and Hispanic counterparts. Older nonfamily members formed the largest single category of abusers for black preadolescents, and "other father-figures" were the largest single category for Hispanics. For whites, abuse by family members predominates (Ruch-Ross, Stucki, and Musick 1990).

The causes of ethnic differences in the various dimensions of sexual victimization are complex. Some may be the result of structural family factors, such as what men are in and around the girl's home. Other ethnic differences may reflect variations in family dynamics and living conditions. Still others may have to do with cultural differences related to gender socialization, male-female relations, and sexuality. For example, Kelly and Scott (1986) note that some groups have a strong sociocultural tradition that values sexual innocence in females. De-

8. It should be noted, however, that, like Wyatt (1985), we did not find significant differences between African-Americans and whites in the overall severity of abuse nor in the diversity of abusive acts.

scribing a group for female adolescent sexual abuse victims at Los Angeles County Hospital they observe: "Parents of some of the Hispanic group members were opposed to the incorporation of sex education as a treatment component. Despite the fact that their daughters had already been sexually abused and were confused about what had happened to them sexually, these parents still believed that their daughters' sexual ignorance was more important than the resolution of their confusion through education" (161). Unraveling the meanings of ethnic differences in sexual socialization is a formidable task, but one thing is known: there are universal human standards which cannot be violated without heavy personal costs. The psychological antecedents and associated problems of too-early childbearing are the behavioral embodiments of these costs.

In investigating possible links between sexual victimization and adolescent pregnancy, we found that nearly one-quarter (23 percent) of the victims reported becoming pregnant by the perpetrator and that 91 percent of these pregnancies resulted in live births. We found that sexual abuse increases the likelihood of early (14–16 years of age) pregnancy. The findings were clear for both blacks and whites, but somewhat less so for the Hispanic respondents (Ruch-Ross, Stucki, and Musick 1990).

The fathers of the adolescents' children were usually friends or boyfriends; seldom were they immediate family members and only very rarely were they strangers. It is important to keep in mind, however, that many were considerably older than the girls.

Interestingly, 23 percent of the sexually abusive experiences were found to be coercive acts in voluntary situations. That is, the girl may have consented to have intercourse but felt forced or coerced into taking part in or allowing other sexual acts, such as oral or anal sex. The structured data and additional comments from the survey suggest that much of what is known about the sexual attitudes and actions of girls who become adolescent mothers needs to be seriously reconsidered. Although a young woman willingly engages in some sexual activities, she may be coerced or tricked into participating in others that she finds repugnant or debasing: "A guy blackmailed me into having oral sex. He done this twice. At the time I was too young to realize that his threats wouldn't hold water." Such remarks also offer a sense of the psychological context in which many of the children of teens are conceived. They speak eloquently to the character of the relationships themselves.

The findings of the study tend to validate the clinical perceptions that for a sizable group of adolescent mothers, contemporary social and sexual relationships with males may be reenactments of patterns established earlier in life: lessons of victimization learned all too well. The comments of these young women reveal feelings of humiliation and grief that extend beyond the victim to her sisters or other intimates who know or strongly suspect what is happening but feel powerless to stop it. Years later the wounds are still there, leading to ways of thinking and acting that will be very hard to change, even when the girl recognizes how self-destructive and self-limiting they are.

> I was told then to keep my dad from prison I said it was all a lie, but it did happen, my mom couldn't trust me about anything for years after and I was totally rejected by my dad. I wanted a father-daughter relationship. . . . Kids shouldn't have to deal with such a deep thing. . . . When it happened I reached an orgasm, and since then I've had problems in that area of my sex life.

> My uncle did this and when I told on him my mom and dad made me tell him to his face that I told on him. My mom and her sister don't speak any more because of me—but I had to tell.

> One of my male cousin(s) tried to have sexual intercourse with my cousin and she was only 4 years old and he was 18. Every time she sees him she would cry.

> I had to have sex with a pop bottle or the person said he would hurt [me] bad so I did. I was very scared. Ever since the first person I have been scared of most men.

> I was scared to tell anyone. I was afraid of what might happen and no one believing me. I hated myself for it and I did blame myself.

I feel sorry for all these young kids. It happened to me and I know the pain they are going through. I told my grandfather if he ever done something like this to my daughter I will kill him.

It hurts too much to rememory it for me and there are times that I have flash backs of those times.

Something like that take control of your body.

These experiences cause more than emotional vulnerability. The victimized girl learns ways of thinking about men and sex that interact with emotional vulnerability to make her highly prone to repeated victimization. She learns patterns of passivity and helplessness in relation to men. For instance, when asked what they thought they could do to protect their own children from such experiences a number of respondents expressed fatalism or futility in regard to their ability to prevent such occurrences.

I don't know any ways to protect my children because it can happen anywhere.

Ain't nothing I can do.

In their journals the girls wrote that they hope what befell them will never happen to their children. Yet over and over they tell us that it has already happened or may be happening.

i have a little girl named Stefany and it frightans me to leave her with anyone because when I was 5 years old [I was] sexually abused and then as I got older I ask myself why it had to hapen to them [her children].

When it happened to my daughter [her 15-month-old daughter was raped by her boyfriend] it all came back again.

I had a boyfriend who I really trusted. It was really hard for me to believe that he really hurt my daughter.

Can adolescent mothers protect their children if they cannot protect themselves? What will they be able to teach their children when they understand so little themselves? There is another point about sexual exploitation that is critical to understanding the apparent ease with which many young adolescents move into sexual activity. Repeatedly the sexual abuse victims say, "I didn't know there was anything wrong. He said it was a good thing to do." This distortion of personal reality is more profound than it initially appears, because most girls will also tell you that they always had a funny feeling, a lingering suspicion that something was wrong. If the girl dared to voice this concern, the abuser would generally tell her she was mistaken: "It's just a little game." He might threaten to harm her or those she loves, or to shame her in some way should she tell anyone: "No one will believe you, everyone will think it's your fault." "I'll hurt your sister." "I'll beat the hell out of you and your mother." When this happens the girl is effectively cut off from other sources of reality testing. Girls subjected (often repeatedly) to such traumatic and mind-twisting experiences enter adolescence confused about what is and what is not appropriate sexual behavior.

Interacting with an ultimately self-injurious way of thinking is the emotional burden of having gone along with something they sensed might be wrong, the burden of having kept shameful secrets. Despite the high incidence of sexual victimization, especially repeated victimization, 39 percent of the victims had never told anyone about their abuse until the survey, whereas only 18 percent had never reported attempted abuse. Possibly shame or guilt for having allowed themselves to be mistreated keeps abused girls from reporting their experience, whereas those who successfully fend off an attempt feel no such emotions.

> I never felt that I was able to tell anyone about it. For fear of embarrassment and shame I felt as if I were alone.

versus:

> When no one was at home my uncle wanted me to have sex with him. I refused and told my mother and she talked to him and it stopped.

One of the effects of sexual abuse may derive from the victim's sense of complicity in her own victimization, the feeling that she had brought it on herself. A feeling like this is hard to cope with. If the abuse was perpetrated by a trusted older person, the child cannot accept that the act was his fault. To do so she would have to admit that someone in whose care she was entrusted was bad. Instead she begins to alter her self-concept in the direction of badness and helplessness. As Summit (1983) has aptly observed: "Much of what is eventually labeled as adolescent or adult psychopathology can be traced to the natural reactions of a healthy child to a profoundly unnatural and unhealthy parental environment" (184). Altering self-concepts is only one of the many ways sexual victimization thwarts development and murders the soul (Shengold, 1989).

Psychological Consequences of Sexual Victimization

I have some questions. (1) Is it possible for something to happen to you, and no matter what someone say you can't remember? Well, . . . I only remember as far back as when I was 12 yrs. old. I don't remember anything before that! Could it be possible? (2) And is it right for a mother to blame her daughter for being sexually abused at the age of 2?

Dear Diary, I have sort of a little problem which doesn't get in my way that much but—yes it does. . . . It all happened when I was about 7 yrs. old, my uncle sexually abused me. I remember that . . . he would come into my room and as I would sleep he would wake me up by touching me like I didn't want him to. But if I would tell him to stop he wouldn't and if I would tell him that I was going to tell my mom or dad he would threaten to kill me so I had to stay quiet. . . . I also used to stare at the light wishing to call for HELP! But nothing would come out. This went on until I was about 12 yrs. old, then I told my parents but the only thing they did is write a report on him. . . . Sometimes when I see him he tries to be nice to me but I just HATE HIM!

The developmental and psychological effects of sexual victimization depend on the victim's age; how frequently it occurred; how long it lasted; the nature and severity of the acts; the girl's relationship to the abuser; the responses of others (especially her mother); whether force, coercion, trickery, or threat was involved; and whether or not she "participated" (Lusk and Waterman 1988). Another important mediator is the emotional climate of the child's life prior to the abuse (Steele and Alexander 1981; Emslie and Rosenfeld 1983). In this section, I have selected and synthesized the clinical and empirical data that are most relevant for understanding a disadvantaged girl's sexual and reproductive behavior and her desire and capacity for change.

The psychological consequences of sexual victimization are great and varied. Finkelhor and Browne (1985) believe that the combination of four "trauma-causing factors" under one set of circumstances distinguishes sexual abuse from other sources of trauma: traumatic sexualization, betrayal, powerlessness, and stigmatization. Stigmatization is caused, according to these authors, by the blame put on the child by the abuser, her family, the legal system (should matters get this far), or the child herself. Although the effects of events that occur after the abuse is revealed have been documented (see, for example, Rogers and Terry 1984; Tufts New England Medical Center 1984), it has not been demonstrated that the reaction of others is the chief cause of the negative consequences of sexual abuse (Haugaard and Reppucci 1988). Even without overt stigmatization by family, peers, or society, however, girls may self-stigmatize, especially if they had suspected that what they were doing might be wrong or if they had derived some emotional or physical pleasure from the sexual activity.

Each of the factors identified by Finkelhor and Browne "alters a child's cognitive or emotional orientation to the world and causes trauma by distorting the child's self-concept, world view, or affective capacities" (Finkelhor 1987). Such altered concepts of self and others are the result of adaptations and compromises that were necessary for psychological survival. Because of the functions they once served in reducing conflict and anxiety, these concepts and their accompanying actions are likely to be strongly maintained and resistant to change. Embedded in the girl's character structure, they color and control her interactions with males. They are deeper and more complex than attitudes or values.

If embroiling a girl in sexually precocious behavior confuses her about what is and what is not appropriate behavior, the invasion of her body makes her feel powerless. Repeated violation of personal boundaries is a kind of brainwashing. It saps the will, destroys self-efficacy, and leads to a perception of self as a victim. People who feel like victims and think of themselves as victims tend to act like victims. Time after time they find themselves in a one-down position in their relationships. The people most likely to find themselves in this position are females, and the relationships in which they feel this way are most commonly those with males.

> My boyfriend is much older than I and I sometimes feel like if he really abused me, I knew what was happening between us but I was always afraid to say no to him, but I think that I love him very much, but then again when our Heart-to-Heart groups started and I learned that it was about child abuse I started to kind of hate him for what he done to me, but yet I know that I still love him deep down inside.

Females have stronger affiliative needs than males do and greater vulnerability around relationships. Adolescent females have love relationships that are more intense and interpersonally oriented than those of adolescent males (Maccoby 1984). Beginning in adolescence, girls have more problems in such areas as body image, self-esteem, and depression (Petersen and Hamburg 1986; Petersen and Ebata 1987). This combined with manipulation of trust and vulnerability, disregard for her well-being, lack of support and protection from those who are supposed to support and protect her, invasion of body territory through force or trickery, and fear and helplessness (Finkelhor and Browne 1986; Hartman and Burgess 1988) results in a significantly heightened vulnerability to males. An increased salience of sexual issues,[9] misconceptions about sexual behavior and norms, and confusion of sex with love and care-giving—all hallmarks of sexual victimization—further set the stage for precocious and compulsive sexual behavior. It seems probable that in a self-perpetuating, person-

9. There is evidence that for some girls, heightened sexual activity is counterphobic, serving to make them feel that they are in control rather than merely passive victims (DeYoung 1984). In other cases heightened sexual activity seems to be the result of having been prematurely eroticized (Yates 1982).

ally damaging cycle, later sexual behavior that replicates previous exploitation could potentiate and exacerbate effects that might otherwise subside over time. Is this promiscuity, or is it a form of revictimization?

One might say that an adolescent surely knows what is happening and should be able to resist an exploitive advance. Yet the capacity to resist is poorly understood, and there is plentiful evidence of an association between childhood sexual abuse and adolescent sexual activity, at least within high-risk populations. For example, Polit, White and Morton (1990) found that adolescent girls who have been sexually abused are significantly more likely than others to engage in voluntary sexual intercourse. They hold more sexually permissive attitudes, are younger at first intercourse, and have intercourse more frequently than adolescents from the same population who have not experienced such abuse.[10] Other researchers have found that girls who have been sexually abused are generally more sexually active and engage in a wider range of sexual activities (Herman 1981; Silbert and Pines 1981; Brooks 1982; Fisher 1983; DeYoung 1984; Fromuth 1986). The self-hate many victims feel is translated into self-punishment in a variety of ways (Lusk and Waterman 1986). Women abused as children appear to be much more susceptible to later sexual and physical violence than those who were not abused (Briere and Runtz 1987; Russell 1984). Findings linking child sexual abuse and later sexual acting-out appear in a number of retrospective studies of prostitutes (Spencer 1978; Vander Mey and Neff 1982). It would not be surprising if a history of sexual fondling by a significant (and often beloved) father-figure could lead some girls to seek out similar experiences, and to confuse love and sex. Clearly, intervention needs to be aimed at helping such adolescents to differentiate the two—not a simple task.

So let's say you have a boyfriend and you're 15 years old and he tells you he loves you and is always gonna be here for you and finally you let him talk you into having sex and he leaves you. Is that abuse?

10. These authors remark that the findings of their study need to be replicated since their high-risk sample (teenage girls receiving child protective services because of abuse and neglect) was not representative of a general population of adolescents.

Other consequences of early sexual exploitation create challenges for programs attempting to bring about change in sexual behavior or relationships with males. These consequences also help to explain certain connections between problems in interpersonal domains and in the worlds of school and work. In what Hartman and Burgess (1988) call the "trauma encapsulation phase" (445), the child uses certain coping and defensive mechanisms to regulate the anxiety, fear, and danger invoked by the abuse. Defenses such as dissociation, denial, repression, fragmentation of a sense of self, arousal disharmony, and splitting are called on to help her regulate her often overwhelming responses to what is happening.

If left to her own devices, over time the victim will reformulate the events and her reactions to them using the defenses she has called on to cope with the trauma. Hartman and Burgess (1988) comment that subsequently there is "disturbance in the self-comforting, caring and protective functions of the child's self-system. Attachment to others, social values, and the ability to take pleasure are weakened" (447). Defensive silence insulates the child from the emotional pain of the abuse, sealing it off from her everyday life, keeping it out of her awareness. Although she may no longer feel the pain, it rules many of her most significant actions and interactions. She cannot easily change what she does because she does not truly know what she does, let alone why she does it. What is out of our awareness is by far the most difficult for us to change (see, for example, Main and Goldwyn 1984; Egeland and Erickson 1990; Egeland, Jacobvitz, and Sroufe 1988).

The emotional energy required to suppress severe emotional trauma depletes the girl's psychological resources. It does more than simply distort her sense of right and wrong; because the chronic psychic drain interferes with her ability to focus and concentrate (Conte and Schuerman 1987), it disrupts her cognitive and academic development. In looking at the effects of sexual abuse, Johnston (1979) and Shaw and Meier (1983) found that school-aged children who had been sexually abused had shorter attention spans and more difficulty concentrating on tasks. At the same time, these children feel powerless, perceiving a lack of control in many situations (Jiles 1981). Summit

(1983) observes that sexually abused children tend to develop a "help-less victim" mentality that carries over into other aspects of their lives.

The combination of scant psychic energy for the normal tasks of childhood and adolescence, poorer attention capacities, and "learned helplessness" (Seligman 1975) could be hypothesized to lower cognitive and academic potential. By distorting the young person's internal working models of self and others, sexual exploitation drives her toward self-defeat and away from self-competence. Although the expressions of fatalism and problems of organizing themselves for the purposes of reaching educational or vocational goals so often noted with disadvantaged young women are not solely the outcomes of sexual victimization, they seem to be at least in part the result of having been used by others as a developing child. Thus, the consequences of deviant sexual socialization can go beyond the realm of sexual behavior to influence functioning in the worlds of school and work.

Dependency and Affiliative Needs

When a girl has been unprotected in her family and socialized into sexuality prematurely and inappropriately it is not surprising if she later, during adolescence, feels helpless and unable to control that aspect of her life. It seems plausible that this learned helplessness in combination with a heightened vulnerability to males is implicated in failures to resist sexual advances.[11] Unmet dependency or affiliative needs create additional vulnerability by supplying the affective "glue" that fixes such behaviors, binding them to the young person's developing character.

One of the premier tasks of adolescence is to relinquish the early

11. A failure to contracept can also be viewed as stemming in part from a sense that one's body is not really one's own. The capacity for self-care is largely derived from the internalization of experiences of being cared for and protected by caring others. Insistence that a partner contracept is predicated on the ability to assert oneself and to stand up for one's rights. The diminished sense of personal worth and generalized hopelessness that characterizes many former victims would mitigate against such self-care and assertiveness. This same hopelessness and lowered personal efficacy may also manifest itself in a later inability to protect her child from harm at the hands of boyfriends or other temporary surrogate fathers.

parent-child relationship. Although the bond between child and parent remains strong throughout life, and although the adolescent still requires nurturance and guidance (for example, Blos 1979; Grotevant and Cooper 1983; Muus 1988), the parent-child relationship is normally transformed during these years. This transformation, built on the earlier relationship, enables the adolescent to move toward greater independence and adult life goals and relationships. Many needs that were previously fulfilled by the parents must be given up so that new modes of relating can be established. Under even the best of family circumstances, this transformation is experienced as a separation, signifying a potential loss. Thus, it can be understood as a normal but nonetheless powerful stressor that contributes to a sense of disequilibrium as it interacts with the biological and social changes that are the hallmarks of this transitional period.

What will be the nature of the adolescent individuation process when earlier dependency needs were inadequately met? Weissman and Klerman (1977) and Rutter (1986) report that the incidence of depression increases during adolescence, particularly for girls. If adolescent girls normally have heightened psychological vulnerability during this period, how much more vulnerable might they be when burdened by unmet dependency needs? How are they to manage the challenges of these years while carrying such burdens?

The teenage mothers I know are a heterogeneous group, yet they share certain common qualities that cut across geographic, ethnic, and, to some extent, economic lines. Chief among these qualities is a profound psychological neediness, the legacy of severe and often protracted emotional deprivation, beginning early and continuing through the adolescent years.

> I felt I was a failure at everything. Exspecially as a daughter. My mother and I never got along and probably never will. Because my mother wanted a boy first and was really disappointed when they said "Mrs. D. you have a beautiful baby girl." I was told that my mother try to smother me when I was just a few months old. My grandma caught her and threw her off of me. I will never live that tragedy down.

I would be scared for . . . Brian [her son] to love anybody. The
reason is because everyone I've loved I've lost. I don't want him
to have a life like that.

Whereas in past generations many poor, young, unmarried women
were able to mother their children adequately—with a great deal of
family assistance—for a variety of reasons this is far less often the case
today. It is surely not the case for most of the adolescents in Ounce of
Prevention Fund programs, who have family histories marked by multiple separations from mothers (and often grandmothers), multiple
caretakers, and insufficient nurturing for as far back as they can remember. Frequently this continues into adolescence. As children
these girls had to share the limited attention of their young single
mothers with other children, boyfriends, and so on. They recollect
their mothers as chronically worn out, depressed, or totally preoc-
cupied with their own lives—that is, emotionally unavailable or ne-
glectful and frequently perceived as perpetually angry at her children.
Was this because she saw them as burdens or as victimizing, robbing
her of her youth, her freedom, her future? Clearly the normal needs of
children, especially young children, can seem overwhelming when the
parent has a scarcity of psychological as well as material resources.

Depressed, angry, or unavailable mothers; multiple separations;
multiple caregivers—this picture of childhood cannot possibly bode
well for developing a robust sense of self or feelings of personal worth.
More advantaged teens from troubled homes, with substantial economic and social resources to buffer the effects of family disruption,
discord, or dysfunction, bend and break under the pressures of this
transitional period, involving themselves in harmful behaviors in their
struggles to fill unmet dependency and affiliative needs. How can we
realistically expect poor adolescents to negotiate the tasks of these
years successfully when they lack so many of the structural supports
available to middle-class teens? For poor adolescent girls, psychological vulnerability is far more dangerous. Without the mitigating effects
of social and economic supports, without other paths to self-worth,
they will find the pulls of potentially harmful behaviors virtually irre-
sistible if they promise to satisfy unfulfilled longings and to make up

for past hurts. Young females arriving at early adolescence with unmet dependency and affiliative needs are at considerable risk for exploitation and early initiation of sexual activity. How can these girls resist men's sexual advances if there is the implicit (or explicit) promise of love, closeness, or being cared for? Unfortunately, as described above, many girls meet the tasks and temptations of adolescence with even greater potential for exploitation because of the nature of their past (and often continuing) relationships with males in their families and social networks.

The Message for Interventionists

If, as seems to be the case, a sizable group of girls have already experienced some form of sexual exploitation before they reach their teens, do the currently proposed programs and interventions address the real problem? Can we reasonably expect family-life education, school-based health clinics, or "increased life options" programs (such as job training, skill building, education) to change sexual behaviors and attitudes acquired through developmentally inappropriate sexual socialization? Does it seem likely that what has been learned through traumatic sexualization can be easily unlearned?

Girls who have unresolved childhood issues around dependence and affiliation are poorly prepared to negotiate the complex developmental tasks of adolescence, particularly those that revolve around relationships. Continually seeking the care and nurturance denied them as children, they have difficulty detaching from their mothers and individuating in developmentally appropriate ways. It is difficult to relinquish what one has never really had. Hope keeps one searching, perhaps for a lifetime. Sexuality presents one possible arena in which to act out ambivalence about growing up and psychologically separating from the mother. At the same time it seems to offer the girl, especially the girl who has been without a caring father or father-figure, the chance to be part of a loving, need-fulfilling relationship. When forces within the home and community create and then feed on psychic and developmental needs and vulnerabilities, and when structural factors close off other viable, psychologically satisfying routes for self-expression, sexual behavior may be the only arena available to the girl. Under these conditions, the active avoidance of early sexual activity places an enormous burden on her personal strengths and inner resources, a burden that frequently proves to be too great. This is more likely to be the case for adolescent girls made especially vulnerable by premature, exploitive sexual experiences.

One does not have to look very far to find evidence of possible factors in the home and community that potentiate other vulnerabilities and promote early sexual involvement. In addition to the considerable pressure from males to engage in sex (Anderson 1989), there are the examples set by a girl's sexually active mother and older siblings, activities of which she may be all too aware because of the crowded living quarters characteristic of poverty. Another and perhaps more developmentally relevant problem is the lack of direction and guidance in regard to sexual decision-making and behavior, both before and during the adolescent period.

Although few parents are fully comfortable in the role of sex educator and value setter, the consequences are more serious for disadvantaged young females. More advantaged families live in environments that provide a variety of safeguards not available to poor families. More often there are two parents in the home or at least a divorced father willing to share the burdens of childrearing with the mother. There are also fewer external pressures for early, unprotected sex, a far broader range of community activities for young people, better schools, more counselors and therapists, greater opportunities, more and better after-school jobs, more easily reachable goals and hopes for the future—all of which help to keep adolescents on track or to get them back on when they fall off. In middle-class communities, everything does not rest on the shoulders of the parent as it does in poorer communities. Poor mothers today have to be far more than "average expectable" parents in order to keep their children out of trouble; they must be exceptional (for example, Clark 1983; Comer 1988; Hans, Musick, and Jagers 1992). In poor communities even exceptional parents often cannot protect their daughters from becoming teenage mothers. The reality is, however, that many a 14-year-old is being raised by her barely 30-year-old mother, a mother who is having numerous difficulties in her childrearing role because of the strains of day-to-day survival, her unresolved conflicts around men, and her too-early parenthood.

Effective intervention strategies will need to be like exceptional parents; not merely good, but very good. This means they must somehow offer restorative as well as supportive relationships, nurturance as well as knowledge. If we hope to transform young people's lives we are clearly going to have to deal with sex more consistently and straightforwardly. But interventions must go beyond that. In order to prevent or change self-injurious ways of behaving and relating, we must also present adolescents with new models of relating and give them firm guidance around the relationships they seek. Growth-fostering interventions, like caring families, must have well-articulated expectations for young people and provide the means to internalize and fulfill these expectations. Finally, like good parents, interventionists must be prepared to do this when these young people are children, when they are preadolescents, and when they are adolescents; over and over and over again.

To increase the chances for the highest-risk girls, interventions not only must increase quantitatively (for example, longer or more frequent interventions); they will also have to change qualitatively. In addition to the multiple noxious influences of growing up in poverty, the gender schemas of many girls who become or are at risk of becoming adolescent mothers are rooted in repeated experiences of personal harm at the hands of those who should be their protectors. These gender schemas—interpretive frameworks, ways of seeing and thinking about self and others, especially males—contribute not only to feminine identity, choice of partner(s), and sexual behavior, but to the decision to have a child and to the desire and willingness to strive for a productive life. In order to alter such schemas, practitioners, whether they are educators, vocational trainers, health or social service workers, need to incorporate techniques and approaches that are more therapeutically informed. Psychological defenses—such as denial, fragmentation, and dissociation—that have been used to deal with the anxiety, fear, and danger provoked by abusive upbringing are antithetic to forward movement in terms of breaking cycles of self-defeat and self-destruction. A childhood of mistreatment disrupts development of the integrative personality functions that afford us knowledge of ourselves—especially of why we do what we do. For those who are already off to a bad start, there can be no genuine change without such knowledge.

No strategy will be able to significantly alter an adolescent's self-defeating sexual, interpersonal, or reproductive behaviors unless it offers her developmentally appropriate and emotionally meaningful ways to be different from what she is and to do differently. No strategy can make her into a sexually and socially responsible individual until it provides realistic alternatives that are as psychologically satisfying as the modes of feeling and behaving she is being asked to give up— modes of feeling and behaving that are like those of her mother, her sisters, her friends. At present we do not fully comprehend the emotional costs for the girl of changing the way she relates to men, the contingencies of such change, or the circumstances under which it can be initiated, sustained, and internalized sufficiently to have a positive effect on her life. This is what is meant by a "motivational challenge": enabling a young woman to take the considerable social and psychological risks entailed in choosing and sticking to her own upwardly directed path.

Adolescents' sexual and reproductive behaviors—the target of so many intervention efforts—are both cause and consequence of the constraints and influences of life on the fringe. The life of a young woman whose identity (and thus her energy) revolves around pleasing and appealing to males will be governed by these relationships. This girl is truly a prisoner of love. Such a concept may have a less ominous side when we look at the life of a more advantaged woman, one who has the skills and education, the resources and supports, to make it in other spheres of functioning. She may be a woman who "loves too much," but she is also a teacher, a doctor, a woman out in the broader world. For girls who lack such personal, social, and material resources, there are effectively no other spheres of functioning, there is no broader world.

a lot of girls I've seen, when they're teenagers and they start out they fall for the first guy that gives them the line that they love em and they treat em right . . . and you fall in love with them and everything else don't matter to you. All that matters to you is you and him and having his baby and that's it. That's all that matters.

Most of my friends they all have the same relationships that me and Miguel had. We all end up getting beaten up and hurt and left and gone back with them again.

My body, I'm not lying, it's gone! Messed up already. . . . [My mind] it's blocked, you know, and it's so affected my relationship that I'm still with this person that gave [gonorrhea] to me. . . . I don't know why, but I'm just still with him.

Brian has hurt me for the last time. (I think.)

Five

Wanting a Baby, Having a Baby

Insidiously, unhurriedly, the beatitude of pregnant females spread through me. . . . This purring contentment, this euphoria—how give a name either scientific or familiar to this state of preservation?—must certainly have penetrated me, since I have not forgotten it and am recalling it even now, when life can never again bring me plentitude.
—Colette, *L'Etoile Vesper*

O little one,
making you
has centered my lopsided life.
—Erica Jong,"For Molly"

I made you to find me
—Anne Sexton, "The Double Image"

I n this chapter the focus shifts from the psychology of adolescent sexuality and relations to men to the psychology of adolescent childbearing—that is, to the roots of the desire for a child and the emotional benefits of becoming a mother. The emphasis will be on first-time parenthood; repeated childbearing, in certain ways a separate phenomenon, will be examined in chapter 7.

> You know by it being the first one. . . . I mean, if a person already have a child, two or three to them it's just another child, I guess. . . . But by it being your first one, you are kind of thrilled and excited about having it.

A girl's pregnancy is the result of her sexual behavior, yet the motives that govern sexuality and male-female relationships are not the same as those that govern the bearing of children. This is one more manifestation of the complexity of adolescent childbearing, one more reason it cannot be prevented by simple means. Examining the emotional logic behind an adolescent's desire for a child helps us understand why other life options pack so little motivational punch for these young women. Even if one does not hold to the notion of a mothering instinct (Benedek 1973), ovulation clearly signals that females are primed for reproduction. If no motivational barriers intervene between a girl and her reproductive potential that potential will be fulfilled—sooner, rather than later.

Psychological Factors and Intervention

Evidence to date indicates only minimal success at interrupting cycles of teenage childbearing (Dryfoos 1990), and while certain social and economic conditions have clearly worsened in recent years (see, for example, Wilson 1989; Ellwood 1988), failures to prevent or reduce the incidence of adolescent childbearing cannot be attributed solely to these structural variables.[1] Social and economic theories do not address the factors in a girl's psychological history that draw her to early

1. In this chapter I am concerned primarily with factors that affect the *conceptualization* of interventions; those that influence the *implementation* of interventions will be examined in chap. 7.

parenthood, nor do they explain why some intervention strategies are promising whereas others barely scratch the surface.

If theories concerned with larger social issues are not directly useful in explaining why girls want to be mothers at 14, 15, or 16, or in designing interventions that persuade them to want to be something else, neither are the more sophisticated and comprehensive ecological models of behavior (for example, Belsky 1980). These models, which are more psychological and developmental in nature, encompass a multitude of influences, from the most micro (individual) to the most macro (societal). However, as Crittenden and Ainsworth (1989) observe, such models, "replace naive simplicity with infinite complexity" (433). Noting that it is probably impossible to specify all the causes in a single case, let alone for large numbers, they comment, "What is needed is a way to narrow our view to a workable model that can both explain the pattern of occurrences and nonoccurrences and describe the process by which [it] is transmitted from one person to another" (1989, 433–434). These authors see a need to focus on "critical causes"—that is, on factors which, if changed, would lead to improvements. If, to date, we have been largely unsuccessful in interrupting cycles of teenage childbearing, it is at least partly because we lack meaningful theories of its critical causes. Although Crittenden and Ainsworth are writing about the relationship between insecure attachment and child maltreatment, the critical cause approach holds promise for the issue of adolescent childbearing as well. Indeed, child maltreatment, attachment problems, and adolescent childbearing are in many ways interrelated and overlapping phenomena, both in terms of the way the young mother performs her childrearing role and in terms of the reasons she was drawn to motherhood in the first place.

The Desire for a Child

If adolescents did not want babies, they would not have them. But they do want them. Indeed, many seem to fear infertility, craving pregnancy and motherhood.

> I like it when people notice I'm having a baby. It gives me a good feeling inside and makes me feel important.

Baby will be here any day now And I will be a proud Teen Mom with my head held high.

When I was about 11 or 12 I was very lonely so then I went to having sex and then I got pregnant and that was my way of curing my loneliness [by] having kids. That's the best thing I have in this world and that's my kids.

I love being a mother. I want to have a couple more.

You're not really messing your life up when you get pregnant. . . . You can still do a little of this and that

I mean, just the thought of it. It's just yours. Nobody can take it from you.

Being pregnant is great. I feel sorry for men because they can never feel what a woman does when she's pregnant.

Dear Kimmie, I lov you. You make me feel special and needed. With out you my life was boring and almost meaningless.

If I didn't want him he wouldn't be here in this world.

This desire to be pregnant and to have a child makes the prevention of adolescent childbearing a formidable task. Although it is not the primary cause of adolescent motherhood, it is one of the strongest threads in the fabric of early fertility. And so the questions become: What is available to disadvantaged young women that is as emotionally satisfying as the idea (if not always the reality) of motherhood? What is worth the struggle and risks entailed in trying to be something else? What other pathways lead so directly to achievement, identity, and intimacy? These are motivational questions, psychological questions. Although it may be influenced by such external factors as restricted occupational opportunities, the desire for a child is very much a psychological issue.

Whenever young mothers or mothers-to-be speak of their wish for a child or describe their feelings, they lay before us the psychology of adolescent childbearing, revealing the psychological rewards of early pregnancy and parenthood. These rewards stem from the gratification of deep and powerful human needs, needs that are particularly salient during a developmental period that reverberates with issues of change, separation, and potential loss. The psychological forces that promote and perpetuate adolescent parenthood are strengthened through interaction with the social and economic circumstances that characterize the lives of poor young women. At a time when a girl feels as though everything is uncertain, motherhood promises to reduce emotional conflict and to resolve issues that seem to be unresolvable.

Within the motivational tapestry of adolescent childbearing there are striking diversities as well as patterns. Developmental tasks differ for each of the subphases of adolescence (Diamond 1983), and individual life experiences vary from girl to girl. The psychological benefits of teenage motherhood will therefore be felt differently. Through pregnancy and parenthood, an adolescent girl can, for example, recreate a close mother-child bond to heal the pain provoked by conflict with her own parents (Brazelton and Cramer 1990); take on adult status but avoid the potentially fragmenting experience of individuating and becoming too psychologically separate from her mother (Musick 1987); obtain the emotional sustenance she didn't get as a child; extend her dependent bond with her mother through identification with her baby (Osofsky, Osofsky, and Diamond 1988), whom she fervently hopes her mother will love and care for; find opportunities for competence in a new and highly valued role around which she can reorganize herself (Hamburg 1986; Burton 1990), developing a new identity through the process of becoming a parent (Bibring et al. 1961; Benedek 1970; Shanok 1990); and fulfill her mother's spoken or unspoken desire for the "second chance" provided by grandparenthood (Ladner and Gourdine 1984; Burton 1990). By giving her child what she did not get, she hopes she can redo the past, master its pain, and loosen its hold over her life. Now she will have someone of her own, someone whose childhood she will make happier than hers was, someone who will return her love.

These are only a few of the psychological benefits that can accrue to an adolescent mother. There is also the comforting feeling of being like her mother or her sisters and friends, many of whom are already pregnant or raising young children. By bearing a child, an adolescent girl can also avoid the considerable risks of change. She can escape the psychological penalties of attempting to "do it better" or differently than most of the emotionally significant people in her life. Again a question: What do social programs offer that is worth the emotional costs of such change?

Psychological factors play key roles in creating and later intensifying risk for disadvantaged adolescent females, leading them down dangerous roads where emotional comfort is won at the cost of personal growth. Although these factors may influence sexual and reproductive behavior at various levels and across various domains, they serve some of their most critical and potentially damaging roles in governing the desire and capacity for change. In a milieu where adolescent childbearing is ubiquitous and other avenues for self-enhancement are absent, questions of whether and when to have children—and especially more children—represent developmental and psychological moments of truth. From a psychological perspective, having a baby can be viewed both as a reaction to fears of ego-threatening change and as a concrete means of gaining a respite (if only a temporary one) from the psychic pain of these fears. Bearing a child can be the adolescent's way of saying, "No thanks. I'll just stay as I am . . . at least for now."

Deciding to "Keep"

Well, when I found out I was going to get an abortion, because at 17 years old and havin sex and then turn around and have a baby and I've got two more years of school, I just wasn't ready. But then, I don't know what came over me, but you know it's not right. It's not the child's fault that it shouldn't have the right to live. So the mother's gonna kill it. So I just kept it.

It's hard not to love and want your child after you have carried it and gave birth to him or her.

It was easy for me. My grandmother said "You give the baby away and you leave home." So I'm keeping mine. [laughs]

They tried talking me into getting an abortion. . . . I mean you just can't like go and get an abortion and just put it out of your mind cause you go and get it and then you're going to sit after it's done and you're going to think about it and then you're going to start feeling bad. I'll tell you me and my family are strictly against it. I came once to try to get an abortion one time but I couldn't go through with it.

Approximately one million adolescent pregnancies occur each year. In 1987, 36 percent of these ended in abortions, 14 percent in miscarriages, and the remaining 50 percent in live births (Forrest and Singh 1990). Once a birth has occurred, very few adolescent mothers will opt to relinquish the child for adoption (Musick, Waddill, and Handler 1984; Bachrach 1986).[2]

People often express surprise that so many adolescents elect to keep their babies, considering how few pregnancies appear to have been planned. Although young mothers may initially say they were very upset to find themselves pregnant,[3] later, as they come to know you

2. Only a handful of pregnant adolescents seriously consider adoption, let alone go through with it (Musick, Waddill, and Handler 1984; Bachrach 1986). For example, sources estimate that 93 to 95 percent of all unmarried adolescent mothers elect to keep and raise their children, a percentage that has increased substantially in the fairly recent past (Hayes et al. 1987; Kalmuss, Namerow, and Cushman 1991). There has been a dramatic decline in adoption placements since the late 1960s, but precise estimates of the number and proportion of teenagers who elect adoption are impossible because there is no national system for collecting this information (Hayes et al. 1987). Also, as Kalmuss, Namerow, and Cushman (1991) point out, "The estimate of babies placed for adoption may be biased downward, as some women who have placed may not report those pregnancies in an interview. This selective underreporting of pregnancies that result in adoption is similar to that of pregnancies resulting in abortion" (17). Although precise figures are not available, the legalization of abortion and the increased social acceptance of unwed motherhood appear to have made adoption a relatively rare event for both white and black adolescent mothers. Data concerning adoption of children born to Hispanic adolescent mothers are not available (Hayes et al. 1987).

3. Michaels (1988), commenting on a 1981 Guttmacher Institute finding that only 9 percent of pregnant adolescents report having purposively decided to have a baby, observes that strong motivation to have a child can exist in the subjective experience of an adolescent who would not make a deliberate decision to have a child. And, "even if motivational processes do not play a major role in the conception, as the pregnancy progresses, motivational processes are certainly involved in decisions about pregnancy outcome (i.e., whether to keep the baby, place the baby for adoption, or have an abortion)" (39). Furstenberg (1976) found that among a sample of low-income urban clinic patients, only 20 percent of the adolescents reported that they were pleased to learn of their pregnancy. Another 20 percent had

better and trust you more, they often change their story, conceding that they are glad to be having a baby (Dash 1989). Some pregnant adolescents tell you they are surprised but nonetheless pleased to be having a baby, while others say they are upset but behave as though they are pleased. Usually their facial expressions and body language give their not-so-secret secret away. For a variety of reasons, pregnancy and parenthood are highly valued by adolescent mothers and mothers-to-be, at least while their children are babies.[4] An unplanned child is not necessarily an unwanted one.

The literature on adolescent childbearing is filled with references to the tendency of adolescents to deny their pregnancies until it is too late for an abortion.[5] The absence of other realistic or meaningful life roles has been implicated in the choice to have and raise a child. The preference for keeping the infant is thought to be most common among girls

---

mixed feelings, and the remainder were disappointed or upset. There are many reasons that adolescents might say they were upset even if they were not. They might also act upset, but for those electing to continue the pregnancy, this generally lasts briefly, often only until they have told their mothers. Age and developmental stage differences can be expected to affect this variable as well, with younger girls feeling more actual distress and panic. It is hard to know, since there has been so little research on this topic.

4. There is some evidence that as the children get older, less cute, and more mischievous, some mothers indirectly express regret at having had children so young. For instance, Osofsky (personal communication 1990) found that some adolescent mothers report that the pregnancy was planned while the baby is still small but, when asked the same question a year later, many will say that it was unplanned.

5. Sandven and Resnick (1990) found that half of their sample of fifty-four teen mothers reported that they had not realized they were pregnant until the second trimester. Although menstrual cycles may be irregular, particularly in early adolescence, such self-reports should be regarded with some skepticism. It is more likely that some of these teens suspect they might be pregnant but are ashamed to admit it. Acknowledging pregnancy somehow makes it seem to have been planned. The defensive style of adolescents also needs to be taken into account (Hatcher 1973; Blum and Resnick 1982). There is no doubt that a number of girls who might consider abortion do not have access to abortion services (Guttmacher Institute 1991/92). However, this was rarely the case among the two samples upon which this book is based. Almost none of these young mothers and mothers-to-be said they had their children because they could not get an abortion. On the contrary, many spoke of having set up an appointment for an abortion and being unable to go through with it.

with poorer basic skills and histories of school failure (Hayes et al. 1987; Dryfoos 1990). In this view, when these girls get pregnant, they opt for motherhood because it offers them a ready-made role and ready-made functions, a sense of what to be and what to do. This accurately describes the situation of a large group of adolescent girls, but it has only limited utility in explaining why some talented and competent girls get pregnant in their early teens and choose to keep their babies. Nor does it fully account for the fact that some adolescents continue to choose childbearing and childrearing when they have what appear to be viable life alternatives.

Cultural issues are frequently said to influence the decision to keep a child, specifically the aversion to abortion among Hispanic and some religious African-American families and the reluctance of African-American families to relinquish a child for formal adoption:[6]

It is the most beautiful thing in my life to have a child. Many people think differently. They think it is O.K. to have an abortion. We think God will punish us. [Hispanic mother]

We believe God has given us this child and you must have it.

Cultural prohibitions against abortion or adoption commonly manifest themselves as pressures from adult family members, particularly the girl's mother or her grandmother, to keep a child. Such pressures emanate from deeply held cultural values that, in essence, convey to the girl, "The family always takes care of its own," or "*We* don't believe in abortion. Nobody should ever get rid of a child." Particularly among African-American families, pressures to keep a child frequently find expression in such seemingly punitive sayings as, "If you can lay down and do it, you can lay down and have it," or "You made your bed hard, you're going to have to lay in it."[7]

6. It is important to remember that until quite recently very few couples were willing to adopt black infants. Pregnant girls and their families were justifiably wary that a child given up for adoption would spend his or her life in a series of foster or institutional placements. In addition, African-American families have traditionally relied on informal adoption (Ladner 1977; Martin and Martin 1978; Sandven and Resnick 1990).

7. Barbara Bowman (personal communication) sees the grandmother as sending a double message when she says these things to her daughter. In one sense such a

Cultural prohibitions may explain why some girls keep their babies while others do not, but it is also possible that such prohibitions serve merely as excuses for a young woman to do what she wanted to do anyway. Views about the role of social or cultural sanctions in the adolescent's decision to keep the child generally exclude the girl's longing for a baby and the enhancement of self that is conferred by motherhood. They are a part of the picture, but only a part.

Adolescent mothers frequently say that they had a child to hold onto a boyfriend or that they declined abortion or adoption at their boyfriend's urging. Still, the direction of male influence is anything but certain. We do not know if pressure from males is predominantly direct, indirect, or some combination of both. Since many of these girls are so acutely sensitive to male desires, it may in some cases simply be intuited. For instance, Dash (1989) found that females appear to initiate unprotected sexual activity as often as their partners, basically, he believes, because of their desire for a child. If this is so, pressure from males to keep rather than to adopt or abort could be conceptualized as supporting or buttressing a decision the young woman has already made.

Interviewer: Did you think about an abortion?
Adolescent mother: At first I did, but my boyfriend, anyway, he wasn't gonna let me get no abortion anyway.
Interviewer: Do you think he wanted you to have a baby?
Adolescent mother: Oh, he didn't. But, no, he said he didn't. He said it was a mistake I guess, but I don't think he wanted me to get it . . . pregnant.

From a somewhat different perspective, Anderson (1989) portrays disadvantaged young men as pressing girls to have babies in order to prove their manhood, not an unexpected response considering their lack of family-sustaining jobs or job prospects. In his view, girls obtain

---

remark is meant to be hurtful, even punitive. It is saying, "You will have to go through with this and face the consequences of your actions." In another sense, the grandmother is saying, "You are going to be able to do this. You *can* master this challenge." These personal messages from mother to daughter are embedded in the larger, impersonal, cultural message that says that abortion is wrong.

a sort of secondary or indirect benefit from succumbing to boys' promises of love and security. Although "they often end up pregnant and abandoned, they are eligible for a limited but sometimes steady income in the form of welfare which may allow them to establish their own households and at times, attract other men in need of money" (59). It is possible that when welfare assistance is available, a pregnant adolescent is more likely to choose single motherhood over adoption or abortion (Moore and Caldwell 1977; Hayes et al. 1987). But financial assistance may simply serve as one more reason for her to have the baby she has already set her heart on, in much the same way that pressure from the child's father reinforces but does not create her desire to raise the child she has conceived. This seems highly probable when one considers that pressure from male partners for adoption or abortion may be experienced as painful or annoying but is repeatedly ignored.

> My baby's father kept me upset because he wanted me to give up my baby. . . . We broke up after I refused several times to say yes I agree lets put it up for adoption after I have it.

Weakening the argument for male influence as a primary or central force in the decision to keep a baby is the fact that girls break up with the fathers of their babies with great regularity, often while they are pregnant or soon after the birth. Although we tend to think that the father abandons the teenage mother and her child, the reverse can be true as well. In one common scenario, the new mother or mother-to-be quarrels with the baby's father over minor issues, often with advice and encouragement from her mother. This helps to destabilize a relationship that is probably not very secure to begin with. Eventually the girl ends the relationship, or it ends by mutual consent. How then do males exert power over females' choices in regard to adoption or abortion if they are so frequently and so quickly out of the picture? Perhaps it would be better to conceptualize male influence as being less direct, serving more as an after-the-fact rationalization or as an added reason for keeping the child.

Boyfriends appear to be less influential than grandmothers-to-be in decisions about pregnancy and parenthood, especially in regard to a first child. In some families, Burton (1990) found, "Grandmothers take over the mother/father role before young men have a chance to get out of the starting blocks" (21). This is particularly true when men are financially unable to contribute to the maintenance of the family (Hogan 1987; McLanahan 1988). As the primary identification figures and the initial and still principal transmitters of values, grandmothers (or grandmothers-to-be) may directly or indirectly set up psychological barriers to their daughters' seeking need gratification outside of parenthood. Certainly the mother-daughter relationship is strongly implicated in many of the motivational processes that promote early childbearing and turn girls away from alternate means of need satisfaction. These processes render other options psychologically unavailable to certain teens, no matter how objectively available they may seem to us.

The Values of Having Children

> When values of having children are strong enough and no alternatives are available, individuals will go to considerable length to have children.
> —Gerald Michaels, "Motivational Factors in the Decision and Timing of Pregnancy"

The "value-of-children" theoretical model (Hoffman and Hoffman 1973) addresses the question of why an individual wants to be a parent. Extensively studied both in the United States and abroad, this model puts forward a set of nine basic values or satisfactions children may provide, functions they serve, or needs they fulfill for the parent. Each value is based on an underlying psychological need. At the same time all are influenced by cultural, social, and economic factors (Michaels 1988). The model also includes an "alternatives hypothesis," which predicts that individuals or groups with limited access to alternative means of gratifying a particular need will value children more highly for this quality. According to this hypothesis the extent to which one holds a particular value will depend on the intensity of the felt need underlying the value, the extent to which children are viewed as potential sources of satisfaction of that need, and the availability of alternative sources of need satisfaction (30). By bringing together sociological and psychological views of the motivations for parenthood, the model acknowledges the complexity and multidimensional character of the issues. Thus, it is a good place to begin an examination of the adolescent's wish for a child.

The nine values of having children as put forward by Hoffman and Hoffman are:

1. Adult status and social identity. The need to be accepted as a responsible and mature adult member of the community.

2. Expansion of the self. The need to have someone carry on for oneself after one's death, as well as the need to have new growth and learning experiences and to add meaning to life.

3. Moral values. Need for moral improvement, including becoming less selfish and learning to sacrifice, making a contribution to society, or satisfying one's religious requirements.

4. Primary group ties and affection. The need to express affection and attain intimacy with another person, as well as to be the recipient of such feelings from someone else.

5. Stimulation and fun. The need to experience the interest and excitement that children provide.

6. Achievement and creativity. The need for accomplishment and creativity that come from having and raising children, and watching them grow.

7. Power and influence. The need to have influence over another person.

8. Social comparison. The need for the prestige that comes through the favorable comparison of one's children with the children of others.

9. Economic utility. The need to have children to help with the parent's work or to contribute to the family income. (Michaels 1988, 29)

In their research on the usefulness of this model for understanding adolescents' motivation for pregnancy and parenthood, Michaels and Brown (1987) added several new value items specifically relevant to adolescents: "to create life," "to establish independence from your parents," and "because it is part of being an adult." Further, these investigators replaced the Hoffmans' original item 4 (primary group ties and affection), with two items: "because you can have someone to love," and "because you can have someone love you." For the national sample of adult mothers studied by Hoffman, Thornton, and Manis (1978), the strongest value was stimulation and fun (item 5), followed by achievement and creativity (item 6) and primary group ties and affection (item 4). Adolescents ranked power and influence (item 7) fourth highest and adult status and social identity (item 1) sixth highest, whereas in the Hoffman, Thornton, and Mantis sample this pattern was reversed.

Transformational experiences that add meaning to life, stimulation, achievement, social identity, love given and received, and something to call one's own are all fundamental human requirements. They become troublesome only when they cannot be satisfied in ways that our society values and rewards. It is true that such socioeconomic factors as a limited opportunity structure, low income, and unemployment can and do act as barriers to seeking other forms of need satisfaction, yet these factors do not wholly account for the motivation for early parenthood. Even when a resource is objectively available, there is no guarantee that it is psychologically available to a given teen (Michaels 1988). Thus, if a girl has been socialized from early in her life to view motherhood as the principal arena in which she can expect to satisfy her basic needs, she may be unwilling or unable to seriously consider other opportunities. This socialization pattern may be exceedingly potent if the girl's mother began childbearing at an early age, because seeking gratification through early motherhood is modeled by the adolescent's primary attachment figure (Michaels 1988). Under these circumstances, the psychological costs of the alternate route may be too high, and the journey too lonely (Musick 1987).

Socioeconomic factors also fail to explain the difficulty many teens have internalizing and deploying newly gained knowledge and skills to move ahead (Musick 1987). Psychologically governed variables underlie the striking variation in capacity for change among groups of disadvantaged adolescents and are strongly implicated in the differential effectiveness of various intervention strategies. It is not simply a matter of more or less skill, but rather of more or less motivation to utilize that skill.

In considering this issue, Michaels and Brown (1987) examined psychological as well as demographic barriers to seeking alternative need satisfaction outside of parenthood. They predicted that for adolescents, four demographic variables—being poor, being black, living in a rural setting, and being unemployed or not fully employed—would be associated with higher values of having children. They also predicted a positive relationship between the strength of an adolescent's values of having children and the age at which her own mother gave birth to a first child, hypothesizing that even when an adolescent is oriented toward the possibility of other options for need satisfaction she might lack the self-knowledge, social competence, independence, and goal-directedness needed to take advantage of these opportunities.

In imparting a sense of the elaborate, densely woven fabric of teenage childbearing, Michaels helps us to better appreciate why an adolescent would want a child:

> Quite early in life cultural and demographic factors set lifelong limits on available sources of need gratification. Then, within this overall context, such socialization experiences as having an identification figure who became a parent at an early age herself may more directly influence the adolescent to look to having children for primary need gratification. Finally, the adolescent's individual level of social maturity may limit her ability to attain the alternative need satisfactions that her culture and socialization experiences have made available to her. During adolescence, gratification of psychological needs through having children may seem to be easier to attain than long-range sources of need gratification. In this light, the social maturity measure, which generated the strongest findings, may reflect both the adolescent's ability to formulate long-term future goals that require extended preparation and training and her ability to delay gratification now with the confidence that long-term gratification will follow later. (45)

Beyond the broadness of this conceptual framework, the value-of-children model is an appropriate starting point for a psychological analysis of the desire for motherhood because it concentrates primarily on motives that are overt or conscious. It is a logical first step toward the less conscious, less direct motives underlying adolescent reproductive behavior. The value categories set forward in the values-of-children model refer to motivations that exist within the individual's awareness. That is, they are the reasons women give for wanting children. The interview data from the two main samples on which this book is based reflect an array of these reasons for having children,

[When I have my baby] I'll be more independent, more smarter. . . . I'll have to sometimes make my own decisions.

You've got somebody to care for and a responsibility.

I got my mom and dad to realize that I'm not a baby anymore, and they know I'm grown up.

[The baby is] something you made, you and your husband or boyfriend.

It is reasonable to suspect, however, that out-of-awareness motivations are also implicated both in the genesis of attitudes and behaviors that lead to early childbearing and in their resistance to change.

The Other Reasons

The diaries reveal or hint at more complex unconscious reasons for having children. Obviously, an individual will have both levels of motivation within her personal psychology. As Anna, a young mother of two, wrote in her diary: "You've never been truly loved until you've been loved by a child" (value: primary group ties and affection).

Reflecting on her behavior before she became pregnant with her first child, at age 16, Anna reveals other motives of which she may have been less aware at the time:

Ever since I was little I felt a lack of love. My youngest sibling is my sister Maria and we're 7 years apart. She was their favorite. They were always hugging and kissing her, showing her love but never me.

And:

> My parents didn't love each other. They were having problems
> and I . . . thought that by me having my baby would keep my
> parents together or at least bring out their love for me by seeing
> where they went wrong and give me the love I wanted. But I was
> wrong.

Note the connections between these diary entries. Anna says children are valuable because of the special love they give. And, as she looks back on her life in her family, she describes those features of her psychological history that have led her to feel that way and to seek a new partner with whom to replay old relationships (Brazelton and Cramer 1990).

In analyzing the content of the interviews and diaries I was also struck by the number of allusions to the value of having power and influence over another person (item 7). This value is frequently paired with themes of ownership, signifying that for many adolescents a primary and less conscious motive is to have someone whom they can control.

> You have something that really really belongs to you.

> Cause it's going to be my baby and I get to spoil it and tell it what
> to do. I can spank its butt and not have to worry about somebody
> say "Don't whup my child." [I can] teach it things, good and bad
> parts of life.

It is no wonder that these young mothers, who feel powerless in many aspects of their lives, crave a sphere of influence of their own, a domain in which their needs come first.

Ownership of a child also offers the girl the chance to be better at something that is highly valued; better than others she has observed (values 6 and 8). Because this enhances her sense of self it is powerfully reinforcing on an unconscious level.

> You know you got to do it better than you see other people do
> their child.

And, as the words of these two very young mothers illustrate, ownership provides stimulation and fun (item 5).

I want a girl cause I love combing hair. I comb my little cousins' hair even if they just got it done.

[I want to] have a little child of my own, that I can hold it, I can take care of it, that I can buy clothes for it.

Just like a baby doll!

Many of the motivations underlying an adolescent girl's desire for a child have their source in her need to resolve certain universal developmental tasks revolving around issues of intimacy, identity, and achievement. According to Steinberg (1989, 1991), the resolution of these developmental tasks is exceedingly difficult in contemporary society because of age segregation and the loss of adult protection and supervision, adolescent rolelessness and loss of purpose, and the specific dangers of pseudomaturity because of its present association with such high-risk "adultlike" behaviors as substance abuse and sexual intercourse. The transition to adulthood is fraught with difficulties and dangers for everyone, but as Steinberg remarks, it is more so for some than for others, especially poor, inner-city, and minority teens.

For many poor adolescent girls, early motherhood is attractive because it promises to resolve issues of identity, intimacy, and achievement better than anything else in their experience. Motherhood settles certain fundamental questions about who the girl is and whom she relates to, what she does and what she can do well. Parenthood is a role, a career, a defining activity. As such, it influences identity. At the same time, parenting is an intimate, evolving, and demanding relationship. Thus, it affects intimacy as well (Shanok 1990, 6).[8] Motherhood and mothering confer a sense of accomplishment. In the absence of other pathways to proficiency, the fact and functions of childbearing and childrearing are visible, tangible achievements. They provide a new opportunity for mastery and a new arena for competence. Although Shanok (1990) is concerned with adult parents, her comments

8. Unlike such theorists as Benedek (1959), Shanok does not view parenthood as a developmental stage for the parent even though it is tied to the child's development. Rather, she conceptualizes it as a "marker process," an event that marks adult development, challenging the individual and calling for him or her to adapt to its long-term and shifting impact.

about intimacy and identity have relevance for adolescent childbearing as well. As Erikson (1963) has written, normal life crises are turning points around which issues such as identity and intimacy are negotiated, modified, and consolidated. Becoming a parent is one such turning point. By becoming a parent, a teen is, in a sense, using this transition to psychologically work through (or avoid) the transitional challenges of the adolescent years. How this takes place will vary not only according to her life experiences but also according to where she is in the adolescent developmental process.

Developmental Issues

The variation found within populations of adolescents mirrors the variation in adolescence itself. Early, middle, and later stages each have their own social, psychological, and intellectual challenges, their own developmental tasks. Unfortunately, few studies of adolescent childbearing have taken this diversity into account. When adolescents of widely differing developmental stages are compared to one another, research findings are compromised. It is always valuable to consider developmental stage when discussing adolescent attitudes and behaviors, but it is imperative do so when considering the unconscious motivations for behaviors and attitudes.

If adolescents have babies in order to resolve important developmental issues, and if developmental issues vary from stage to stage within the adolescent era, it is logical to expect that the motives for adolescent childbearing will vary from stage to stage as well. Taking psychoanalytic theory as their developmental model, Osofsky et al.(1988) have done precisely that, examining the stage-specific psychological meanings of pregnancy across the early (ages 12–14), middle (15–18), and later (18–21) adolescent years.[9] In examining the

9. These authors remind us that age ranges given for the various stages of adolescent development are only estimates since adolescence is a physiological and psychological process with enormous variation in timing. Thus the psychological meaning of an adolescent's pregnancy reflects the specific conflicts and tasks of her physiological, psychological, and cognitive age as distinct from her chronological age (210).

developmental aspects of motivation, the accent is on childbearing before age 19, since that has been the major focus of public debate on this topic (Furstenberg, Levine, and Brooks-Gunn 1990). Obviously, the late adolescent is developmentally closest to being ready for motherhood. Additionally, in communities where adolescents expect to go directly from high school to work, motherhood at 19 and 20 may be normative. Especially in the rural areas and smaller cities in the Southeast and Midwest, from which my samples are drawn, working-class and working-poor girls often begin childbearing in their late teens. Many of the white and Hispanic girls will marry early as well.

Early Adolescence

The early adolescent era encompasses both preadolescence (before the emergence of secondary sex characteristics) and puberty (when the somatic changes actually occur, culminating in the menarche).[10] During this period, the girl's primary psychological task is to renegotiate her relationship with her mother, shifting from her earlier dependent attachment to a more individuated, more autonomous affiliation. The purpose of this psychological separation is to pave the way for mature heterosexual relationships (Blos 1962), as well as to enable her to begin to function more independently in other spheres of her life. The task is twofold: she must renounce her early (or infantile) maternal dependence and, at the same time, identify with her mother as a reproductive prototype. Thus, as the girl enters the middle adolescent stage, she should be less childishly dependent on her mother and should consciously or unconsciously perceive herself to be similar to her. If she is successful in accomplishing this, she will have relinquished one form of maternal closeness for another.

According to psychoanalytic formulations (for example, Deutsch 1944), heterosexual activity in the preadolescent part of this stage does not represent true feminine sexuality. Rather, it is a defensive attempt to ward off or deny the early dependent (same-sex, and thus homosex-

10. The psychoanalytically oriented framework for normal adolescent development advanced in this section is based on the formulations of Osofsky, Osofsky, and Diamond (1988). The interpretation and extension of the framework are my own.

ual) longings for mother. The young adolescent may become pregnant both as a way of fighting her regressive longings for her mother and as a way of extending her dependent bond with her mother through identification with her own infant. In terms of the latter motivation, it is as if the girl is saying symbolically: "I'm too big now for my mother to love and take care of like a baby, but when she loves my child, it feels like she's loving me too."[11] Indeed, in such cases the baby's father may be experienced as an intruder in the mother-child dyad rather than a supportive figure.

Childbearing during the early adolescent years appears be on the rise nationally. Whereas the overall numbers of teens becoming parents has decreased slightly over the past years, births to teens under age 15 have increased (Hayes et al. 1987; Moore 1991).[12] In contemplating the role of unconscious motivations in early childbearing, several factors come to mind concerning the psychological effects of inappropriate sexual socialization. Adolescent mothers with histories of childhood sexual victimization are most likely to have this experience at the beginning of puberty or immediately preceding it (Gershenson et al. 1989; Butler and Burton 1990). Sexual exploitation during this time of heightened psychological vulnerability can be expected to increase a girl's potential for sexual acting out in response to developmentally engendered conflict. Further, it can be expected to promote the tendency to engage in unprotected sexual activity, since contraception as a form of self-care is predicated on a sense of entitlement vis-à-vis one's body. The sense that one has the right to protect one's body is not well developed in girls who have been repeatedly subjected to abusive or exploitively tinged sexual socialization experiences. As noted in the chapter 4, if it is hard for adults to practice rational

11. One might also wonder if the deepest desire is not to have a baby but to be a baby oneself.
12. For a decade, the birth rate among U.S. teens has remained nearly constant, at a level much higher than that in comparable Western countries. Data for 1988—the most recent year for which national figures are available—show no decline. In addition to the rise in births to girls *under* age 15, a small but significant increase (10 percent) occurred in births to teens aged 15 to 17 between 1986 and 1988 (Moore 1991).

prophylactic behavior, how much harder must it be for children and adolescents subjected to nonvoluntary sex (Moore, Nord, and Peterson 1989, 110).

Other aspects of sexual exploitation could be anticipated to lead directly or indirectly to the birth of a child in the early adolescent years. A female with a history of repeated sexual exploitation may come to believe that her value to males lies almost exclusively in her ability to fulfill their sexual needs. Such vulnerability to males explains why so many sexually abused girls become promiscuous or turn to prostitution (DeYoung 1984; Fromuth 1986; Herman 1981). In turn, greater sexual activity obviously brings with it a greater risk of pregnancy, especially during the early adolescent period, when contraceptive practice is irregular at best (Zelnik and Shah 1983; Hayes et al. 1987). The poor sense of self that accompanies sexual maltreatment leads many victims to search for comfort, pleasure, and diversion from the anxiety that threatens to overwhelm them. Pregnancy and the creation of a new family promises at least temporary distance and relief from emotional pain.

There is another connection between sexual exploitation and the desire for a child: the use of pregnancy as an escape route from sexual abuse. For the younger adolescent especially, having a baby may be a way to extricate herself from an intolerable life situation she feels powerless to change, a way of running away from home, even if it is only a symbolic or psychological leave-taking. As one young girl said about her early pregnancy (by a boyfriend):

> I was so happy to be pregnant. I thought he [her stepfather] would leave me alone if I was having a baby (Butler and Burton 1990, 3).[13]

The teen mothers I have studied speak similar words, words that say, in effect, "He didn't leave me alone until I got pregnant." In this

13. In a related finding, Rutter (1989) notes that family circumstances were very important with regard to childbearing for girls in his inner-city London sample. After returning home from institutional care, 93 percent of those in discordant families had a child, versus only 30 percent of those in nondiscordant families. One might fairly assume that sexual exploitation is more prevalent in discordant homes.

way, pregnancy can be interpreted as a signal the girl has sent, generally to an older man, to keep his hands off her. Beyond saying symbolically, "Look at how sexually unattractive my body is. You wouldn't want to touch a body like this, would you?" it is also a notice that she has been spoken for, that she belongs to someone else. "Now," she seems to be saying, "will you leave me alone?"[14] Behavior that results in a pregnancy can include motivations at various levels of consciousness. For the young adolescent in a sexual predicament, pregnancy can be both a means of gaining independence from the perpetrator and a way of unconsciously pleading for her mother's attention and help. It should be emphasized that a longing for pregnancy and motherhood in early adolescence, for whatever reason, is seldom acknowledged as such. Because of the defensive style of this developmental stage, girls tend to isolate and distance themselves from their feelings, denying their wish for a child more often than admitting it, and certainly more often than the older teen.

Finally, it is useful to recall the cognitive style that typifies early adolescence. Still tied to the concrete, the 13- or 14-year-old is not fully or consistently capable of hypothetical thinking, not always able to anticipate the consequences of what she does. If she is sexually active, she is less likely to be aware of the risk of conceiving, less likely to take the precautions necessary to avoid it. Beyond this, because the younger teen is likely to be less capable of making reasoned choices and less able to recognize the effect a child will have on her future, she is more inclined to act impulsively—a dangerous propensity in an environment that offers too few safeguards and too many opportunities to work out her problems by way of motherhood.

Middle Adolescence

Osofsky et al. (1988) portray the middle adolescent girl as needing to mourn the loss of her childhood attachment to her father while seeking appropriate substitutes for this tie. To establish appropriate heterosex-

14. Historically (and perhaps even today in certain communities—e.g., Rutter's London sample) early marriage and parenthood served a similar function in helping a girl to separate herself from a situation she found unbearable but felt powerless to escape.

ual relationships outside the family, the girl must relinquish the fantasy of being the primary female in her father's life. This mid-adolescent challenge is annexed to that of early adolescence when she was required to give up her childlike dependence on her mother. According to this model, the girl falls in love to replace the former ties to her parents, filling the emotional void of this separation with new loves and new relationships (212).

During the middle adolescent years, the girl's sense of self is still affected by the need to view herself as a worthy rival to her mother. If pregnancy is used as the means of asserting herself as her mother's rival and gaining independence, she may experience it with pride but also with guilty feelings. The middle adolescent's guilt may interfere with her ability to attend adequately to her health needs during pregnancy. Indeed, many pregnant teens avoid or delay seeking prenatal care. That this seemingly self-destructive behavior may be a manifestation of unconscious guilt is another indication of the psychological complexity of adolescent childbearing and the self-defeating behaviors that so frequently attend it.

It is open to question whether the specific developmental tasks put forward by Osofsky et al. are the same for girls from dissimilar social, ethnic, and economic backgrounds. Undoubtedly some of these tasks are more sensitive to cultural and other environmental influences than are others. The developmental task of relinquishing childhood attachment to a father (or father figure), for example, is quite different when he has been absent or only minimally involved and the mother (or grandmother) has been head of the household. On the other hand, issues that concern the adolescent girl's relationship with her mother may have greater universality across cultural and socioeconomic boundaries.

Although in some ways overlapping with the unconscious developmental motives described above, the mother-daughter relationship has a separate and preeminent place in the motivation for a child in one's teens. Because a mother's behavior has greater effects on her daughter's ego development and individuation efforts (Powers et al. 1983), adolescent girls often fear their mothers' power over their lives. As one young woman in Apter's (1990) study of mothers and daughters during adolescence describes it, "When I'm angry with my father, I want to punch him; but when I'm angry with my mother it's as though something's ripping me up inside" (95). Mother-daughter relations—both negative and positive aspects—are forces to be reckoned with in teenage childbearing.

Mother-Daughter Themes

In her wish for a child, a woman experiences a unique form of *double identification.* She will simultaneously identify with her own mother *and* her fetus, and thus will play out and work through the roles and attributes of both mother and baby. . . . The reemergence of the relationship to her own mother is a very intense process during pregnancy. It can be revealed in dreams, in fears, and in a *rapprochement* to her mother.

—Brazelton and Cramer, *The Earliest Relationship: Parents, Infants, and the Drama of Early Attachment*

Adolescent: I didn't want no children to tell you the truth about it. Every time my Momma would ask, "When you gonna have children?" I said, "I ain't planning on having no children." . . . and the next year I was pregnant.
Interviewer: How old were you when your mom said that to you?
Adolescent: I was 16.

The diaries and interview data that form the core of this book are laced with themes testifying to the power of the mother-daughter relationship: universal childhood themes that ring with loss and longing for love ungiven;[15] universal adolescent themes of attachment and

15. For the unmarried, childless college woman, wanting a child seems to be related to loving memories of her own mother (Gerson 1980). As with Benedek's (1959, 1970) emphasis on positive early mother-child experiences as underlying motivation for parenthood, this finding suggests that it is mainly women whose childhood needs for maternal love were fulfilled who wish to be mothers themselves. Yet many adolescents seem drawn to motherhood as a means of compensating for what they failed to get from their own young, burdened, or depressed mothers (Horwitz, Klerman, and Jekel 1991).
We must be cautious in our interpretations here, however, since when teens relate their wish for a child to maternal deprivations, they are generally speaking

ambivalence toward the mother, of rivalry and desire to outshine her, and of dread of the possible consequences of doing so. Repeatedly one encounters elaborate stories and personal myths around the subject of "telling Momma" (about the pregnancy). These accounts sometimes speak of the apprehension felt before telling her and, most significant, of the enormous relief experienced after having done so. If the girl feels guilty for acting-out her rivalry with her mother ("See, I can be a mother too!"), she may be relieved to find that she has not permanently alienated her. If she has unconsciously wanted a child to validate her mother's lifestyle choices, she may be relieved to find that she has correctly intuited what her mother also desired, consciously or unconsciously. Frequently a girl will say that her mother "already suspected I might be pregnant 'cause she had a dream about it." Often the grandmother-to-be is upset at first but soon comes through, making up with her daughter and preparing for the baby to come. Such moments have extraordinary emotional force. Told and retold as stories, they become part of the personal narrative the adolescent constructs about herself, as a mother and as a daughter. The narratives about telling Momma and watching her reaction illustrate the ways a pregnancy can effect a rapprochement between a mother at her wits' end and her rebellious adolescent daughter, defusing a potentially explosive situa-

---

retrospectively—that is, after their childbearing career has begun. There are problems with prospective as well as retrospective measures of motivation for parenthood. Although it is true that memory distorts past events and emotions, some reasons for wanting a child cannot be foreseen by a person before she becomes a parent.

Although it is difficult to know the precise mechanisms linking early mother-daughter relationships with later childbearing patterns, issues of emotional loss, depression, and yearning for closeness appear to play significant roles in the intergenerational transmission of adolescent parenthood. Further, such issues are likely to involve grandmothers as well as mothers. For example, Horwitz, Klerman, and Jekel (1991) found that while many of the offspring of young mothers did not become parents by age 19, those who did were most likely to be female and to report depressive symptoms. Of those children—both male and female—who did become young parents, many had been removed from their grandmothers' homes before the age of 2, when their adolescent mothers moved out of their mothers' homes. Thus they experienced the loss of caregivers intimately involved in their physical and emotional well-being. These researchers also found that many school-age parents were the offspring of women suffering long-term depression.

tion. They speak of how a pregnancy can relieve traumatic anxiety for mother and daughter at a point of separation and threatened loss for both and of how it can offer the grandmother-to-be a second chance to do for a grandchild what she was too young or stressed or burdened to do for her daughter. Gradually assimilated into the childbearing chronicle the young mother creates and recreates, the story of her mother's response may play a part as meaningful as the birth itself.

> It's a joy to them. That's what my sister said. You'll be surprised you and your mother can be the worst enemies. Well when you have a baby she said that's the closest time you can get. Since I've been pregnant you know, me and my mom, well me and my momma get along better than my momma and sister do.

> My father had me crying and always upset when I first found out I was pregnant he would say things that would kill a dog if it had human feelings. . . . He hurt me so bad I want to leave home, but my mother she stood by me and still is standing by me. . . . Thank God my mom loves me . . . she's easy to talk to and to relate and I can talk to her day or night anytime. Really she's my best friend.

> My mother . . . is very special to me. We have gotten closer and closer since I had my son. We were close before, but during my pregnancy we got very close.

> I was just, like I was a wall. I didn't know what to do. About a week later everything was OK, cause me and my mom we was like sisters.

> For a while she didn't speak to me. But she like it now. She's alright, and they already told me she got me a baby bed for Christmas.

> *Interviewer:* What will it be like when the baby is first born?
> *Pregnant adolescent:* My mom holding it all the time [tone is almost cooing with love].

> They thought I was having an abortion and my mom said "no", cause this is her first grandchild. I believe that's why she wanted it. She's excited about it.

My mother she was sittin' in the room, so she said, "You are pregnant" . . . like that. So my momma, she looked at me, and I felt her looking, but I didn't look back at her. She just said, "Well ya'll have a baby to take care of." But I feel like she was happy because by the next month she was goin' buyin' the baby this, gettin' the baby that.

Mother-daughter relations are highly complex, as complex as the individuals themselves. For example, Ladner and Gourdine (1984) found the grandmothers in their sample of African-American families to be suffering from an abundance of unmet needs. Lacking alternative (or more traditional and acceptable) means of gratification, they look to their children as potential sources, rather than recipients, of nurturance; they sometimes use them to fulfill unmet needs.[16] Ladner comments that these women did not welcome their daughters' pregnancy. Many of the grandmothers were quite young, still in their childbearing and childrearing years. Some were fatalistic in outlook, feeling that the matter is out of their control.

(My mom) fussed for awhile and finally when she accepted it, it was allright between us. . . . It's too late to be mad now. They accepted it now.

No, they wasn't mad. It's over with now. Ain't nothing to be done. That's why my momma didn't fuss.

It is also likely that some women feel a need to make up for past failures by reworking unresolved parenting issues with a new generation. A woman might seek to give to her grandchild the time and emotional energy she was too busy or burdened or immature to give to his mother. In this way the grandmother can make amends to her daughter, expressing her love for her through her love of the child she has produced, redoing and (she hopes) undoing the past.

16. There appears to be a higher level of dependency (or interdependency) between African-American mothers and their adolescent daughters (Fu et al. 1984; Goldfarb 1965), perhaps because there are considerably fewer males to fulfill roles as either mates or fathers. We do not know if such a model would apply to other ethnic groups where conditions are different (Sandven and Resnick 1990).

The nature of a girl's relationship to her mother, past and present, plays a significant part in determining how successfully she meets and masters the developmental challenges of adolescence. For example, it is more difficult to negotiate adolescent tasks around separation and individuation if the earlier mother-child attachment relationship was unsatisfactory or incomplete. The physical and psychological changes brought about by adolescence tend to reawaken strong wishes to be nurtured by and close to a mothering figure.[17] Regressions of this kind can make the normal challenges of the adolescent transitional period formidable, if not insurmountable, when there is a history of troubled mother-daughter relations. In these cases, early fertility can be conceptualized as one way for the adolescent girl to fulfill her need to be psychologically connected to her mother, to recapitulate her experiences, and to wrest some sorely needed comfort and emotional sustenance from her. It is not at all unusual for a pregnant teenager to discuss this wish quite openly, articulating her hope that the pregnancy will occasion some change of heart in her mother by focusing attention on her plight and in this way eliciting the maternal care of which she feels deprived. Quite often it does precisely that. The mother may initially act angry or distraught but will eventually come around. The emotional rewards will be forthcoming, at least for a while.

Clinical observations of teen parents (for example, O'Leary, Shore, and Weider 1984) indicate that pregnancy can indeed lead to a moratorium in adolescent turbulence, bringing a rebellious young woman closer to her mother and allowing her a vehicle for separating in a more modulated way. It affords her the opportunity to assert her autonomy without sacrificing intimacy, especially if she knows or intuits that her mother would like a grandchild. The impending birth may help to resolve the painful struggles around separation and dependency that are experienced by many teens—struggles that are more highly charged in conflict-laden mother-daughter relationships, where there

17. Anna Freud referred to these essentially normal regressions as being in the service of the ego; that is, they are especially useful in helping the young person to meet and manage developmental challenges (A. Freud 1966). The term "regression in the service of the ego" was first used by Ernst Kris (1936, 290).

are attachment problems or where a mother has been present only intermittently for much of her daughter's life.

Some adolescents do straighten out as their pregnancy advances or after the birth of the child. Motherhood serves as a psychological catalyst for these adolescents, a way to stop them from destroying their lives, a sort of self-administered slap in the face.

I think this baby's wising me up to know I gotta get out there and make it for myself, and not depending on no man or the baby's father.

I got pregnant with Cliffie and that's when I settled down . . . that's how I straightened myself out, by getting pregnant. After all the places that tried to help me, I ended up doing it myself. I'm pretty proud of that cuz I've never went back to my old ways.

Considering the significance of the mother-daughter relationship during the early and middle adolescent years, it is possible that this phenomenon is at least partly a consequence of the twin comforts experienced by the girl in effecting a rapprochement with her mother and avoiding an emotionally tumultuous and precipitous separation for which she is developmentally and psychologically unprepared. With pregnancy and parenthood, the transition to adulthood (or quasi-adulthood) can be managed without the emotional risks of leaving the family behind. The young woman is spared the ordeal of uprooting herself from her family and its history. Therefore, a central task of adolescence—moving toward adulthood—can be accomplished by identifying with the mother and her way of life, a separation without psychological amputation and loss. The adolescent now views herself (as do others) as a changed, more adultlike person, yet one who remains a vital limb on her family's tree.

Concurrent with such events, parenting obliges the girl to take on a new set of duties that require distinctive skills and higher levels of maturity. The successful accomplishment of these duties (assuming that others such as the grandmother have not taken over the care of the child) can provide a sense of proficiency that is highly rewarding, a sense of personal worth rarely experienced before. The concept of "required helpfulness" (Rachman 1979) sheds light on the self-enhancing aspects of adolescent mothering. A person required to meet and master a challenge often becomes more competent and determined as they do so. In this way, a "helper" who successfully rises to the occasion may find that she has grown in the process.

The concept of required helpfulness as a possible motivation for motherhood provides another example of the interplay of individual (psychological and developmental) variables with those that originate in broader socioenvironmental forces. Describing the experiences of adolescents from impoverished families, Elder depicts a downward extension of "adult-like experience" (1974, 80). Although he is reviewing the lives of children growing up during the Great Depression, Elder's observations have relevance for disadvantaged young people today. Secular or structural changes such as those brought about through deindustrialization (Bowman 1987) and radical demographic shifts in urban communities (Wilson 1987) have resulted in major changes in role performance and functioning in the family (see also Steinberg 1991). For countless poor young women this has meant the premature assumption of caretaking roles, beginning in the early middle school years (and in some cases even earlier). Many first-born (or oldest female) preteenage and teenage girls spend most of their out-of-school time caring for younger siblings. If they are especially mature or responsible, they may also function in a caretaking role vis-à-vis their own immature or poorly functioning parents. [18]

Although the consequences of these role reversals are complex and

18. Research on female high school dropouts indicates that adolescent girls provide inordinate amounts of caretaking for their families and lose out on school as a consequence. Michelle Fine (Valentine Foundation, unpublished report) comments, "They survive at the 'public/private' boundary, while their schools erect a partition between these ostensibly separable worlds, asking young women to make a choice. And so they do. They choose kin and relationships, and sacrifice their academic lives in the process." In a similar vein, Ianni (1989) observes, "From about fourteen years of age . . . urban minority girls exhibited the least satisfaction with their schooling . . . the feminine conflict of family versus career had already begun to demand some resolution in terms of a future orientation to one or the other, or required some balancing to avoid decentralizing identity. This suggests another possible dimension of teenage pregnancy, as an acceptance of which way the future is likely to go and an early decision to escape role confusion" (246).

varied, the heightened sense of competence accompanying required helpfulness should not be underestimated. Making a psychological virtue of the particular necessities of her life, a girl may derive a sense of mastery from her role as caretaker. A young woman in these circumstances might well say to herself, "I'm taking care of *her* kids; why not have my own?" Indeed, one adolescent recalled her pregnancy as her only way of escaping from her mother's house; she told me that if she had to scrub floors and change diapers, they were going to be her floors and her kids' diapers. In such instances, early parenthood provides the adolescent with the means to leave her mother's house, at least symbolically. It gratifies her need to see and to present herself as an independent person. Nonetheless, even if she really does leave her mother's house, this type of autonomy is one of appearance only. By repeating her mother's pattern, the teen avoids the emotional rupture of psychological separation. Instead of being independent she remains psychologically connected to her mother.

Conclusion

The psychological rewards of fertility are based on some of the deepest, most powerful of all human motivations (Erikson 1964). The promise of these rewards can be very enticing during a developmental period that reverberates with issues of change, separation, and potential loss . Early childbearing is not simply multidetermined, perhaps even overdetermined, for disadvantaged girls. Rather, the forces, both environmental and psychological, that foster the desire to become a mother are essentially unopposed by equally strong forces fostering the desire to do otherwise. Therefore, these forces can be very hard to resist during a developmental epoch in which the need to do and be like others has heightened salience. In this way an issue such as the influence of peers or sisters comes to prominence—not as the principal or dominant causal factor, but simply as one of many forces that promote, reinforce, and reward early parenthood for certain girls.

I was the last one of the whole group to get pregnant . . . there were about ten of us. Now they each got one or two babies.

That was the year for teenage pregnancies. It seems you know like when a new style comes in and everybody tries to get it? That's what it was. Everybody got pregnant. . . . As soon as one got out of the hospital, another one went in. It was just like a train.

The adolescent who succumbs to these forces is one who, for a number of reasons, is more vulnerable at this time; a girl for whom motherhood serves as the central adolescent rite of passage (Gabriel and McAnarney 1983). For this young woman, the dream (and sometimes the reality) of parenthood answers the unanswerable question of what to do about the future. It fits best with the internal working models she holds of herself, her internal representations of who she is and what she can safely do with her life. Whether or not she will be a good (or even adequate) parent is an issue of a different order—she very badly wants to be a parent, and to be a good one as well. She yearns to love and be loved by her children, and—in spite of possible protestations about not having wanted or expected to get pregnant— she most probably did want to. Although some adolescents freely admit their longing for a child, others do not consciously know or feel free to acknowledge it, nor do they always understand how or why they got pregnant. All the same, there is a not uncommon reaction after the initial uproar over an unplanned pregnancy has subsided. That reaction is relief. They have done it.

This fits with a concept of early parenthood as an adaptive pattern for certain adolescent girls, specifically those for whom the probability of eventual marriage is relatively low (Wilson 1989) and the alternate routes to competence are blocked by poor basic skills and lack of role models, appropriate educational experiences, and job opportunities. Furstenberg, Levine, and Brooks-Gunn (1990) point out that the availability of abortion has changed the composition of the population of adolescent mothers. "Once pregnancy occurs," they note, "fewer teenagers today are forced to become parents, making early parenthood, relatively speaking, a more voluntary act. We believe that this has had the effect of filtering out of the population the more ambitious and successful teens, who more often elect to terminate their pregnancy rather than jeopardize their chances of further schooling" (28). Girls such as these might have become teenage parents a generation ago.

It would be incorrect, however, to conclude that adolescent mothers are always girls with the lowest basic skills and academic potential. In disadvantaged communities young women with considerable potential are sometimes drawn to early parenthood, or at least to having a first child during their teen years. These girls may be bright but socially less mature, or they may lack the social skills necessary to seek and utilize alternate sources of need gratification (Michaels 1988). Our theories must be able to account for early childbearing in this relatively small but significant population as well.

> They all looked up to me cause I was the one, the head of the group; I was the leader. . . . All of them cried, "Why did you get pregnant? You said you wasn't gonna have any?" And I said, "Well, it happens."

> My dad had big dreams for me. . . . He said "I didn't expect that from you," cause he knew what I wanted to do. And I said I didn't expect anything like that from me either, it just happened. Til this day I don't even know how it happened.

> Everyone was disappointed because I became pregnant in my sophomore year in school. . . . My rank was third in my class. Everyone said I wasn't going to amount to anything. At 15, God! But I've earned my respect.

These more competent adolescents may also be troubled emotionally or may have greater difficulty maintaining psychic equilibrium during what is often a turbulent period of life. As Osofsky et al. (1988) have noted, "Adolescents become parents in an effort to resolve important age-related developmental issues" (227). That promising young women are also unable to resist the pulls toward early childbearing speaks to the vigor and complexity of the forces at work in promoting teenage parenthood when there are obstacles to envisioning, let alone becoming, other "possible selves." In several instances teens said that girls who proclaimed that they would never be adolescent mothers were those most likely to become one soon. "Them the ones that gonna be next."

> I was disappointed in myself cause that's not what I wanted. I wanted to go to college first. . . . I said I'm going to be married and out of college and have a good job and I guess that's why I got pregnant because I was bragging all the time about what I was going to do.

Does such boasting by the more competent girls reflect the pressures they feel to have a child? It surely speaks of their ambivalence and perhaps their hope that if they protest loudly enough it will (magically?) somehow pass them by.

Not all adolescents will succeed in resolving core developmental or psychological issues by becoming parents. Although for some girls pregnancy and parenthood serve as catalysts for positive change and "enhancement of the maturational process," many others "find that their action has not made their conflicts disappear" (Osofsky et al. 1988, 227–228). All too soon, the baby showers,

> They're excited now. I got over half the school coming to my house. . . . There's alot of my friends gonna throw me baby showers. [jokes] Probably have to leave town for a few days.

and the attention,

> I get more attention. From my boyfrind. That's what I like about it. But I get more attention from my mother and sisters too.
>
> I get spoiled. Anything I want I get. If I don't want to walk home from school my grandmother picks me up everyday and takes me every day.

and the entreaties to rest and eat right and take special care of herself are over. When the dreams and illusions of yesterday give way to the unanticipated realities of motherhood, many a girl is left emotionally alone with her baby, disenchanted, depressed, and more vulnerable than ever. Without prompt and appropriate intercession, these girls will continue to regard motherhood as the only journey beckoning them, as the only identity imaginable.

Its weird to think back at the false ideas I had about kids. When I was 13–14–15–16 I would say I wanted a kid. . . . I just knew I would have a girl and . . . she would have curly blond hair and blue eyes. I would picture myself walking around with this little tiny baby and she would never get heavy or never need a diaper change. . . . I know there are alot of those girls out there with the same false ideas I had who think having babies will be glamorous. And I wish there was some way I could help them. Everyone I know has babies now and 16 years old is way to young for having babies.

If the strategies for preventing or ameliorating the problems of adolescent childbearing are not matched developmentally and psychologically to the complex nature of these problems, a significant subgroup of disadvantaged females is going to persist in their efforts to resolve core developmental and psychological issues by becoming mothers in their teens. Some will do so just once, but others will do so over and over and over again.

My baby
flowed out around me
protecting me
in her own radiance
for nine whole months.
I did not fear death.
The baby within
& the spirit without
were one,
& I was at peace.
Then she was born,
& fear reclaimed me.
—Erica Jong, "The Protection We Bear"

Adolescents as Mothers:
The Being and the Doing

What I had to give to a child Rayona got, and what I needed she gave. You hear of people who want to live their lives through their children, who dream their kids can avoid every mistake. I didn't expect that much. I wanted to go back and do Aunt Ida's [the narrator's mother] part better, and mostly I did. I set aside special times for Ray and me early in the mornings and fixed her healthy breakfasts. I wasn't ashamed to let her see me cry or to let her know I cared about her. I never lost my interest in her life. I never expected her to be perfect. I never wished she was anybody else but who she was.

—Michael Dorris, *A Yellow Raft in Blue Water*

Even though my baby is only five months old I read my baby bible stories every night before she go's to sleep because it seems like she understands what I'm saying, and although she will not be perfect I want her to have a better life than I did.

—Yvonne, an adolescent mother

W h a t kind of mothers are adolescents? There is no single answer to this question; some are good and some are not so good—much like adult parents. In their diversity, adolescents mirror their adult counterparts, and yet they are also distinctive.

There are extremely competent and extremely incompetent adolescent mothers; there are some who need almost no help beyond what is given by their families and others who seem to be beyond reach or help. Most adolescents fall somewhere in between these extremes, functioning adequately or even very well as parents but at some cost to their own development in other spheres or, conversely, realizing their own developmental destinies but at the cost of those of their children. Balancing motherhood with selfhood calls for maturity, psychological strength, and a full complement of family and external supports. To be a student and a worker, a daughter, a friend, a girlfriend, and a mother is demanding at best. To do so at sixteen, in a milieu where there is little margin for error, requires extraordinary talent and fortitude. When an adolescent is also a mother, someone unavoidably is going to be short-changed. Quite often that someone will be her child.

Today I did something I felt bad about. . . . I hit my daughter in the face because she was crying and I could not take it any more. I don't know but I find myself yelling at her all the time, getting her scared of me and I don't want that. I need to love her I think I just need a little more time to myself because now that I am having another baby I don't want her to feel alone or not loved. . . . Ever since she was born she been like this crying for everything. She had colic and I had a very hard time. If it wasn't for my mother I don't know what would have happen.

I'm scared Lord. Scared that I can't handle them. Scared of losing them. Not enough strength, that is what I lack, and patience. Something I do not have. I have all the love in the world

for them, but I'm not sure it is enough. Please Lord, God, help
me, help them.

Although some, perhaps a good many, young mothers and their
families do an inspired job of childrearing, for those intimately ac-
quainted with teens and their children, the overall picture is a sobering
one. Observing adolescents interact with their children and hearing
them recount the ongoing trials of their daily lives, it is hard to escape
the clinical impression that certain dysfunctional patterns of raising
and relating to children are more characteristic of these young parents
than of their adult counterparts. Products of who they are as developing young people coping with demanding life circumstances, these
patterns tend to be surprisingly unyielding, at least during the initial
years of motherhood. And, as might be anticipated, the more disordered these patterns are, the less tractable they are.

Intervention experiences gradually reshaped my ideas about teens
as mothers, raising questions I still grapple with today. Why are some
adolescents better parents than others? What patterns of caregiving
and relating to children are more characteristic of adolescent mothers
than of their adult counterparts, and why? Why is it that only some
young mothers are able to utilize counsel or support to enhance their
mothering?

How are such questions to be answered? How does one determine
what is most significant about the experience of being raised by an
adolescent mother? Plainly we cannot walk in her child's shoes or
know how he perceives his young mother's caring in the context of all
the other events of his life. Similarly, observing what his mother does
and listening to what she says about what she does are not the same as
knowing what she feels—even she may not be aware of that. We can
rarely have complete faith in the reflections of any parent. Who we are
as parents is too closely meshed with who we are as persons to be easily
accessible and open to self-scrutiny. No one wants to present (or see)
herself as a "bad parent," least of all an adolescent whose identity is
intimately connected to her role as a mother. Understanding the pressure young mothers feel to keep up appearances, I tend to view with
some skepticism certain statements they make about themselves as

parents, especially when they are very young or when they have already exhibited serious caregiving problems.

If self-report techniques have obvious limitations, so do more empirical, scientifically precise approaches, which seem predisposed to miss the subtler issues of premature parenthood—what really counts about being raised by a teenage mother. To discover what matters we must find ways to get beneath the surface to analyze what it means—for the mother and for the child—to swim each day in the stream of experience her early parenthood has created. A search for these "true essences" is the key to understanding and constructing the conditions for change. Ethnographic studies and qualitative and clinical data are all essential to such an inquiry (see Norton 1990). In developing my ideas about adolescents as parents, I have integrated the theories, research, and clinical findings of others with my research and practice with adult, as well as adolescent, parents.

In a sense, a young child's parents are much like a ship in which he journeys from a place of absolute dependency to the distant shore of greater autonomy and maturity. When the seas are rough, the craft must be steady and seaworthy, well-equipped and provisioned for the voyage ahead. Without considerable support, an adolescent mother today is like a vessel that has slipped her mooring; adrift in turbulent waters, she is ill prepared for the crossing ahead.

Parenthood

Parenthood is a role, a career, a defining activity: parenting is an intimate, evolving and demanding relationship of deep impact. Parent*hood* affects identity: parent*ing* influences intimacy.
—Rebecca Shahmoon Shanok, *Parenthood and Personhood*

Making the Transition: A New Role and a New Identity

First-time parenthood is a turning point, a "normal life crisis" involving opportunities as well as challenges (Bibring et al. 1961; Erikson 1963). The resolution of this crisis depends on the objective challenges of the situation as well as the parent's material, social, and psychological resources. Nonetheless, since parenthood presents a crisis that can never be fully resolved, it has unique qualities. Such "marker processes" (Shanok 1990) present continuing demands, adaptational challenges to be mastered again and again, at different developmental levels, as child and parent change over time. [1]

Most of the research on the transition to parenthood since LeMasters' landmark 1957 study of "parenthood as crisis" has focused on married, middle-class, white adults. This transition might raise a separate set of issues for very young parents or for those from other ethnic, social, and economic groups (Goldberg and Michaels 1988). For example, most research on middle-class populations has found the quality of the marital (or couple) relationship to be the critical factor in adjustment to new parenthood. Yet in cultural groups where extended-family living arrangements are the norm for young single mothers, an adolescent's relationship with her child's father may be much less important to her adjustment than the supportive relationships she has with other family members. [2]

Any new mother, no matter what her age, reorients and reorganizes herself as she adapts to this new role. Because the central issues of adolescent psychological development are so often those of identity [3] and because becoming a parent signals a shift in identity, we might expect to find an adolescent element in the young mother's response to her new role. That is, when the transition to parenthood takes place during the transitional phase of adolescence it will have a characteristically adolescent flavor. In assuming the role of parent, a girl may use this particular transition to resolve issues of identity. [4] According to

1. I have found the work of Rebecca Shahmoon Shanok with older parents to be very useful to my thinking about adolescents as parents. See "Parenthood: A Process Marking Identity and Intimacy Capacities."

2. In the Mexican and Puerto Rican families I have worked with, this arrangement may hold, at least for the earliest years of childrearing, when the young mother is married to her baby's father.

3. Clearly, identity formation is a lifelong development (Erikson 1980, 122). Identity themes surface and resurface throughout adulthood (Shanok 1990). Nevertheless, they have heightened salience during the adolescent years when a person may be more powerfully affected by them because of his or her youth and lack of maturity.

4. Applying James Marcia's extension of Eriksonian theory (1966, 1980, 1988) to adolescent childbearing, the resolution of identity issues through early parenthood can be interpreted as a case of "identity foreclosure" rather than identity achieve-

Beatrix Hamburg (1986), "Black adolescent mothers use their first years of parenthood to consolidate their own growth and solidify their networks." She goes on to remark that, for some young mothers, early childbearing is "a strategy that promotes personal and social development and cultural survival given their socioenvironmental contingencies" (122).[5]

Early fertility leads to membership and greater participation in adult society and helps prepare these young women for heading their own households. In Hamburg's view, early parenthood serves an adaptive purpose for certain disadvantaged young women, particularly those poor, urban, black, older adolescents who are more mature and less emotionally troubled.[6] The role of mother confers a distinct and highly valued identity, serving as a catalyst for psychological reorganization and, in its wake, self-advancement.

This scenario is most likely to unfold, I suspect, when an adolescent's motives for motherhood also involve the need to be like emotionally significant females in her life—or, more specifically, not to be different from them. When a girl feels psychological pressures to validate the lifestyle choices of others,[7] the symbolic value of the role may be enough to enable her to move ahead once she has attained it. Having achieved the role of motherhood, a girl with potential may be psychologically freed to do what is necessary to realize it. By first choosing motherhood, she symbolically says to those close to her: "See, I'm not trying to set myself apart from you. I'm just like you where it counts." And to herself she says, "Now that I've gotten that out of the way, I can

---

ment. According to Marcia's taxonomy, the foreclosure adolescent is one who has already made commitments without having experienced an identity crisis. These commitments, however, are not the result of personal searching and exploration but are handed ready-made to the young person by others.

5. As discussed in chapter 5, scholars such as Joyce Ladner and Linda Burton have come to similar conclusions.

6. I have seen it do the same thing for Hispanic and white adolescents, who come from small towns and rural areas as well as from cities. For example, the teen quoted in chapter 4 who credits motherhood for straightening her out is a white girl from a small town.

7. Females are also more sensitive to others' emotional needs—perceived as well as real—and more likely to feel pressured to meet them (Gilligan 1982; Belenky et al. 1986; Gilligan et al. 1990).

go on and live my life; I can achieve in *my* way." Now, no matter how far she travels, no matter how much she accomplishes in worlds beyond family and friends, something special will always be shared— the role and identity of motherhood.

For a promising girl drawn into early parenthood, becoming a mother may actually work. At worst, it diverts or sidetracks her for a time, facilitating a temporary "regression in the service of the ego" (Kris 1936) or simply allowing her to regroup her psychic resources. If she is fortunate enough to have substantial emotional and practical support from her family (or from a good program), and if she has the opportunity to prepare herself educationally or vocationally, she may do well in the long run. Under optimal circumstances, her role as a parent will not be in serious conflict with her other roles as student or worker or as girlfriend or wife. What is more, her personal victories will not have to be won at the expense of her child. If it can be said that any child of an adolescent mother is fortunate, it can be said of the child of a mother such as this.

Balancing Different Roles, Serving Different Functions

The trouble is, most adolescent mothers are struggling to balance three fundamental and sometimes conflicting roles: parenthood, partnerhood, and work (or education as preparation for work, or education and work). This sets limits on the kind of parent she can be, no matter what kind she may want to be. Moreover, there are likely to be continuing struggles with parenting itself as the young mother becomes aware of the *doing* as well as *being* dimensions of her new role. There are certain distinctive lifestyle and psychological qualities in adolescent motherhood that inevitably shape the kind of childrearing environment young mothers establish and maintain for their children.

If an adolescent mother is single, as she is quite likely to be and to remain, she begins, at least symbolically, to assume the additional role of lifetime breadwinner. The more future-oriented and conscientious she is, the sooner she will recognize the need to provide for herself and her child. Although she may rest on a cushion of family support or welfare until she finishes school or finishes occupational training or finishes growing up a little, it is virtually certain that before long she will be required to support herself and her child and to continue to do so for years to come—perhaps for as long as she lives. In the short term she may choose not to work, but over the long haul the choice between motherhood *or* work will seldom be hers to make. If she wants to get out and stay out of poverty, always, unremittingly, it will be motherhood *and* work.

An increasing number of middle-class mothers are balancing maternal and economic roles, some by choice, some by necessity. In general, however, more advantaged women are not obliged to juggle these roles while they are still very young and inexperienced. Chances are that, in addition to her greater social, material, and child-care resources, the more advantaged mother (married, unmarried, or suddenly single) has already acquired her education and at least some occupational expertise by the time she becomes a mother. If she is divorced or widowed, she can realistically conceive of remarriage and the possibility of some relief from unceasing role strain. This is a far more remote possibility for the average adolescent mother. Read the words of 17-year-old Roxanne, mother of a 2-year-old, after her car has broken down for the last time:

> I decided to just save the rest of my money and try and buy me something cheap and to get me around. Because there was no way that I could get a ride to both jobs everyday plus take CeeCee to the babysitters. When I got off work I went to get CeeCee and I found out that she had been real sick all day. I just cry[ed] because I feel bad because I couldn't be there with her when she needed me. . . . I have to be a lot but I know that I can make it. I am going to [college] and make it better for CeeCee and me. I just got to keep on my self about getting that GED and going to college.

Another example is 18-year-old Lou, a married (unhappily) mother of a 1-year-old, seven months pregnant with her second child, who provides daycare for another child and works part time:

> I get so tired. I have a 1 year old and a 2 year old all day plus try to cook and clean, school at night and selling Mary Kay.

A teenage mother needs (and wants) to fulfill roles other than parenthood, for developmental as well as practical reasons, and ultimately it is in her best interests to do so. Doing this entails psychological tasks involving relationships (especially with her own mother) and role-related tasks involving school, preparation for work, and a social life that includes boyfriends. Conflict is unavoidable because the adolescent process is an egocentric one, focused on developing and consolidating intellectual and interpersonal skills, whereas the parenting process is other-directed, focused on fostering the development of another. Adolescence is selfish, parenting is selfless and requires an abundance of precisely those emotional resources that the normal, self-centered tasks of adolescence are likely to deplete. As Hetherington (1984) perceptively observed, "The needs of children and parents are not always the same . . . a solution that contributes to the well-being of one may have disastrous outcomes for the other" (12). She is referring in this case to the consequences of divorce (and, by implication, to adult parents), but her point is doubly relevant to the conflicting needs of adolescent mothers and their children. Because so much of the adolescent developmental agenda is centered on concern for self,[8] solutions that contribute to the adolescent's well-being and eventual success are likely to be developmentally costly for her child. This is one way that adolescents are at a disadvantage vis-à-vis older, more mature mothers.

Another contrast between adolescent and adult mothers can be observed in the tendency of younger mothers to want children but to reject childcare after they discover what it entails. That is, adolescents may value and desire the role of mother but not the functions that accompany it. Few parents, no matter what their age, fully realize what is involved in childrearing until they have children. Still, it is reasonable to assume that this is especially true for adolescent mothers, if only because of their relative immaturity.

8. It is true, as I have pointed out, that female adolescents are very much other-directed in terms of the desire to please and to be close to significant others (Gilligan 1982; Belenky et al. 1986; Gilligan et al. 1990). However, these motives appear to stem from the more self-oriented adolescent need to take emotional care of one's self rather than from the more mature, adult desire to take care of another person.

More than her adult counterpart, the adolescent mother is primed for disappointment once she awakens to the inescapable discrepancies between her fantasies of motherhood and the realities of taking care of a dependent infant, day after day, month after month, or coping with a 2 year old's struggles for independence. The motives behind her maternity and her images of the psychic and social rewards of motherhood have ill prepared her for the trials and sacrifices of these new situations. No matter how often she has heard her sisters or friends complain about the hardships of childrearing—lack of sleep, cranky babies, no time for oneself—no matter how many toddlers she has seen getting into everything, throwing their food, or having tantrums in public, she is still thunderstruck when it happens to her. Over and over I have heard (and read in the diaries) some version of the statement, "I thought it would be different with my baby." To the extent that a young mother's motives for wanting a child have to do primarily with the being of motherhood rather than the doing involved in mothering, there will be problems in this domain.

Functions of Parenting

The psychological issues that swept the adolescent toward motherhood in the first place affect her modes of relating to her child. Faithful companions during her transition to parenthood, these "ghosts in the nursery" (Fraiberg 1980; Brazelton and Cramer 1990) are the interior analogues of what she actually does to and for her child. Because they are products of her need to adapt to the circumstances of her life, these inner models are not easy or quick to change. Because they set psychic rules for relating to her child, they set limits on her parenting capacities. And the more limited a mother's childrearing capacity, the more serious her parenting problems, the less likely she is to change enough to improve her child's developmental chances. Although intervention programs are able to help some adolescents improve the care they provide for their children (see, for example, Polit 1988), these mothers generally have greater potential to begin with. As the late Bruno Bettelheim said, "The parent equipped to make good use of child-rearing advice hardly needs it, while the parent unable to evaluate and reevaluate the overall situation correctly cannot use advice intelligently and successfully" (1987, 6).

The theme of intervention is woven throughout this book. Here it reappears as a concern with the difficulties inherent in attempting to alter complex, multidetermined human relationships, a concern with the personal and other barriers to eliminating harmful childrearing practices. Parenting embodies a set of skills, but it is not merely a set of skills; it is a relationship. As such, it cannot be taught or retaught if it has not been learned well initially. Although at certain times child-rearing may feel like a job, it cannot be trained for like a job. One can learn to diaper and feed a baby, but how one does so is not easily changed.

What must all parents do? What must poor parents do? Are there childrearing universals, aspects of parenting that all children must experience? Are there universal childrearing rules that adolescent parents somehow violate?[9] Studies of parents and children across diverse cultures and contexts indicate that a list of hypothetical universals would be arbitrary at best, trivial and misleading at worst. It is more useful to consider the ways adolescents organize certain universal human experiences for their children, especially those regarding self and other. As Stern observed, "The self and its boundaries are at the heart of philosophical speculation on human nature, and the sense of self and its counterpart, the sense of other, are universal phenomena that profoundly influence all our social experiences" (1985, 5). When looking at a teen as a parent, we should ask: How does she arrange the developmental building blocks of human experience, universals such as language (Bruner 1975; Brice Heath 1983) and time (Stern 1985; Norton 1990), which are foundations of the developing self? Is she able to provide a useful scaffold for the construction of a coherent framework for living and acting in the wider world (Norton 1990)? What sort of

9. I am speaking here, of course, of needs that parents meet beyond the most basic ones for nourishment, rest, and protection from harm. (See Musick and Stott 1990, for an analysis encompassing middle as well as early childhood.) Because this book is about adolescent mothers, it tends to emphasize what the parent does rather than how the child experiences it. In reality, however, these are complementary perspectives.

"other" is an adolescent as a counterpoint for her child's developing sense of self?

To understand adolescents as parents, we must ask about the specifics as well as the universals of parenting, and particularly about the specifics of parenting in a high-risk environment—the kind of environment in which most teenage mothers live. In these contexts, what are the most essential functions of parenting and what purposes, beyond the obvious ones, do they serve? How capable are most adolescents of carrying out such functions?

The Critical Role of Parents as Mediators

There can be little doubt about the need to consider the total ecology of risk, including the influences of extended family, community, and the broader society; of limited financial and material resources; and of unemployment and social isolation (Bronfenbrenner and Crouter 1983; Belsky and Vondra 1989; Wilson 1989). Although acknowledging the impact of these more macro-level variables, those who work directly with families recognize that during the earliest years (and even longer in the highest-risk communities [see, for example, Clark 1983]), parents are the most significant aspects of their child's environment.[10] All parents act as mediators between the world and their young children, but within the context of severe poverty, where there is danger and chaos, their role is literally, as well as symbolically, a lifesaving one.

> She wants to come home by herself. Like I maybe let her get a little head start because she thinks that she's doing something big. "I came home by myself." And I stand on the porch, and I watch her. When I see her get about right there, I hit the steps. So when she gets there I say, "You walked all the way home by yourself! Didn't you?" Sometimes I let her come all the way up.

10. For example, there is clear evidence, from multiple sources, that a close and secure parent-child attachment relationship in the earliest years of life serves a critical protective function, especially where social risk is high (Anthony 1987; Farber and Egeland 1987; Fisher et al. 1987; Musick et al. 1987; Werner and Smith 1982; Cicchetti 1989; Werner 1990).

My husband's standing downstairs. He don't see me. I'm standing up on the porch.

I let him go to the store a couple of times by hisself, but I was like hiding, watching. And I mean, he was prepared. He knew how to watch before he crossed the street. . . . Look out for cars. Look both ways. All this. But I really wanted to see could he really do it. But I was like right there. He didn't see me though. [11]

When no one else will safeguard her child's emotional well-being, a parent's role can be a mind-saving and soul-saving one as well. An example is this conversation with the mother of a successful kindergarten child in a very low-income community (Hans, Musick, and Jagers 1990):

I'm not going to let nobody run over my kid. . . . I went to the dentist. . . . Ellie is terrified of needles. Cause when she was 3 she had to have surgery in her mouth and that's a lot for a little 3 year old to understand. I guess he touched something and it scared her and she turned her head and he went off. He said "Kids should not be allowed to make decisions. You should make decisions for them. Take them in the washroom sometimes and pat them on the behind." I said, "Hold it. Wait a minute. Hold it! Hold it! I said number one, you don't know why she's like this. And you don't tell me how to raise my kids." . . . I didn't like the way he said what he said, as if kids don't have any rights. . . . You know, this is my kid. This is my child and I know her. I know her ways, and I know what's going on, "I don't

---

11. What might be considered growth-thwarting childrearing practices in middle- and upper-income families may be the opposite for families living in dangerous environments. Extreme restrictiveness—making children stay indoors or very close to home, regulating their friendships, rigidly punishing infractions of family safety rules—is often the only way poor parents have to keep their children from harm. Although environmental factors such as child safety are associated with parental control, there is nonetheless considerable variability among low-income parents in terms of their disciplinary attitudes and practices. See, e.g., Kelley, Power, Wimbush 1992.

need you to tell me that. Now if you want to do this work in her mouth, fine. But, if you don't that's fine too."

Because the care of children still falls primarily to the mother in our society, the role and functions of mediator will be hers as well—no matter how immature or unprepared she is. Unless the adolescent's mother or other adult takes over this role, she will be called on to mediate the effects of poverty, of harmful or antisocial community values; she must shield her child from the consequences of social pathology and dysfunctional relationships within the family. Risk factors such as these impinge directly upon the parent who then transforms and transmits them to her child or shelters him through her caretaking. In this way, a young child's mother *is* his environment: her well-being and his are interdependent.

The various interlocking components that make up the social context of risk sometimes act directly to harm children. Caught in the cross-fire of drug wars; cruelly used by parents (and others) who have been pushed beyond their psychic limits; born addicted, infected, or otherwise damaged, children are regularly sacrificed in the homes and streets where intractable poverty resides. Often, however, the harm is more subtle and indirect: the death is that of mind and spirit rather than body.

Findings of longitudinal studies on the children of the Depression (Elder 1974; Elder, Liker, and Cross 1984; Elder, Van Nguyen, and Caspi 1985) and on the "vulnerable but invincible" children of Kauai (Werner and Smith 1982; Werner 1989, 1990) offer unmistakable evidence of the ways in which parents filter and give meaning to such experiences as economic disaster, family and community problems, and turbulent times. Serious stresses have profound effects on parents' perceptions and thus on the way they interact with and raise their children—effects that may last for generations.[12] It is naive to expect an intervention—even one that improves a family's economic circumstances—to undo in one generation the pernicious effects of past deprivations.

12. Note also the multigenerational effects of the Holocaust—on the concentration-camp survivors, on their children, and now on their grandchildren.

Even when conditions improve, as they did for those who lived through the Depression, even when children's lives are objectively better than those of their parents, some psychological effects remain. Internalized by parents and offspring, these effects imbed themselves in the tissues of the family; they will not be easily and quickly reversed. Unfortunately, conditions appear to be worsening for many poor families today (Wilson 1989). For middle-class parents, "the mistakes we make in rearing our child—the errors often made just because of the intensity of our emotional involvement in and with our child— must be more than compensated for by the many instances in which we do right by our child" (Bettelheim 1987, ix). But unless the life circumstances of our most disadvantaged families improve— markedly and soon—being a good enough parent will not be enough to give a child a fighting chance to make it. When a child's parents are virtually all he has, they must be more than merely good enough; they must be much, much better. This is not a reasonable expectation for most adolescent parents.

Making Good Use of Motherhood

I have a wonderful and healthy son. His name is Paulie. He's 15 months old and very bright. . . . He has made me a better and stronger person. . . . I love sharing time with my son, and taking care of his needs makes me very proud. I attend high school and I'm looking forward to graduating this year.

For some adolescents, the role of mother, once attained, is enough to initiate a phase of reorganization and positive change. For other teens, it is not so much the role as the functions of motherhood that take center stage, providing opportunities to develop and deploy new skills and to be good at something that is personally meaningful. Feelings of competency engendered by doing well as a mother may generalize to other domains, serving as the bridge to success in school or work. If her own mother or some other relative has not taken over the care of her baby, the teen will suddenly be faced with and forced to take on a new set of obligations and duties that call for different skills and a new measure of maturity. The successful fulfillment of these

obligations provides a feeling of accomplishment that is highly rewarding for some young women, a sense of mastery and personal worthi-
ness seldom experienced before. Rachman's notion of "required helpfulness" provides a useful explanation of this phenomenon and the
changes that often accompany it: "Under the incentive of high social
demands, helpers often act more effectively and more persistently
than at other times. The execution of successful acts of required helpfulness may lead to enduring changes in the helper himself" (1979, 4).

> I came a long way from being on aid and whoring. I'm a really
> good mother. I really love my kids.

The daily care of a small child also furnishes the opportunity to
experience a new and intimate relationship, one which recalls other
intimacies of the past.

> Her first glance of me she smiled. That smile made me feel loved
> from the inside out.

In reexperiencing past intimacies and attachments, the adolescent
mother may also rework and begin to resolve important issues, ones
that have haunted her or held her back. As Brazelton and Cramer
(1990) observed: "A new child is never a total stranger. Parents see in
each baby-to-be a possibility of reviving attachments that have been
dormant for years, a new opportunity to work them through. The
feelings contained in these previous relationships will once more be
played out, in an effort to resolve them" (15).[13]

The satisfactory resolution of issues through bearing and caring for
children frees some young mothers from a kind of self-limiting psychological imprisonment, enabling them to move ahead and succeed in
other areas and roles. There is a catch however. The adolescents who
manage to put motherhood to good developmental use almost always
have substantial support from others and substantial personal and
social resources themselves. Whereas girls like these may rise to the
occasion of motherhood, others, devoid of such resources, plunge to
the depths, dragging their children behind them.

13. Brazelton and Cramer see the beginning of this process during pregnancy as
the "prehistory of attachment."

Mothering in Multiproblem Families

> I've been getting depressed lately alot, I've just had my third child,
> I have two girls Gloria Louise who is 4, Julia who is 2 and my son
> who is 2 months. . . . My boyfriend I've been with him 4 years in
> December. We had a hard time before I got pregnant with my son
> but now it's kind of getting better. He is really insecure, he doesn't
> trust me as much as he wants to. He is 14 years older than me but
> he don't act like it. . . . I don't have my first daughter because they
> took her away. . . . I guess maybe that's why I've been depressed
> alot. She got heart and the way she got heart they say thats not how
> she got her injury . . . now they say I won't get her back unless I
> tell them how she got hurt. so now deep inside I know I'll never
> get her because I don't know how she got hurt so they
> don't want her with me.

At the opposite end of the broad continuum of parenting aptitude and ability is the adolescent for whom the bearing of children, often many children while still quite young, is simply further evidence of a life that is out of control and spiraling downward, a life marked at all turns by disorganization and self-defeat. For these adolescents—most of them from chaotic, dysfunctional, and often abusive families—neither rapid, repeated childbearing nor serious parenting difficulties constitute the defining issues. Such problems are merely the modes through which psychiatric illness, character disorders, and other mal-adaptations manifest themselves. Although they are teenagers and mothers, teenage motherhood is not their fundamental problem.

These women, whether adolescent or adult, all too frequently make life a living hell for their children—not always by what they do to them directly but by what they indirectly allow or enable others to do.[14]

> When I had my first child I had a apartment with me and my
> boyfriend. I left the house and he beat my son and wen I got

14. For research and description of such multiproblem parents, see Pavenstedt 1967; Pavenstedt and Bernard 1971; Egeland, Jacobvitz, and Papatola 1984; Stott, Musick, and Cohler, 1984; Stott, Cohler, and Musick n.d.; and especially the volume on child maltreatment by Cicchetti and Carlson 1989.

home I call the police and wen they came we went to the hoptl [hospital] to take my son and they take the father to jail my son was bad lee hurt he had mark on his leg arms face his head was swolling he had balood clogs [blood clots] on his head he had to have stiges I did[n't] think he was going to make it but good [God] was with us there. . . . the father only got 6 months in jail he should have got life becaus the baby was only 9 month old his [he] did[n't] now right frome rong. they ask why did he wope [whip] the baby he said that the brad[t] wont stop crying.

Mothers like this one periodically (and sometimes permanently) lose parental custody because of child abuse or neglect. Still, they repeatedly and extravagantly declare their love for their children. Here are the journal entries of three mothers whose children were removed by the state child welfare authority:

They are my world and my life. I don't know what I would do without them. I love them so very much.

When Tiffy was taken away from me I felt like my life was over. . . . I want [her] to have everything that I didn't, especially love.

I love her quite alot and I wish she was at home because we miss her quite alot. . . . [She] is so very important to me. I love her so very much. She is very preshuss to me and my husband.

How, one might ask, can a mother say she loves her children so much when she hurts them or allows them to be to hurt by others? Though based on findings from an intervention study conducted in the 1950s and 1960s, Stein's (1967) description of multiproblem parents in Boston's North Point area applies to the adolescents quoted above: "They are able to bear children physically, but they cannot bear the emotional responsibilities that being parents to children presupposes. Yet once they bear children, they become addicted to them, and like any addict, spend their lives hating and craving the objects to which they have become compulsively attached" (315). Often these troubled young mothers seem genuinely unaware of how they repeatedly embroil themselves and their children in harmful situations.

Now [protective services] is talking about taking away my rights
[to] my kids. Why are they doing this to me?

Related to this issue, McCool (1991) found that increases in anxiety
during pregnancy were associated with positive, rather than negative
parenting outcomes as anticipated. This is not surprising: anxiety is an
appropriate reaction, both to impending childbirth and to the demands and life changes that will accompany motherhood. The pregnant and parenting teen who reacts with increased anxiety is indicating
that she is aware of what is happening to her, not denying it. Denial of
the realities of parenthood is the harbinger and companion of some of
the worst childrearing and relational problems (see Main and Goldwyn 1984; Main and Hesse 1990). In discussing his findings, McCool
speculates that a certain degree of heightened reactive or anxious state
may be beneficial for the woman about to become a mother, and that
rising levels of anxiety during pregnancy may indicate a healthy development from being "woman-without-child" to "woman-and-child."
Indeed, it signals a shift from the idealism that characterizes so many
adolescent mothers to the realism of what is required to adequately
perform the tasks of childrearing and to form and maintain a real, as
opposed to an idealized, relationship with one's child. I have found
that adolescent mothers who cannot move beyond this idealism are far
more likely to have serious—and lasting—parenting problems. Women who speak of the joys of motherhood while their children live out
the horrors often show remarkably little anxiety or worry about childrearing; they deny or play down their parenting problems and act as
if they have few stresses or concerns in that regard.

Turning the care of the teen's child over to other family members is
often the best resolution for serious caregiving problems. By providing
stable care and more positive models of identification, a child's grandparents or aunts and uncles can serve as significant buffers of stress
(Furstenberg 1976, Furstenberg et al. 1987; Kellam, Esminger, and
Turner 1977; Farber and Egeland 1987; Musick et al. 1987; Werner
1990). Unfortunately, within-family alternative care is not always a
feasible solution. In the most disorganized, most pathological families,
substitute caregivers are apt to have only marginally less severe, and

sometimes even worse, problems with childrearing than the adolescent mother.

If neither the adolescent nor her family are able to provide acceptable care for the child, should programs strive at least to prevent subsequent births, which increase the burden on an already fragile caretaking system? In theory this appears to be a sensible goal. In practice, however, it is rarely a reachable one. These young mothers have too many friends and relatives in similar situations and too little sense of personal control or choice.

Rachel: Cause if I can stop having babies long enough then I could go back to school and graduate—cause my little boy, my first one is 2, he'll be 3 in February and this one is 7 months, but now I'm pregnant again. I'm 18 to 20 weeks, and I didn't just find that out until about two weeks ago. This is my third child.
Interviewer: How old are you?
Rachel: 18. My cousin has five children and she's 20 and [now] she's having twins.

Terminating a mother's parental rights may not offer a satisfactory or lasting solution either, especially if she is in her early childbearing years. Take away one child and she will most likely get pregnant again soon, reasoning that, "They are not going to get my new baby away from me." As a noticeably impaired and incompetent mother once told me, "If I lose custody of this one, I'll just have another." The addictive quality of the need such mothers have for children, the vital roles their children play as narcissistic self-objects (especially when they are still small and docile and dependent), and the fact that motherhood makes them feel less marginal and more like other women converge to make it very difficult to resolve the problem by removing their children from their care.[15] In addition, many seriously inadequate mothers assiduously avoid contact with anyone they feel wants to "steal" their chil-

15. In addition there are far too few foster or adoptive homes, much less good ones, for children from multiproblem families. More often than not, these children have a variety of developmental and physical problems that make them more difficult to care for and less attractive to potential adoptive or foster parents.

dren away from them and fight with every means available to them to prevent the children's removal or to have them returned. As Pavenstedt (1971) comments:

No matter how negligent, how devoid of contact or communication with them, how abusive they may be, these mothers cling to their children.

The statement of a mentally retarded, alcoholic, promiscuous, and sometimes violent mother of nine children has stayed with me. . . . Once she came home before her children had been returned. [from foster care]: "I didn't know what to do with myself. I sat there smoking, feeling helpless and useless. Without the children I had no life."

In other words, her children were her only link to reality or perhaps even constitute her reality. They fill her life with activity, no matter how disorganized; their empty stomachs punctuate her day. Without them, she is faced with emptiness and passivity; her self-disparagement becomes unremitting (65).

The dangerously deficient caregiving environments provided by young mothers in multi-risk families present dilemmas for which there are no immediately apparent solutions.[16] When children receive at best only sporadic protection from destructive influences, when decent surrogate care is unavailable within the family, and when baby follows baby in rapid succession, the outlook for the children is bleak. There is no way to determine precisely how many children of adoles-

16. Developmental day care and nursery programs provide respite, support, and guidance for the mother and a nurturing, organized, alternate reality for her child (Provence and Naylor 1983; Greenspan et al. 1987; Seitz and Provence 1990; Shonkoff and Meisels 1990). Unfortunately intensive preventive and therapeutic programs are quite scarce in relation to the number of families in need of service. Most are relatively small and, because of the vagaries of funding, relatively short-lived (Schorr 1988; Musick and Halpern 1989, Halpern 1990). As Werner (1990) notes, if we cannot extend such services to all young children, we must set priorities and make hard choices. Among the various priority groups she would target for service are "babies of single or teenage parents with no other adult in the household" (112). One might expand this category to "no acceptable alternative caregiver"—but who will (or can) define and set standards of acceptability?

cents fall into this category—that is, how many are born to young women embarking on problem parenthood "careers."[17] Whatever the number, it is surely too great—even though the majority of adolescent mothers do not fall within this highest-risk category, being neither very good parents nor very bad ones.

It is one thing to recognize that a parent can either temper or heighten risk for her child;[18] it is another to understand why one teenager does more of the former while another does more of the latter. How is it that some teenage mothers are quite effective mediators and facilitators, whereas others act as risk-makers? What are the pivotal determinants of adolescent childrearing capacity and how responsive might these be to efforts to bring about childrearing change?

Determinants of Parenting

There is a substantial literature on why individuals raise their children the way they do (Belsky 1984; Belsky and Vondra 1989),[19] and a growing body of research and clinical observation on the psychological and social conditions necessary for positive childrearing change (Egeland, Jacobovitz, and Papatola 1984; Egeland, Jacobovitz, and Sroufe 1988; Pianta, Egeland, and Erickson 1989; Beckwith 1990; Musick and Stott 1990; Stern-Bruschweiler and Stern 1989; Shanok 1990; Zigler and Hall 1989; Sroufe 1988; Rutter 1989). Although this literature has been concerned mainly with adult parents, some of its concepts can

17. However, adolescent mothers do tend to come from the lower end of the socioeconomic scale, where there is greater prevalence of environmental risk factors, including serious social pathologies (Sameroff 1987; Sameroff and Fiese 1990).

18. Garmazy (1983, 1985, 1987) and Anthony and Cohler (1987) provide important insights into the processes by which parenting either promotes or blocks a child's self-righting tendencies. Although these investigators have largely been concerned with the risk for psychopathology among the offspring of psychiatrically ill mothers, many of their ideas apply to adolescent parents and their children as well.

19. Much of the best and most recent literature on this topic is concerned with early intervention for children at risk (Beckwith 1990; Sameroff and Fiese 1990; and Greenspan 1990); with the causes and consequences of child maltreatment (Cicchetti and Carlson 1989), and with internal representations (models) of the caregiving relationship (Main, Kaplan, and Cassidy 1985; Stern 1985, 1990; Bretherton 1987; Zeanah and Barton 1989).

help in the construction of a framework for viewing adolescents as mothers, in terms both of their parenting relationships and practices and their capacities for change.

Three major parenting determinants have been identified: characteristics of the child, contextual sources of stress and support, and the psychological well-being and personal resources of the parent (Belsky 1984). These interlocking but distinct subsystems buffer the parenting system against threats to its integrity which might result from disturbances or weaknesses in any single source.

Child Characteristics

In recent years much has been written about the ways a child may inadvertently contribute to or create a childrearing problem because of biological impairments, prematurity, or genetic disorders. Biologically based risk factors such as these act directly by limiting a child's ability to make use of growth-facilitating aspects of the environment or indirectly by interfering with or diminishing his parent's responsiveness to him. Babies with central nervous system damage, physical malformations, biological handicaps, chronic illnesses, or difficult temperaments can present formidable childrearing challenges— obstacles that even the most loving, mature, and knowledgeable parents may be unable to overcome.

Since a substantial minority of disadvantaged infants suffer from the multiple effects of both biological and environmental risk, and since the majority of children of adolescent mothers are disadvantaged, it stands to reason that they may make more than the ordinary demands on their already overwhelmed and underprepared mothers (see Meisels and Shonkoff 1990). Few studies have addressed this issue directly, but adolescents might well have more trouble altering their behavior to be better in tune with a child who was delayed or otherwise demanding (Brooks-Gunn and Furstenberg 1986). In addition to their preoccupation with their own social and developmental agendas, to say nothing of the trials of their daily lives, adolescent mothers generally know less about child development than older mothers and tend to be less responsive to their infants (Field 1981; Marecek 1985) and less affectively attuned to their feeling states (Osofsky and Eberhart-

Wright 1988, 1989). Thus, it would hardly be surprising to find that, without ample caregiving (and other forms of support) from adults, they might provide less than optimal childrearing environments for infants with special needs.

Sources of Stress and Support

Throughout this book I have sought to keep the issues of adolescent childbearing within the context in which they are played out, a context replete with stresses and for the most part devoid of meaningful supports. It is not necessary to spell out, one more time, the negative forces that surround and impinge on adolescents and their children or to dwell on the self-evident fact that adolescent mothers with strong, reliable, caring, supportive networks are more satisfied with their lives (Unger and Wandersman (1988) and better able to relate to and rear their children and to get and stay on track themselves.[20] It may be necessary, however, to point out that sometimes a source of support turns out to be a source of stress as well.

Some young mothers and their children thrive because of support received:

> I know they're in good hands. I can just leave . . . like when I went to Job Corps and I stayed there for half a month. When I came back my kids were healthier than ever. I went because I trusted my mom.

> When I had her I was just a child myself. I didn't know nothing about taking care of no child. I was glad my momma was there, she knew.

> If it wasn't for them I think I would have been gone and left those babies somewhere. But with my mother and father's help I'm doing pretty good.

20. Contextual (e.g., geographic) factors can play important roles in determining the amount and type of family (primarily grandmother) support available to teens and their children. For example, a comparison of Bryant's mothers in the southeastern region of the country with my sample of urban and small city teens in Illinois suggests that there are still more old-fashioned sources of support for single and adolescent mothers in the South, in white as well as black families.

Still others—perhaps an even greater number—pay dearly for such support.[21]

6/18/89

Today was a hard day I had to go back to Public Aid today they always giving me a hard time well when I got home my daughter was driving me craz[y] she was hungry because she didn't eat all day bacause she was sick well a hour went by and she was still crying I told her to sit by herself then I made her go to the room I closed the door and she throw-up all over and pissed all over herself I started yelling at her I put her in the bathtub and took her a bath I started to cry because I scared her I told her I was sorry. I think all my anger comes from my mother-in-law tell[ing] my [me] what to do with my child and I know it's not right about some of the things she tells me I love my daughter so much I always tell her that may-be when we get are own place things will be better. When we are home by are self she is a good girl I don't know what happens to her when every body comes home.

Further, those sources of stress and support most strongly related to adult parenting competence—social networks, employment, and, especially, the marital relationship (Belsky and Vondra 1989)—are likely to have unique connotations for adolescent mothers, although it is difficult to more than speculate about their effects since so little

21. Brooks-Gunn and Chase-Landsdale (1991) report that for families in which early childbearing is an intergenerational pattern, "'generational compression' is reflected in very young ages for grandmothers." One, frequently stressful, consequence for the grandmother is the need to combine the central tasks of middle adulthood with her grandmother role. In cases where the support given is too emotionally, financially, or physically costly for the supportive other, the adolescent and her child may ultimately pay. The indirect effects of these strains can be seen most clearly in the three-generation household where the teenage mother, her child(ren), and the grandmother reside together. Brooks-Gunn and Chase-Landsdale (1991) found that coresidence with the grandmother had a negative influence on young mothers' parenting practices, which in turn negatively influenced their preschoolers' emotional functioning. Not surprisingly, children fared more poorly when both mother and grandmother exhibited less optimal forms of parenting.

research has focused on this topic.[22] What may be of greater consequence are individual differences in two basic dimensions of support-
stress that have special relevance for adolescent parenting, although
they have received only minimal attention in the literature on adolescent childbearing.

One dimension of support-stress for the teenage mother encompasses the time and energy she must spend taking care of people in
addition to her child. She might, for example, feel obliged to care for
an aging grandmother who raised her when she was young,[23] or she
might be responsible for the the psychological, if not the concrete, care
of a mother, father, or other relative with chronic psychiatric or substance abuse problems or antisocial behavior patterns that regularly
involve trouble with the law. In many families an adolescent mother
continues to have primary caretaking responsibilities for her younger
siblings. Multiple caretaking roles and duties can tax the energy of
confident, caring, able adults. Just imagine the strain on a 16 year old;
imagine the effect on her parenting. When such burdens go unrelieved
the effects are wearing and corrosive.

More apparent, and equally significant sources of support-stress
are the relationships young mothers have with the boyfriends (and
husbands) who move in and out of their lives. Several studies have
described how support from the male partner plays a critical role in
affecting the adolescent mother's behavior toward her child (Furstenberg et al. 1983). For example, Crockenberg (1987) found that mothers

22. For an in-depth consideration of the role of support or stress in promoting or
undermining parental competence, see Belsky and Vondra, "Lessons from Child
Abuse: The Determinants of Parenting," in Cicchetti and Carlson (1989). See also
Colletta (1981) and Colletta and Lee (1983) with regard to social support and adolescent mothers.

23. Burton (1990) notes that among some lineages in her sample, the adolescent
mother's role is to take care of the great-grandmother, while *her* mother takes
primary care of her child. This highly structured system of "non-adjacent generational caregiving" appears to work relatively well in the semi-rural setting in which
it has evolved. There the stresses and supports tend to stay in balance with one
another. In other family or community contexts the scale appears to have tipped
toward the stress end, with young mothers—often the most able and competent—
needing to care for older and younger kin while receiving very little assistance
themselves.

whose partners remain involved tend to be less rejecting and punitive in their parenting practices. This is a very interesting finding because, objectively, these men are often only minimally involved with a child. Rather, the mother's subjective sense of being supported seems to make a difference. Perhaps it helps to make her feel less anxious and to reduce caregiving stress if she feels the emotional support of a man. When I have probed for the details of partner support (or the support of the baby's father, who is not always the same person), young women frequently respond by saying "Oh he's really a big help. He always brings a box of Pampers (or some formula, or a toy, or an article of clothing), whenever he comes by the house." Although adult mothers also appreciate and benefit from the support of their children's fathers, the support they receive is usually far more substantial. The fathers of their children are often their husbands and better off economically and socially than the average father of an adolescent's child, better able to provide greater material as well as emotional and social support. Interestingly, many adolescents act as though they have received such support when in reality they have not. Perhaps this subjective sense of receiving more than what is objectively given is partly a developmental phenomenon. Adolescents are more idealistic and even a little support may fit into their dreams of themselves as mothers. And, within the current context of poverty—a context characterized by the absence of father involvement—adolescent females long for the care of a nurturing male.[24] The young mother perceives her partner's gestures toward her child, however minimal, as caring for her. In some instances this benefits her child, and in other instances it clearly does not.

It is true that teenage girls are commonly consumed by their relationships with males: "boy-craziness" is a perfectly normal part of female adolescence. The trouble is, for many adolescent mothers, this normal developmental affinity is augmented and greatly magnified by a more excessive vulnerability to men. When this happens, the psychological cravings that drew her toward early pregnancy take on new and more menacing forms once motherhood begins.

24. As little as one generation ago, fathers—even unmarried ones—were more likely to be involved in their child's lives than is the case today (Brooks-Gunn and Chase-Landsdale 1991).

Like maybe you didn't have your mother and father's love when you were growing up, so you always depend on the opposite sex, as long as they tell you they love you, you put them before anything. You will put them before your kids . . . and why? I mean, you're not talking about marriage, it is just going to be a fling, the kids are there, supposed to be there for life.

He was a bad influence on my son. He would do the gang signals and my son started doing them too. He would roll a joint and curse and my son started doing the same thing. My son would play like he was rolling a joint and smoking it. Then things started piling up and he started hitting me in front of the children. He didn't want me to go to college.

The lives of some young women are ruled by the need to get (and stay) on the good side of men. Repeatedly seeking and involving themselves in self-destructive relationships with males, these psychologically vulnerable teens are victimized again and again.

I feel like a big piece of GUM, the kind that sticks to a shoe and gets stepped on, over and over again. I've tried everything to keep him.

The child of a victim is almost always a victim as well, the unwitting legatee of his mother's enmeshment in volatile, abusive relationships. In her struggle for psychic survival, this adolescent may sacrifice her child to her need for emotional support. The stresses and costs of such support are borne by children as much as, possibly more than, their mothers. Here Laurel writes in her journal about life with her husband Matt:

4/7
Mark wet his pants today. Matt is making him stay in bed all day. . . . I'd rather be a one parent family than let the kids have two parents that act like Matt and I do. . . . Sometimes when we argue I think Matt will hurt me or one of the kids real bad. . . . I don't know what to do anymore. One day Matt drank some Margaritas and we ended up arguing. He smacked me and my

nose bled. . . . I was around 4 or 5 months pregnant. . . . Matt
put his legs around me. I wanted to come home. He threatened
to squeeze me so I'd lose the baby. He didn't want me to leave
with his baby. We fought and argued a lot then. My nose bled a
couple times.

4/10

I'm glad he's leaving. He's not normal I guess. . . . I know I'll
never be alone. I have my kids. Their enough for me. They love
me when I feel sad and when I feel alone. They make me
happy. . . . I don't know what I'd do without them. Its too bad
Matt is the way he is. He'll miss seeing them grow up. . . . All I
wanted was a happy family that stayed together. I'll probably
miss him at first but I have to go on with life. . . . I'm going to
study for the literature quiz tomorrow and go to bed. . . . Matt
came home and said he's leaving Saturday so I'll need a new
sitter. . . . He says I'm a failure. I was doing my homework
beside him before I went to bed and he got mad. I can't concentrate on my schoolwork. I'm going to bed. It seems like our
arguments are a lot worse now.

4/16

Matt decided to stay.

4/23

He sometimes is rough with the kids. Two weeks ago he slapped
Claudia across her face. He did this around 1:00 in the after-
noon. When I came home from school I noticed the marks . . .
she had broken veins on her face. . . . I hate Matt because he is
mean. When Matt left in April it was the kids and me. We were
happy. . . . Now if I do a lot of things and play with the kids a
lot, Matt says I'm ignoring him. He's jealous. A family isn't
supposed to be like that. I don't know what's wrong with our
family that makes it like it is. *What can I do ?*
. . . I want my family to be better. That's why I'm go[ing] to
college. I want a career that will be financially secure. I want my
children to have a good future. I think of tomorrow and the
future. I try anyway. Matt doesn't seem to care.

4/29

. . . my husband and I are going through counciling. This is helping us a lot. . . . We are working to be better parents.

And here Marta describes a scene with Luis, the father of her son Gabriel, when Gaby was about 2 years old:

The worst time was when me and him had broken up. . . . I was walking . . . and he came by in the car and I didn't want to talk to him at all and he got mad and he got out of the car . . . and I was like "I don't want to talk to you. Get away from me." So he pulled the baby away from my arms . . . and I grabbed the baby and I was screaming at him, "let him go you're hurting him." Cause he had his legs and he kept pulling him . . . and the baby is screaming. And he got mad and . . . started pushing me . . . he just kept hitting my face and I was covering the baby and one of the punches just slipped to the baby's head and busted his ear and I got mad and I seen the baby bleeding from his ear. . . . He remembered for a while. He kept telling everybody the story. "[Daddy's] in jail. He hit mommy."

When asked about her friends' relationships with men, Marta responds that most of them are the same as hers:

They're afraid to leave the guys because if they do the guys threaten to hurt them and they have done it. And they have called the cops, and the cops don't do nothing. So they're afraid . . . you know, that they might end up putting down their kids [losing them to protective services] . . . and their kids is the number one pride of their life. And they don't want anything to happen to them, or they don't want anything to happen to themselves because then they're going to be wondering what's going to happen to their kids. . . . I had a lot of girlfriends who go through the same problem too, and their in the same situation as me . . . they're just in a mess(ed) up apartment with their kids, and their boyfriends are druggies or gang bangers and . . . the guys are putting their lives in danger, not only theirs but their kids . . . and they don't really care.

Physical or sexual abuse, neglect, even abandonment—these are only the most obvious symptoms of young mothers' entanglements with emotionally needy, domineering, or outright dangerous men, and these are only the most readily apparent effects. But the psychological pressure, indeed the compulsion, to please a man—to gain and retain his support—may take myriad forms, touching virtually any parenting function and affecting the quality of the parenting relationship. When asked to "write some positive thoughts and compliments about your child," 16-year-old Leila wrote:

Dear Lindsey, Today Mommy felt really bad about Rusty treating me wrong and I didn't feel like hearing you cry, but you know that I really love you and care about you. [Rusty is her 32-year-old boyfriend.]

Where there is adolescent overdependence on men, new risk is added to an already risk-laden childrearing environment, depriving the children in greatest jeopardy of the benefits most likely to prevent, reduce, or remediate developmental damage. Consider, for example, how an adolescent's relations with men may influence that earliest and most basic of parenting functions, feeding—specifically the choice to bottlefeed or to breastfeed an infant. Illustrating the intricate interweaving of social, developmental, and psychological factors, the determinants of this choice exemplify the challenges inherent in creating effective interventions—ones that make sense—for both adolescents and their children. In examining these issues, we cross an imperceptible border between the social and the psychological determinants of adolescent parenting.

Feeding Methods: A Confluence of Parenting Paths

Breast milk provides an ideal balance of nutrients in easily digested form, as well as antibodies and other immune factors that protect against infection.[25] Such protective factors would have significant ad-

25. This section is based on the research of Carol Bryant, Doraine Bailey, Jeannine Coreil, Sandra D'Angelo, and Minda Lazarov (1989). These writers document a number of factors affecting feeding choice. I have selected only those that I felt were most pertinent to issues of adolescent parenthood.

vantages for poor infants who tend, as a group, to be more physically vulnerable.[26] In addition to these health benefits, breastfeeding enhances a mother's attachment to her child and fosters strong emotional bonds (see, for example, Klaus and Kennell 1982). Most economically disadvantaged mothers, however, especially adolescent mothers, choose to bottle feed their infants.[27] Before health or social service providers rush in to promote breastfeeding to teenage mothers, they need to appreciate that the reasons these mothers choose the bottle generally make good sense to them at the time and may make very good sense for them as well.

There are a number of logical determinants of adolescents' decisions to bottle feed rather than breastfeed. They may find it too difficult to balance nursing with work and school activities, and they worry about losing their freedom:

If I breastfeed it, it wouldn't be no way I could go back to school or nothing, you just have to sit there all the time.

They have strong peer pressure to bottle feed and few same-age models:

Cause young people always on the go . . . still in the prime time of our lives. Just take it to a babysitter or whatever and go on.

26. Statistically, disadvantaged and minority children tend to have relatively high rates of neonatal and infant morbidity as well as mortality. A substantial subgroup of children of adolescent mothers are poor or of minority status. Evidence is conflicting as to whether maternal age, apart from socioeconomic background, is a primary risk factor for neonatal and infant death or illness. Thus it is still unclear whether the children of adolescents are at significantly greater risk for health and developmental problems than are other disadvantaged minority children. See Brooks-Gunn and Furstenberg 1986; Chase-Landsdale, Brooks-Gunn, and Paikoff 1991; Osofsky, Osofsky, and Diamond 1988; Schellenbach, Whitman, and Borkowski 1991.

27. For example, Ross Laboratories (1987) reports that in the Southeast Region where breastfeeding rates are the lowest in the nation, less than 30 percent of low-income mothers initiate breastfeeding and only 7 percent continue for six months or longer. Bryant et al. (1989) note that participants in wic (the government's supplemental food program for poor women and children) have even lower rates, with few clinics reporting more than 10 to 15 percent breastfeeding at the first postpartum appointment.

They also fear (with some justification) that others on whom they depend for support will feel left out if they cannot feed the child:

> This will be the first grandbaby. . . . My parents and his parents too would want to be close to him. I just think it would be better if they could help feed it.

As one grandmother put it:

> I said "girl, you ain't gonna breastfeed that baby, you gotta go to school." . . . I said "I'm not gonna be going through that problem keeping the baby, and that baby be wanting you and you not here."

These are rational reasons, given adolescents' educational, economic, social, and developmental needs.[28] A seemingly less sensible set of determinants involves sexuality and, by association, relationships to males. Adolescents, especially young ones, are generally self-conscious about their bodies. This is a developmentally normal response to their bodily transformations.

> . . . everyone's gonna look at you and that's one thing I can't stand is for someone to sit and look at me.

> I'm not gonna have none, especially when you're out someplace and have to feed it, just pull it out.

Adolescent mothers are also afraid to breastfeed around men, worrying that this might be interpreted as seductive, no matter what precautions they take to preserve modesty. Some fear that men will read it the wrong way, become aroused, and attack them sexually while they are in a vulnerable position. Considering the sexual attitudes and behaviors demonstrated by many males in their milieu, these fears may not be unwarranted. As one young breastfeeding mother recounted:

> I was at the store at the mall and . . . these perverted men [said] "Yeah baby you feedin that little baby. Can I have some of that

---

28. In a lighter vein, teens also seem more concerned that breastfeeding would keep them from eating their favorite foods such as fries, chips, soda, burgers, and other "junk": "I like to eat a lot of spicy foods and they were saying that the things give the milk a funny flavor" (Bryant et al. 1989).

titty you got? I want some milk, I'm thirsty." I said thank God my husband ain't here he would have went off on them.

These girls are not overreacting when they say, "Raping is so big" or "I might be on the bus and this man is looking at my breast."

Mothers in Bryant's study described their breasts primarily as sex organs, serving to attract and please men.[29] It is hard to reconcile this view with the nurturing image of breastfeeding a child: "The breasts are men's play toys, they're not for baby to nurse on."Some teens said they didn't breastfeed because their partner was jealous of the mother-child intimacy or unwilling to "share" their woman's breasts with a baby.

My fiancee don't want me to breastfeed . . . he don't think that these belong to the baby, they belong to him. . . . He thinks they're for a sexual thing [more] than it is as far as a health thing.

Or, as one teen's boyfriend said to her infant son:

Boy you gonna have to stop sucking on them breasts. That's my breasts you up there gettin horny on em.

Others said that their partner didn't approve of breastfeeding because his male friends might see it and get "turned on."

My baby's daddy said . . . "you're not going to get out there in public and pull your breast out so everybody can see it."

Because breasts are associated with adult sexual intimacy, the notion of offering them to a child is highly objectionable to some mothers—analogous to incest: "People think it's perverted . . . when you let a child suck on your breast."

Sexual connotations such as this are overwhelming for young women who are already disgusted and offended by the thought of exposing their breasts or suckling a child. For them, crossing this boundary is tantamount to a moral transgression (Bryant et al. 1989). And for

29. Bryant's target population consisted primarily of economically disadvantaged women in six southeastern states: primiparous and multiparous; black and white; urban and rural; teen and nonteen. In using data from this study I have tried, wherever possible, to separate teens from nonteens.

adolescents who have been victims of sexual abuse, intimations of incest may be experienced as doubly threatening and repugnant. Barriers to breastfeeding that involve sexual and relationship issues exert particular force for still developing, not-yet- mature young females, and one must think very carefully before trying to overcome them. No matter how well intentioned, misguided efforts may hurt rather than help. For psychological as much as social or economic reasons, we should not automatically encourage adolescent mothers to breastfeed, regardless of the potential benefits to their children. At 13, 14, 15, and 16 years old they may be mothers, but they are not yet women. It is not appropriate to pressure a girl to breastfeed, and to pressure her to do so for a child conceived through force or psychological manipulation is cruel.

Breastfeeding is only one of many domains where there is potential conflict between the needs of an adolescent mother and those of her child. Balancing these different needs is more than a simple intervention problem; it is a complex psychological problem. Psychological factors play a major role in the genesis of caregiving and parental relationship difficulties for all parents. They are the internal barriers to change. Beyond this, psychological factors play a preeminent role in adolescent parenting difficulties because of unique developmental and relational issues in female adolescent life. Unfortunately, too few health, education, or social service workers are equipped to intervene in such complex issues.

Psychological Determinants of Parenting

The three major parenting subsystems do not exert equal influence on parenting. As Belsky and Vondra observed, "If something goes wrong in the parenting system, optimal functioning (defined in terms of producing competent offspring) will occur when the personal resources of the parents are the only determinants that remain intact" (1989, 188). This means that a mother with greater psychological capital is better able to overcome or modulate risk characteristics of her child, to be a more effective mediator and raise him well in spite of the constraints of limited financial or environmental resources. Psychological structures are "the most influential determinants of parenting not simply for their direct effect on parental functioning, but also because of the role they undoubtedly play in recruiting contextual support" (191). In other words, a mother with more substantial personal resources elicits and makes better use of whatever supports are available to her. Indeed, she is able to create supports where none exist (Hans, Musick, and Jagers 1992), transmitting to her child a sense of self-efficacy, a belief that despite numerous obstacles personal effort will engender success. On the other hand, a mother who feels defeated by life and powerless to control her own destiny may transmit this to her child through lower expectations of what he is capable of accomplishing in school (Clark 1983; Comer 1989), which are often evident as early as preschool or kindergarten (Hans, Musick, and Jagers 1992); by her depression, emotional unavailability, and insensitivity to his needs (Ainsworth et al. 1978; Fraiberg 1980; Sameroff and Emde 1989; Stern 1985); or through a self-imposed social isolation that denies him access to alternative sources of guidance and support (Stott, Cohler, and Musick n.d.). Finally, she passes on a legacy of futility and impotence each time she declines to assert herself on his behalf or fails to protect him (Gershenson et al. 1987).

Growing out of a parent's personality and psychological makeup, such behaviors do more than create educational, psychological, or physical jeopardy; they communicate certain long-lasting messages about a child's worth to those closest to him and, ultimately, about his worth as a person. A child constructs his sense of self from these messages, experiencing the meanings he holds for his mother—her internal representations of who she is, who he is, who they are together, and how their relationship fits into the larger social world (Bowlby 1980; Bretherton 1987; Main, Kaplan, and Cassidy 1985; Zeanah and Barton 1989; Stern-Bruschweiler and Stern 1989; Brazelton and Cramer 1990). It is not so much who he is and what he does as how she sees him and interprets his actions—what their meanings are for her. Even when she knows what these meanings are, they are hard to change.

For more than two years I have had the burden of thinking about being sexually abused by my son's father. He really put me through hell and I will never forget the pain he has put in my heart. At the age of fifth-teen he forced me to have sex with him . . . he hurt me mentally and may I add that he hurt me a great deal. . . . I still have the pain in my heart of being beat and raped over and over again. . . . I would just like to add that alot of the time when I look at my son I see his father in him and I feel like hurting him, but God helps me to deal with this. I hope one day I can be able to afford counseling for my son and me because I don't want to hurt him the way I have been hurt.

The meanings a parent attributes to her child have their origins in her personality, psychological history, and responses to the major relationships and events of her life. Ghosts from her past—such as her relationship with her mother (Fraiberg et al. 1975; Fraiberg 1980; Main and Goldwyn 1984; Ricks 1985; Brazelton and Cramer 1990)—shape the way she perceives, interprets, and thus responds to her child (for example, Broussard and Hartner 1970, 1971; Cohen and Beckwith 1979; Meares et al. 1982; Cramer 1987; Emde 1987). As she attributes meaning to what her child does, she begins to label his behavior (and often him as well) as good or bad, smart or stupid, destined for success or for trouble, and so on. According to Brazelton and Cramer (1990) a hidden scenario emerges in which she acts out imaginary interactions with her child (135). Perhaps he represents someone important in her past or some aspect of her own unconscious. Perhaps their relationship reenacts past ways of relating. Whatever the origin of a parental fantasy, we can be sure that children "will realize in their behavior roles that their parents expect them—unconsciously—to play" (Brazelton and Cramer 1990, 141). That is, whether a parent's perceptions are accurate assessments of the child's objective behaviors and characteristics or distortions and exaggerations which generate self-fulfilling prophesies (Stott, Cohler, and Musick n.d.), the child will tend to adopt self-perceptions congruent with his parent's expectations.[30]

30. Other psychological factors, such as emotional disturbance, may interfere with a mother's capacity to carry out childrearing functions (Rutter 1987c; Rutter and Cox 1985) apart from any inherent lack in parenting skills or relationship qualities (Rutter 1989). For example, depression seems to affect a mother's percep-

As Brazelton and Cramer note:

> When the mother begins to recognize the life of her fetus, she
> will unconsciously put herself in its place, identify with it. . . .
> This fantasized "return to the womb" allows for yet another
> working through of unfulfilled dependency needs and symbiotic
> wishes. . . . This regressive trend can also activate conflict and
> pathological reactions. . . . If the mother's need for dependency
> is too great and unfulfilled (in some teenage mothers, for exam-
> ple), she will experience her fetus—and later, her baby—as a
> rival, and may treat the infant as an envied sibling. In this case,
> mothering will seem a heavy burden and even a frustration of her
> own needs. (1990, 21–22)

The adolescent voices in this and previous chapters speak of the variety
of special meanings that children hold for young mothers, some of
which are distinct from those shared with mothers who are older.
These separate meanings—as much as adolescent immaturity per se,
lack of knowledge of child development, difficult life circumstances, or
child characteristics—determine what a teen will actually do as a
mother. An adolescent's child is more likely to be encumbered by his
mother's relationship problems with her mother and her unconscious
expectation that he will be the main provider of love (Brazelton and
Cramer 1990). He is more likely to be burdened by her unrealistic
dreams and hopes, unconsciously blamed and treated harshly (or re-
jected) for failing to solve her developmental problems; for failing to
provide a magical cure for her unhappiness and self-doubt. And, during a developmental era distinguished by the reemergence and reworking of attachment-separation issues, an adolescent's earlier losses or

---

tion of her child, *independent of his objective characteristics* (Cohler et al. 1983;
Friedlander et al. 1986; Panaccione and Wahler 1986; and Rickard et al. 1981),
causing her to exaggerate his problems and be less satisfied with his social and
affective development (Kochanska et al. 1987). Mothers with recurrent or chronic
depressive disorders tend to be less appropriately responsive to their children, less
likely to sustain positive interactions, and less able to control the children (Mills et
al. 1985; Pound et al. 1985). There is, however, no evidence that adolescent mothers
are more depressed than older mothers in similar economic circumstances (Brooks-
Gunn and Furstenberg 1986).

abandonments may be replayed or recapitulated with her child. Because an adolescent mother is psychologically still something of a child, she is less able to modulate her impulses and emotions, less qualified to provide the consistency and direction that are the first rungs on the ladder up and out. Still so young, how can she actively lead her child beyond where she is? How can she actively foster his development when she is so caught up with her own? Not fully developed, a 16-year-old may "play mommy" yet be incapable of a genuinely reciprocal parenting relationship; she may be too narcissistic to permit let alone enable her child to be himself, free from her desires and projections.

Indeed, what often seems to be neglect or pathological distance from her child may actually be the manifestation of a teen mother's symbiosis with her baby, her inability to differentiate his needs from her own. It is not unusual to hear some variation of the following exchange between an adolescent mother and her baby's childcare provider:

Caregiver: Why isn't he wearing a jacket today?
Adolescent mother: I'm not cold.

And, unless he really fusses, he may not be fed until she is hungry.

What empirical evidence do we have that adolescent mothers behave in ways that are systematically different from adult mothers? Very little that is not equivocal.[31] The existing research tends to be concerned with parenting infants rather than preschoolers and school-aged children, and most has focused on what Brooks-Gunn and Furstenberg (1986) call the "prototypical adolescent mother: black, urban, poor and unmarried" (34).

The available data indicate that teens are more inclined to use physical punishment with their infants, especially when they fail to meet developmental expectations (DeLissovoy 1973; Field 1980), and

31. For discussion and reviews of the research in this field, see Osofsky, Osofsky, and Diamond 1988; Osofsky and Eberhart-Wright 1988, 1989; Brooks-Gunn and Furstenberg 1986; Brooks-Gunn and Chase-Landsdale 1991; Chase-Landsdale, Brooks-Gunn, and Paikoff 1991; Schellenbach, Whitman, and Borkowski 1991.

display more hostile (and childlike) behaviors such as teasing and pinching (Osofsky and Ware 1984).[32] Adolescents spend less time talking to their infants than do adult mothers (Field 1981; Sandler, Vietze, and O'Connor 1981; Osofsky, Osofsky, and Diamond 1988). This may be evidence of their greater self-absorption, not only their apathy, or lack of knowledge about the importance of talking to young children.[33] Whatever its cause, the fact that they vocalize less and offer less stimulation in general to their infants may be key factors in these children's later depressed cognitive functioning (Chase-Landsdale, Brooks-Gunn, and Paikoff 1991).

Much of the data on teens as parents is anecdotal. It comes from the observations of experienced clinicians such as Rosalie Streett, founding director of Friends of the Family, Maryland's family support program initiative, who work with adolescents and their children. Ms. Streett, who designed and ran programs for adolescent mothers for many years, worries about how they relate to their children: "I have found that one often has to allow a teen mother to be a child herself before she can provide adequate care for her own child. I remember having to hold a very young mother on my lap—she was so upset with her child. She sat in my lap and cried, and sucked her thumb, while her child sat in her lap sucking his."

I used to observe child-development specialists teaching groups of young mothers how to teach their young children to play with Play Doh. The mothers were frequently unable to think about giving this or

32. Culture and social class, however, strongly determine the meaning of teasing behavior. Thus, the socializing context in which teasing takes place must always be considered when interpreting this behavior. For example, Miller and Sperry (1987) observed that urban working class white mothers deliberately created teasing situations in which their daughters could practice defending themselves. Given life's harsh realities, these mothers believed that it was important to teach daughters early to be strong, to suppress hurt feelings, and to stand up for themselves when wronged. Brice Heath (1983, 1987) also discusses this issue, noting that in the southern black community she has studied for many years, teasing is used to socialize boys: "As soon as they could toddle, boys became public objects of verbal teasing, and successful verbal retorts could command attention from spectators on several porches" (9).

33. Where is the need to talk to her baby if he is not experienced as a separate being but only as an extension of herself?

other playthings to their children until they had played with them for quite a while themselves. Some could hardly bear to part with these delightful, never-before-experienced things; if they had no toys of their own, they might well grab and keep their child's toys for themselves. Mother love: you can't give it if you need to get it yourself.

Many adolescents give the appearance of having little tolerance for their children's developmentally appropriate demands or attempts to explore and assert themselves. They tend to speak very critically and negatively to their children, handle them roughly, and terrorize them one moment and smother them with kisses the next. They spank and slap babies when they cry or spit up or spill food, attributing willful naughtiness even to very young infants—"He's just trying to get me!" Their responses seem insensitive and inappropriate, unconnected to who their children are and what they need. These same sorts of interactional problems have been observed in older, troubled mothers by clinical investigators (for example, Fraiberg 1980; Greenspan 1981; Musick et al. 1987).

The quality of adolescents' play with their infants tends to be less reciprocal and poorer than that of adult mothers (Culp et al. 1989). Clinically it might be described as being mother- rather than child-focused. Certainly it is rougher, more physical, and more intrusive than one finds with older mothers. The teen's greater physicality may derive from her perception of the infant as a toy, something to be played with when and how it suits her without regard to how it feels to him.

Childrearing patterns such as these cannot be without negative consequences, especially when they are a part of the daily experience of children already in jeopardy because of poverty and its attendant risks. I was sharply reminded of these consequences some years ago as I listened to a talk by Lawrence Steinberg in 1987. Summarizing research on characteristics of families who either promote or inhibit their children's development, he cited parental rejection as the most harmful parenting practice. It may be that one of the most pernicious effects of teens' problematic childrearing practices is that they imply parental rejection. They imply that the young mother has failed to engage with the child she said she so badly wanted or has disengaged from the role she had envisioned herself as enjoying. Even if such practices are not meant to be rejecting—and in many cases they are not—a sensitive and vulnerable child may construe or perceive them to be so.

Sometimes I can be some mean old bag to my children, but then I can be nice. I am mean a lot, especially to David. . . . I love my two kids. I wouldn't give them up for anyone or anything. . . . It is complicated.

The psychoanalyst Therese Benedek once said that the capacity for motherliness is dependent on a mother's having enough psychological distance from her child to enable her to move in the direction of making the right choice for his sake (1970). Can we say that an adolescent—a girl with only one foot out of childhood herself, who is drawn to early parenthood to make up for other things she hasn't had and fears she may never have—can we say she has that distance? Is she developmentally and psychologically capable of making such choices consistently? Time and her own efforts may markedly improve her mothering and life circumstances (Herr and Halpern 1991). Positive parenting "discontinuities" (Rutter 1989) can improve her child's chances as well (see Brooks-Gunn and Furstenberg 1986; Brooks-Gunn and Chase-Landsdale 1991; Chase-Landsdale, Brooks-Gunn, and Paikoff 1991). Yet, if completing her education, getting a job, moving to a better community, sending her child to a better school, and having a more stable life—if these things (done on her own, or with the help of a program) allow her child a second chance, her parenting problems were probably less serious or deeply rooted to begin with. As the young mother above put it, "It is complicated."

Adolescent Parenting and Change

In the case of adolescent motherhood, the issue of change is an especially important one, interwoven with—indeed, inseparable from—the issues of adolescent parenting. Though they may be modified in any number of ways, many of the forces that drew her into early parenthood will influence her as she takes on the functions of mothering. These forces will regulate her childrearing abilities and determine her motivation and capacity for change in this domain. Parenting change has multiple manifestations and meanings. For one parent it takes the form of being markedly better than her parents were when she was growing up, of breaking patterns of dysfunctional parenting enacted and reenacted across generations within her family. For another, it means improving how she relates to and takes care of her child after an initially unpromising or even a disastrous start. For one mother, change is wholly self-generated, vows made and kept to spare her offspring the childhood anguish she remembers so well:

> I don't believe in whooping my kids. Because when I was coming up it seems that the least little thing that I done, I got a whooping for it. And I had said that if I ever had any kids I wouldn't whoop my kids, because I know how it feels to be whooped. So I don't whoop my kids, I mainly talk to them.

For another parent, change comes only with long-standing (perhaps ongoing) external, professional guidance and support (Egeland and Erickson 1990), including therapy for herself and her child (Fraiberg 1980; Provence and Naylor 1983; Greenspan et al. 1987; Greenspan 1990). And always, for adolescent mothers, changes in parenting will be linked to the adolescent process itself. As one teen mother put it, "We're growing up together, him and me."

Many theorists believe that the gravest problems of parenting will not, indeed cannot, change unless the underlying, largely unconscious, meanings are altered as well.[34] This is an intervention task that relatively few programs have been ready or able to fulfill. There is much we do not know about changing childrearing patterns, especially when the meanings governing these are markedly distorted or when the parent is still very much a developing, if older, child herself.

34. In particular, I am referring to work by Mary Main, Martha Erickson, Alicia Leiberman, Stanley Greenspan, Joy Osofsky, Rebecca Shanok, Michael Rutter, T. Berry Brazelton, Bertrand Cramer, Daniel Stern, and Selma Fraiberg, much of which has been cited earlier in this chapter. These authors have dealt mainly with the parenting of infants and very young children and, with the exception of Osofsky, have not looked specifically at adolescent parents.

The answer lies not merely in the creation of more programs or in the recruitment and training of more people to provide parenting interventions for young families at risk. This will surely help, but it will not help enough. The numbers and needs are too great. Not every adolescent's parenting problem can be solved, or solved in time to save her child. For the interventionist, the most significant predictors of improved parenting revolve around an adolescent mother's desire and capacity to use help for change. A measure of emotional maturity, a self-reflective nature, personal honesty and willingness to take responsibility for her own actions, openness to the pain of her past, and the desire and tenacity to struggle (and keep on struggling) to create a different and better future for her child—these individual traits of character are authentic sources of personal change.

Allie has brought my life to a stop so I can look back on it so I can raise her like I would have liked to been raise[ed]. My parents made mistakes and were very harsh at times but I don't want to with her. I want to be fair and never punish her becuz I *thought* she *might* have done something wrong. My father used to beat the hell out of me and I'm afraid I'll do that to Allie. I never want to and if I *ever* start I will get help. I know how children feel.

Transformations: Developmental and Otherwise

A few years ago I gave a talk at a conference on adolescent motherhood and self-transformation. After my presentation, a smartly dressed young woman came up and handed me a letter. This is what it said:

> Dr. Musick—
> My name is L. H. I was put in a foster home at the age of approx. 9 months old. My foster parents passed away when I was 10 years old. . . . So I was put in another foster home. . . .
> At the age of 16 I was pregnant with my first child. . . . I had my son in August, missed September out of school, but went back to school in October. I graduated from high school in June of that school year, with my class.

I went to college for about 2 ½ years.

I had my second son five years later. I moved out on my own the following year. I thought that everything was fine. But on November 12, 19__, I woke up to a man in my apartment and was raped, and my children's lives threatened.

After that I felt so helpless, not only for myself but because I was a 21-year-old mother of two and my children's lives were in danger. I went through the year-long trial (because I was able to identify the guy), the postponements, and all the other things that you have to go through when you're going through a criminal trial when you are the victim.

These are just *some* of the things I have been through in my life. I am in my late twenties now. My oldest child is 11, my youngest 6. Both are doing very well in school. I'm working for the Department of Human Resources of P. I start back to school in September. I'm going to the University of P.

I think my life is going pretty well. It could be better because like with anything there's room for improvement.

I had a chance to meet my natural mother. And when I look at how she's living I thank God that I had a chance to have a better life. All my foster parents were very supportive of me even as a young child. I did have a lot of walls to climb in my life. (Some that I mentioned, some I didn't.) But my foster parents made that climb much easier.

I teach my children to *always have hope*. Be the best that *they* can be. Always respect everyone, especially themselves. I think I'm doing fine.

Please excuse my handwriting and how I jumped from one thing to the next. Your workshop was very interesting and now I see that I'm not alone.

Laurie's story and the way she recalled it reminded me of a young mother I had interviewed as part of a follow-up study of former Ounce of Prevention Fund participants. In recalling her grandfather's attempts to sexually abuse her, Sharon brought up other significant experiences in her life, describing her responses to them. Like Laurie,

Sharon overcame many obstacles in her very young life. And, like Laurie, she knew what it is about herself and others that helped her do so.

Oh, it [the sexual abuse] didn't go on long at all. Because I had enough sense to know that it wasn't my fault and there was my stepmother [and] I told her. . . . I had it where somebody would know besides me what was going on. . . . I was so confused, and I felt like I had done something—I'm like, you know, better than that. But I feel like if I wasn't even strong enough to know that, that it would still be going on. . . . It's just that everything that I did was at the right time, but then my father couldn't accept that his father . . . tried, and well, that kinda hurts me a lot too, because my father just, he couldn't accept it. . . . He didn't blame me. He said that if he didn't believe me he wouldn't be there to get me [and take her back to his house], but he didn't tell his father that, . . . it was just, "Okay Dad" and "Okay daughter, I understand" . . . one of those situations, and I couldn't accept that, . . . [I wanted him] to acknowledge . . . that it really happened. . . .

I have lived through a lot of changes when I was younger and I have always been a strong person. There have been some mistakes I have made but I am smart enough not to go to drugs or drink alcohol. I am pretty much a strong person, so there are a lot of things I can accept. [Heart-to-Heart] . . . was helpful. It brought back a lot of old feelings and memories . . . I didn't really want to deal with, but every little bit helped.

I had a type of situation where with my family, they know the type of person I am. I like to sit in my room, that is my privacy, and I did that during high school, and I went places, but I like to sit and read and think. I am a thinking person, period. I only go to work for eight hours a day and be with those people because I have to, but other than that I am a thinking person. . . . You know, I don't like to share too much with too many people, and when I went through a lot of changes during high school, I always said, when I graduate, I am leaving, and that is exactly what I did. I left my mom's house. . . . I did. I think I've done well, I really do. I know what I'm gonna do. It takes a long time. . . . Okay, I spent nine months on public aid, I'm never going back as long as I work eight hours and pay my bills and try to pay for the school and just gradually, I'll make it. . . . It's tough, but I like being able to do it on my own.

Now she is pregnant again and planning to marry the father of this child.

Well, after Billy I just didn't want any more because of the expense. It's always at the wrong time, of course, but . . . he's got a good job, a real good job, two good jobs. He works construction with his dad and then he does food service at the hospital, and he wants to go to school so he can be a respiratory therapist. But when you gotta think about long term goals, and then you got a baby on the way, you gotta prepare for it. It's confusing sometimes. . . . He has always taken good care of my son. . . . When my son was in diapers, he would take the dirty diaper and wash it out in the toilet. I won't even do that, so he's always been a lot of help. . . . [Billy] will be three in November. . . . He is in day care and I don't worry about him any more. And they know I am the type of mom that comes on lunch hour and I want to see exactly what they are doing.

Speaking about the home in which her father grew up, Sharon clearly rejects her grandparents' way of life, contrasting it with that of her stepmother, a woman she admires and looks to as a role model.

So I try to stay away from their life cause they live a different type of life that I don't ever want to live. My grandfather is an alcoholic, my grandmother, she's a gossip, she just didn't teach her daughter anything, and her daughters they have their kids, they go through adoption processes and abortions, and it's just a mess. . . . Now I see my stepmother, there is a lot of things that we did not agree upon but she came from a better family, and her and my dad, she been, she feels she is the type of person, . . . the type of wife that likes to keep her family together, and since my grandmother raised my father that certain way, she's always had to struggle. It's like she had to mold him over, his way of thinking has to be different because she came from a better side of the family that taught her, you know, some morals, and her values were just better than his mom and dad's, so I think that helped me a lot because there were a lot of things that my stepmother and I didn't agree on, but I can say that everything I know she taught me. What my mother, my real mother didn't do, she did. So if I can't appreciate her for anything else, I can appreciate her for that.

The narratives of these two young mothers do more than spell out the grim particulars of growing up at risk. They expose a network of interlocking themes related to change: psychological themes connected to the capacity to meet and master adversity, to achieve as a parent as well as a person, to use whatever is given (or found) to transform and reinvent oneself, and to envision and set about constructing a life that is different from and better than that of one's mother or father or grandparents. Beyond these capacities are the external influences to which they were fortunate enough to be exposed and wise enough to utilize.

Stories such as these help to reframe our concepts of success and of the different routes by which it is achieved. Laurie and Sharon are not the most troubled young mothers,[1] nor are they the "one or two in a dozen" with exceptional talent or motivation (Lynn 1990) or extraordinary families (Comer 1988). For both, pregnancy seems to be something that "just happens." Both were mothers in their teens, and both had a second child while unmarried. Each carries on her struggle to get and stay ahead—two steps forward, one step back.

In this chapter, lessons gleaned from these and other stories are used to highlight the role of psychological factors in motivating, mediating, and sometimes blocking positive change. Lessons from practice—observed encounters between interventions and individuals—are used

---

1. Furstenberg, Brooks-Gunn, and Morgan's (1987) longitudinal study of teenage mothers indicates that approximately one-third of their sample falls into this category. Others estimate similar percentages in their samples.

to examine the numerous facets and forms of change: What makes a person want to change? What helps her take the personal risks involved in doing it differently and better? What helps her to stick with a demanding new task until it is mastered? What are valid markers of change for adolescent mothers—that is, how do we know that meaningful change has taken place? In which domains are changes most likely to occur for adolescent mothers: education or work, relationships with children or parents or partners or peers? Are some domains of change more significant for disadvantaged girls? Are some more developmentally mediated? What are the developmental and psychological mechanisms underlying change, and how do these interact with externally constructed mechanisms like intervention programs? Are there differences between transformations that are solely self-generated and those that result from outside intercession, between those one has sought and those imposed by others? Although personal change is always to some degree self-generated, it is possible that some transformations are more self-generated than others.

Questions such as these address issues beyond adolescent childbearing per se. They also ask: Under what circumstances are new skills and knowledge acquired and used? Under what circumstances do the effects of trauma diminish; under which do they endure and pass from generation to generation? When asking these questions we are speaking about intervention in the broadest sense—not just intervention programs for adolescent mothers but the full range of growth-promoting and healing experiences, relationships and environments that make a difference in how young people develop and live their lives. Intervention experiences have shaped the ideas put forward throughout this book; in this chapter they move to center stage.

The catalyst for constructive change may be a particular event or experience in the young mother's life. It may be the consequence of developmental maturity, of simply growing up and out of her adolescent problems. It may be any combination of these factors and others. Although we can never know precisely why any particular beneficial change has occurred, examining its motives and means is worthwhile. Without analysis we have little way of knowing what part—if any—our efforts may have played in bringing this about.

Obviously not all, perhaps not even most, adolescent mothers are in formal teen-parent programs. Nevertheless, many make use of some type of support during their early years of parenthood, even if it is only in a specific area such as job training or health care or for only brief periods of time. Of course, some adolescent mothers are not motivated to accept, let alone seek, any outside support. Often these teens are the ones in greatest need, but they may not see themselves as needing help or they may be too confused and disorganized to use it.

When an adolescent mother seeks help, we often assume that she wishes to change, but she may not—at least not at first. She may want help in solving an immediate problem, defusing a current crisis, or finding an appropriate educational or vocational training program. She may be looking for child care, health care, welfare, shelter, or temporary respite. She may be seeking a surrogate family to guide her past risks and temptations. She may need a place to go to escape the pressures of her home or the streets—a place to talk and be with others, a place to be herself.

Although personal transformation is seldom the primary goal when adolescents first solicit the support of others, it may be the eventual byproduct.

> It's a place where you can go, put your kids in one room, and you can go in another room. You don't have to worry about your kids falling, bumping their heads, because somebody's there to watch them. You can sit back, get your thoughts together, think about what you're going to do . . . sit and talk. . . . You don't have to be in the street all day long. . . . We had parties, big dinners, pot luck, Thanksgiving parties and stuff. . . . Ain't nothing they haven't told me or planted in the back of my head that I don't know.

Different Paths

> My life is such a *screw up* and I am not doing anything about it.
> I threw my life away and now I am trying to find it.

Adolescent mothers are a highly diverse group, so one finds marked diversity in their individual life paths. Although early childbearing places numerous risks and obstacles in a young mother's way, with time it is possible to overcome a good many of these and go on to succeed as a parent, partner, worker, and member of society.[2] Studies that have followed teenage mothers for twenty years indicate that roughly two-thirds of them have completed school, gotten and stayed off welfare, and noticeably improved their employment status (Furstenberg, Brooks-Gunn, and Morgan 1987; Furstenberg, Levine, and Brooks-Gunn 1990; Horwitz et al. 1991a, 1991b).

Whereas many young mothers eventually do well for themselves, as a group their children appear to be at a developmental disadvantage compared to children of women who delay childbearing into their twenties. These children have more school-related and behavioral problems, especially when they reach adolescence (Card and Wise 1981; Mott and Marsiglio 1985; Brooks-Gunn and Furstenberg 1987) and are more likely to become adolescent parents themselves.[3] At the same time, as a group—like their mothers—they demonstrate considerable diversity, with many doing quite well in school, work, and fertility control. For example, Furstenberg, Levine, and Brooks-Gunn (1990) report that close to two-thirds of the daughters of the adolescent mothers they studied postponed childbearing beyond their teenage years. This finding tells us that daughters of adolescent mothers are not predestined to do as their mothers have done.

Variability in adolescent mothers' lives over time is reflected in variability in their children's outcomes. As the years pass, these children do better if their mothers' lives improve, especially if these improvements involve welfare and marital status (Chase-Landsdale and

2. Not surprisingly, the adolescent mothers most likely to succeed are those who are at grade level when they become pregnant or who are able to finish high school within five years after the baby's birth. These are also those who have few siblings and whose own parents are not on public assistance and have more than a tenth-grade education themselves (Furstenberg, Brooks-Gunn, and Morgan 1987, as cited in Chase-Landsdale, Brooks-Gunn, and Paikoff 1991).

3. This is especially true for those adolescents whose mothers have experienced recent spells on welfare. As Furstenberg, Hughes, and Brooks-Gunn (1991) note in regard to this issue: "Those women who are persistently on welfare undoubtedly have lower education and fewer marketable skills. They have larger families and more crowded households, they may be more depressed and discontent with their lives, they may live in more distressed neighborhoods, and their children may have attended worse schools."

Brooks-Gunn 1990).[4] In most cases, a former teenage mother who improves her socioeconomic status through work or marriage brings her children with her to a better neighborhood with better schools and greater opportunities. In doing this, the upwardly mobile young mother provides a model of initiative, high self-standards, and competence for her children to emulate.

> I'm getting out of this neighborhood, and I'm getting him out too. I don't even want him going to the day camp here this summer. I want him to go to the Park District camp where the smart kids go—the kids whose parents have money.[5]

There is a catch, however. An upwardly mobile young mother may have to expend so much effort to get ahead that she has little time or energy for her children. If no one else (such as the grandmother) is there to provide them with appropriate experiences, they may obtain the material but not the social or psychological benefits of upward mobility.

Forty-one-year-old Phyllis is a former teenage mother. Well-spoken, energetic, and very successful in her work, she struggled for many years to educate herself and launch a career while supporting her four children. None of these children has done well; all have had children as teens themselves. They speak and look like the kind of people Phyllis was so determined to leave behind her as she moved ahead.

Forty-three-year-old Barbara was also a mother in her teens. Equally well-spoken, energetic, and successful in her career, she, too, worked hard to educate herself and launch her career. Unlike Phyllis, however, when Barbara pulled herself out of poverty she brought her children with her in every way, making certain they acquired the social and emotional as well as material tools to succeed on their own.

One source of variability in child outcome thus resides in an adoles-

4. See Furstenberg, Hughes, and Brooks-Gunn (1991) for a discussion of the relationship between maternal marital decisions and child outcome. As these authors note, the relationship is not a simple one.

5. This quote is actually a composite of a number of statements made by participants in the Ounce of Prevention Fund and Project Match. (The latter is a services research program in Chicago's Cabrini Green community. See Herr and Halpern [1991] for a full description.)

cent mother's commitment to—and capacity for—parenting. For whatever reason, Phyllis put all her energies into doing well as a student and later as a worker, and she certainly has done well for herself in these domains. She was far less dedicated to mothering, and it shows.

We can see that some young mothers and their children make it into the mainstream and others do not, and we can see (or at least infer) the processes by which this takes place. Still, we cannot always explain such variability in outcome. In discussing this issue Furstenberg, Hughes, and Brooks-Gunn (1991) remark: "If we know why many youth navigate their way out of poverty, we may be in a better position to help those who cannot. Is it because their needs are greater, their resources less, or are they simply less fortunate in finding escape routes out of poverty" (25).[6]

Some adolescent mothers who succeed as adults have followed a more or less steadily upward-moving path, with early motherhood only a slight detour. In communities where teenage childbearing is an adolescent rite of passage, having a baby in one's teens is a far less deviant behavior than it would be in a more middle-class, mainstream context. Thus, we cannot assume that early childbearing automatically interferes with or diverts all girls from their developmental tasks. For some, motherhood during adolescence is what they are doing to fulfill—albeit prematurely—the developmental task of identity achievement. In such cases, when adolescents begin to show improvement in school or work or relationships with men, it may not be that they have changed but rather that they have simply continued onward to accomplish other developmental tasks. At most, they may need to get themselves back on track after temporary derailments. To question why some adolescent mothers succeed where others do not is one order of inquiry. Another, overlapping area of interest pertains to variability in motivation and capacity for change after one has made a mistake, for redirecting and altering goals and behavior from failure- to success-engendering. Little is known about this type of variability or indeed about the processes of personal transformation for adolescents

6. In this instance the reference is to the children of adolescent mothers. These issues have equal applicability to the mothers themselves and can be found in many of Furstenberg and Brooks-Gunn's discussions of this topic.

at risk—the factors that support or thwart it, the separate domains in which it unfolds, the markers that signify its presence, and the mechanisms by which it takes place.

Domains of Change

> The highest levels of self-esteem are found in individuals who are performing competently in domains that are important to the self.
>
> —Susan Harter, "Self and Identity Development"

> I am an O.K. person. I go to college, work and take care of my house for my son Carlos and boyfriend Jack. I am starting to look better physically . . . so I'm feeling better mentally (a little).
>
> —Mia, an adolescent mother

In addition to adolescents' psychological health and their achievement of developmental tasks, there are specific domains of functioning to consider in relation to change. For young mothers the domains of education, work, parenthood, and relations with men are particularly significant. Although it is important for interventions to address each of these, it is not reasonable to expect adolescents to demonstrate change in all domains at once and still preserve a sense of personal continuity over time (Harter 1990). If adult mothers—even ones who are middle class—find it hard to balance the demands of separate and sometimes conflicting roles, how much harder is it for an adolescent mother? A 16 year old who drops out of school may not be motivated to return until she needs to do so in order to do something else (Herr and Halpern 1991).[7] A 15 year old may not be able to manage anything except school and the still unfamiliar changes of early adolescence.

7. Herr and Halpern (1991) find that many of the participants in Project Match who succeed in making the journey from welfare to work do not initially go back to school. Instead, they first do volunteer or part-time work in community agencies and institutions (e.g., Head Start centers, schools, neighborhood clinics, community centers). Later, they seek further education and training because they wish to qualify for a particular job or career selected during their step-by-step socialization into the world of work. Although the majority of Project Match participants are now young adults, many were mothers in their teens.

Polit, Quint, and Riccio (1988) found that five years after participating in Project Redirection, young mothers were least likely to show positive changes in educa-

Certain domains seem to be more psychologically complex than others, more deeply rooted and resistant to change. As Bonnie, a staff member in one of the Fund's programs, once said to me, "Relationships with men are the last to change." She was referring not only to the teens in her program but to her own situation as well. A former runaway, drug abuser, and teen mother, she has been able to turn her life around in terms of education and work and—to some degree—in terms of the kind of parent she is for her three children. Nevertheless, she continues to be attracted to extremely violent and unstable men. As a consequence, she continues to have a stormy and unpredictable life. Bonnie has moved forward in some very important ways: she is far better off than when she was running the streets and taking drugs. Yet she holds herself and her children back in other critical ways by living with a very troubled and brutal man. Though she is a caring and generally careful mother, her relationship with her partner has already compromised her children's psychological health. In Bonnie's life, the domains of parenthood and partner relations remain closely entwined.

The nature of adolescents' relations with men can magnify the instability of their children's already unstable lives, increasing the chance that the children will be left with a caretaker whose interest in their welfare is marginal or temporary. A young mother's partner relationship represents more than a separate domain, since it often affects her childrearing behavior as well. In addition, disadvantaged adolescents need to be single-minded if they wish to escape poverty's grip; time and energy spent pursuing attachments to men is deflected from pursuits essential for success in school or work. Further, a girl may hold herself back if she suspects that her achievements are going to alienate her partner:

> I know that if I want to make something of myself, I'm going to have to leave him.

tion and family planning and most likely to show them in parenting and employment. They comment that the popularity of program components in these domains corresponded to what was most important to the participants as teens and continued to be important in their twenties: "their desire to be good parents and to improve their financial status" (27).

If the price of success is loneliness, it may be too high.[8] Only if she finds a new self will she be secure enough to lose those who hurt her or hold her back.

> I would always tell myself that Joe would change one day, that he would stop drinking and . . . that soon he would learn patience and understanding but nothing ever changed. So now I'm alone. People ask me all the time how I can handle living in a big house by myself. I like it, I guess. I'm not frightened to be here at night. I guess I enjoy the quiet. I do miss Joe. but why be unhappy and miserable?

Finally, it takes little imagination to see the connection between the domain of relations to men and that of reproductive behavior. All too frequently a young mother has baby after baby so that she can give a child to—and thus hold onto—man after man.

Intervention and Domains of Change

It is a rare program that can devote sufficient attention—with sufficient intensity—to all the relevant domains for all their participants. This is just one of the reasons why social support programs as they currently exist are not a sufficient response to the problems of adolescent childbearing. In spite of the oft-used phrase "comprehensive," most intervention efforts emphasize one domain over the others, generally either school and work (depending on a girl's age and years of school completed) or parenting. Far less attention is paid to reproductive behavior, unless a program is part of a medical or family planning institution, in which case it may neglect the other domains. Few programs devote sustained, unambiguous attention to adolescents' relations with males, although many do encourage discussions about relationships with family members and friends. No matter what their brochures say, prevention and intervention programs typically do most what they feel equipped to do best.

In the typical community-based program for adolescent mothers,

---

8. Joyce Ladner (personal communication) comments that today a successful minority female is "pricing herself out of marital partners."

much of the direct service is provided by paraprofessional (lay) workers who live in or near the neighborhood. Although these paraprofessionals are generally dedicated, warm, and well meaning, relying too heavily on lay staff can present problems. Most obvious is the fact that many of these workers lack easy access to the mainstream institutions and organizations that are vital pathways to success. To make it in the wider world, disadvantaged adolescents need models and mentors to bring them there—literally as well as symbolically. These must be people who are comfortable being there themselves. Equally troublesome, and harder to remedy, lay staff members are more likely to be hampered by their own inadequately resolved problems around sexuality, relationships to men, childrearing practices, family violence, assertiveness, or autonomy. These issues can cause strong psychological reverberations for workers when they threaten to bring to awareness painful feelings that have been denied or repressed. Issues such as these are particularly hard for staff members like Bonnie, who had (or still have) serious problems in these domains (Musick and Stott 1990).

Paraprofessional workers also may be affected by unacknowledged (and unexamined) ambivalence or conflict around personal change, success, and doing better than their partners, family, and friends. After all, many lay staff were once in similar circumstances.[9] Lacking

9. Many of the professional workers in these programs are also former teenage mothers, but most are now middle class. Almost all have graduate degrees, many are married, or were at one time, and almost none still live in the communities where the programs are located.

Paraprofessionals are by no means a homogenous group. For some of the younger staff members, being employed or volunteering in a program is a first step toward a career. There are also middle-aged and older women who want to do something for the young people in their community after having successfully raised their own families.

For some workers, a community-based program is their first job after many years of being on public assistance. Indeed, these jobs are often the ideal way to make the transition from welfare to work. The new worker is still in the community where she feels comfortable and does not have to go abruptly from a familiar to a faraway world. She works with people like herself. She can be herself, surrounded and supported by people who understand her experience, as she allows the work experience to gradually socialize her into a new role and self image (Herr, personal communication). However, if she still has a troubled life herself, the job may be beneficial for her but less so for the young women she is supposed to be helping.

the supervised clinical experiences of graduate training—experiences designed to help professionals manage countertransference[10] as well as other psychological reactions—these home visitors, parent group leaders, community-mothers, mentors, child-care or youth workers are more likely to harm a participant inadvertently or fail to help her because of their own unrecognized feelings.

This is a phenomenon apparent in many interactions between staff and adolescent mothers: certain subjects are not raised, or if raised are not discussed consistently or insistently enough, because they are emotionally or concretely "too close to home" (Halpern 1990a).[11] For example, in a study of attitudes toward the option of placing children for adoption (Musick, Handler, and Waddill 1984), teens remarked that this subject was rarely brought up. Several girls recalled wondering why no adult ever suggested adoption, despite their clearly expressed feelings, or those of their families, that they were not ready to be a parent. I am not suggesting that adolescent mothers should relinquish their children, but it is interesting that this alternative was not mentioned, considering how many teens have serious problems providing adequate care for their children and do eventually relinquish or lose them to the foster-care system—if only on a temporary basis.

It is difficult to manage someone else's unresolved issue if it is your unresolved issue as well; it is hard to bring someone else beyond where you have gone, psychologically as well as vocationally. Confronting domestic violence may be too stressful for a woman who was (or still is) a victim of it herself. Family planning and contraceptive issues may be taboo topics for a woman who was a mother in her teens. If a home visitor disregards a teen mother's harmful childrearing practices because she lacks formal child development knowledge, this is a relatively easy-to-remedy type of problem. If she avoids intervening because of psychological discomfort with the subject, the situation is more complex (Musick and Stott 1990). Perhaps she was raised as the

10. The term *countertransference* is used here to refer to difficulties in maintaining psychological distance or objectivity in regard to the participant. Such distortions or emotional interference on the part of a staff member may result in failures of empathy and failure to notice or understand what is really going on with an adolescent.

11. Robert Halpern calls these "domains of silence."

young mothers in her program are raising their children. "*I* was spanked and yelled at when I was a child, and I turned out all right. (I did, didn't I?)," she may say.[12] Or perhaps she raised her own children this way. As one home visitor said, "You know, I didn't do those things with my kids when they were little [reading to them, playing games with them, talking instead of hitting, and so on], and now I'm wondering if maybe I hurt them."

Many service providers in teen-parent programs are unable (or unwilling) to speak frankly about sexual behavior and values, sexual exploitation, or relationships with men, although a full discussion of these matters is essential for avoiding subsequent births. When observing parent groups or home visits, I have often heard girls say something to the effect of, "I sure hope I'm not pregnant again." Rather than asking a girl what—if anything—she is doing to prevent a pregnancy or talking to her about what else is going on in her life that might make a subsequent pregnancy appealing, the home visitor or group facilitator responds hesitantly, signaling her reluctance to go into it in-depth. She may even change the subject altogether. It probably will not come up again . . . until the girl announces that she is expecting another child.

These kinds of intervention problems are magnified when professional-level staff—directors and supervisors—hesitate to set clear goals for paraprofessionals because they too feel uncomfortable with strongly value-laden topics such as family planning. For example, every year we would ask program directors to send us anecdotal material documenting their successes to be included with our annual budget request to the state. On one occasion, a site forwarded a letter from an adolescent mother in which she praised the program extravagantly for everything it (and its staff) had done for her, and it had done a lot in terms of getting her back into school, preparing her for work, and giving her the emotional support that "helped me to see that I was an intelligent person and I could do whatever I wanted with my life." But the girl had also written, "When I found out I was pregnant for the second time I was scared for health reasons." I found this letter very

12. Similarly, James Garbarino (personal communication) points out that judges who were beaten as children are often very lenient with abusive parents.

unsettling, not so much because it revealed the program's failure to prevent another pregnancy; the psychological and social forces promoting early childbearing are too powerful to make that an easily obtainable goal. Rather, the letter was disturbing because of the staff's lack of self-consciousness about its contents—their denial that an unplanned and potentially dangerous second pregnancy might qualify the success of their "success story," a story destined to be read by state legislators already skeptical about the effectiveness of programs for teenage parents. Yet it is all too understandable: preventing pregnancy is so daunting a task that those who work with adolescent girls tend to concentrate on what they can achieve and to disregard what they cannot, lest they become too discouraged to continue their work.

This incident exemplifies an inherent weakness in many community-based interventions—the ever-present possibility that an adolescent's limitations and vulnerabilities will be magnified by those of her help-givers. When such an interaction occurs, the girl's capacity for change is restricted to (or channeled into) only certain domains. Later, her failure to examine (and alter) her reproductive behavior or relations with men may compromise her success in school or work. The babies she keeps having, or the boyfriends she keeps choosing, will prevent her from getting and staying ahead.

Even girls who are successful in school or work may use subsequent pregnancies to modulate positive change, to keep themselves from moving forward too rapidly, outdistancing—and possibly losing— their family or friends. For a disadvantaged girl, childbearing,— especially subsequent childbearing,—is commonly the vehicle for this "failure at the moment of potential growth," the mode by which she can avoid moving into a strange new world. If a program does not help her find alternative ways to manage her anxiety in regard to change, it indirectly encourages—and perpetuates—her use of baby-making as an escape from problems or challenges she cannot face. It is sad enough when an adolescent's mother colludes with such self-injurious behavior. When those designated to show her a better way do the same thing, it is sadder still. Adolescents hunger for guidance even as they resist it. They crave our direction in their roles as parents and partners, students and potential workers, daughters and friends. When we miss opportunities to provide it, we compound the problems we are claiming to solve.

To help adolescents change, lay workers may need to change themselves. The Fund's Heart-to-Heart and Developmental programs offer promising strategies toward this end. Because these programs-within-programs are designed to be run by paraprofessionals, both have extensive training and supervisory protocols. Because the primary goal of Heart-to-Heart is sexual-abuse prevention for both mother and child, it emphasizes domains such as parenting, victimization, sexuality, and relationships with males. Because the Developmental Program seeks to improve outcomes for the children of teens, it emphasizes the domains of child development and parent-child relationships. Community-based workers and their supervisors are trained to provide developmental screening, referral, education, and support around parenting and child development. Both Heart-to-Heart and the Developmental Program encourage trainees to reflect on their own lives and pay special attention to relationship domains. Both use a training process designed to model the kinds of reciprocal, interactive roles staff will be expected to fulfill vis-à-vis the teen parents, who will then (optimally) be able to act in similar ways with their children. They seek to create a "chain of enablement" (Musick and Stott 1990), fostering positive growth in service providers so that they can foster similar growth in adolescent parents, who, in turn, can use what they have gained to further their own growth and that of their children. As one home visitor describes this process:

It's like a whole new view. Your whole way of looking at things has changed. Now when I make my home visits, the girls run to show me their babies. They know I know about kids, they say "You're interested in my child," and then they become interested too. Before, well the moms and I, we would just talk about everything *but* how they were doing with their kids. . . . I can pick up on little things. I really learned to observe and it generalizes to other things as well. I notice now how a child relates to a mom and vice versa. . . . I went to see one girl who was supposed to be a problem. But her child looked really good. I said to her, "Well, you're doing something right." You know she went then and registered for school and went to get WIC. . . . One of the grandmas called and said, "What did you do?"[13]

Both training programs are interactive, encouraging trainees to participate actively in their own learning process. The trainers (who also give ongoing supervision) offer assistance and support while modeling the critical elements to be acquired. Most important, they enable service providers to come to terms with and effectively use the strong emotions that surface around psychologically sensitive subject matter. As another Developmental Program trainee observed: "It gives you a third eye and helps you not to personalize. It's personal, but it's impersonal and objective too." They help staff to deal with powerful issues and emotions in adolescents by helping them to deal with them in themselves.

The training has been a new and helpful experience. This is the very first time I experienced talking with someone about what I went through. I shared something yesterday that I had never told anyone before. I was sexually abused when I was younger but never told anyone. I was scared, embarrassed and guilty, but I felt comfortable talking about it. . . . I felt much better afterward.

I have read all the books that were on your list, but there was one that impressed me the most. In it there are stories told by women who as children were sexually abused. I related to what they felt and understood. Maybe because I was a victim. Maybe because my mother was a victim. Maybe because others in my family were victims [too]. I sometimes feel angry at this. . . . Well, I can't beat up the abusers but I can stop other girls and boys from being abused. . . . It's no longer a taboo and we can prevent this. . . . These teen moms are the first step. . . . I'll teach them, they'll teach their kids, and their kids will teach their own. We can change this circle of abuse! . . . I am excited, I feel like wonder woman!

13. This entry is a composite of the remarks of several different staff members as they discussed the Developmental Program.

I have a question. When a daughter doesn't have the love of her mother, when she becomes a mother she suffers because of that; is it true that it will affect her emotionally and mentally, do you think she will be able to be a good mother and to have a good relationship with men? I am worried because I have seen this happen two times. Please, I want to know your opinion. This is affecting me, one of the girls in the program is going through this. I am feeling what she felt because the same thing happened *to me.* . . . . I am telling you because I trust you. It's like going back and it hurts.

Dear Journal: It is very difficult to put into words the enormous flood of feelings I have experienced these last two days. For over twenty-five years I haven't allowed myself to feel anything or think about my experiences for fear it would destroy me. I've even thought counseling would help but have not found the courage to admit to anyone the trauma I've experienced. My desire is to be able to talk through my feelings so that I can be free. I've no desire to forgive, some justice has been done that I'm aware of, and I gain some comfort in this. It's difficult to gauge the effect over the years on my ability to lead a productive life. It has not come without a price. I've had to learn to love, not wanting to give anything of myself, not knowing why exactly. This must not interfere with my love for my children, no matter what the cost. The damage done is irreparable, never to be fixed, but this is a start for me to reconcile my feelings and to make peace with myself. So much I can say but am unable to find the words to express. This has helped—Thanks.

The training methods used in Heart-to-Heart and the Developmental programs help in motivating providers to pay more attention to certain neglected domains—and to be more effective in promoting change in these areas. Specifically delineated themes such as parenting, child development, and sexual victimization lend themselves well to direct, tightly focused approaches; adolescent fertility behavior does not. Positive changes in this domain are usually signs or markers of positive changes in other domains. An adolescent mother's conscious decision to postpone further childbearing is a sign that constructive self-transformation has occurred. Having one baby after another is a sign that it has not. This means that reproductive behavior should not be treated as a separate issue but instead should be integrated with change-promoting strategies across all the significant domains of functioning. Thus, when an adolescent mother says, "I *hope* I don't get pregnant again," the program must help her understand the connection between her reproductive behavior and other important things going on in her life. If, as frequently happens, she is using childbearing as a mechanism for avoiding change, staff must help her in her struggle to tip the psychological balance toward positive change.

Markers of Change

It is not easy to tell if an adolescent has revised her life script; the most meaningful changes may not manifest themselves for years. Markers of change are dependent on age and development—the younger the girl, the fewer definitive markers there will be. For example, during preadolescence and early adolescence, positive change may appear in the form of improved grades or conduct; it may be inferred when a girl who is flirting with drink or drugs or premature sexual activity elects to follow a different path. Still, one can never be sure about the internal motivations of such equivocal markers of change, especially in the years before adolescence. During middle and later adolescence and early adulthood, there are markers such as school completion, employment, getting (and staying) off welfare, and avoiding (or postponing) subsequent births. Improvements in her child's health, developmental status, and behavior may also be interpreted as signs of improvement in a young mother's functioning and life circumstances. There are also such common- sense, conventional markers as enrolling her child in preschool or Head Start and making certain that he attends regularly, participating in the events and activities at his school, and so on.[14]

Finally, there are other manifestations of change that can be ob-

14. Or, for somewhat older mothers, doing volunteer work in community organizations and institutions (Herr and Halpern 1991).

served by people who work directly with adolescents and young adults. One group of markers involves the development of self-monitoring skills. Beginning with increased self-awareness ("Am I crazy? It seems like I can do so well, then I don't do so well."), this evolves to thinking before acting and taking personal responsibility for what she does. From an after-the-fact sense of "how did this happen to me," the adolescent gradually shifts to the concept of "I brought this on myself," and from here—ideally—to considering possible consequences before she acts. This is difficult for adolescents, especially younger ones.

For the disadvantaged adolescent, change means traveling to a new land, where she may have little in common with others. It requires the will and ability to identify and become attached to new reference groups; to find and bond to new, emotionally significant others; to, as one girl put it, "look for respect and encouragement to better myself." Change calls for potentially risky transformations in her relationships with family, friends, or partners; she may unconsciously fear that success will estrange her from them. At the same time, if she is determined to move ahead, she may deliberately distance herself from those who she feels are holding her back, even when they are people she cares deeply about. Perhaps also, in her struggle to succeed, she must defend herself against weaknesses in herself. Distancing can therefore be interpreted as a marker of the young woman's sense that she must change partners to change herself—whether these partners are friends, family, or mates. It also signals a need to see herself as different from (and better than) others.

[There are girls in the program] who still want to get pregnant; no job, haven't been back to school, and still get pregnant.

You got some teenagers now just have a baby for the hell of it. . . . You got babies being pregnant now with babies. They think these young males are going to be around, but they [are] not. . . . See, that's what I thought was going to happen, but it didn't. I have learned my lesson.

Ray was immature as far as growing as a person. He didn't want me to grow and I refused to let anyone stop my growth. He didn't want me to go to school. He was real aggressive, he liked to fight. He fought me once and I refused to get into a relationship where I was afraid. . . . He was a fool. I'm glad I didn't marry him.

Sometimes you can just make a mistake and then you regret your mistake after you did it. And sometimes some people just keep on making them same old silly mistakes like wanting to have boyfriends that beat up on you and stuff all the time.

I was telling my mother she needs to move cause didn't nobody like me. That would pull me down . . . they thought I was conceited cause I was going to school. . . . I stay to myself . . . because I'm always on the go. I try to stay away from a bad environment . . . trying to get in school and work. It was only to better myself. I don't want to live over here. I got in school and got a certificate to work computers. I won't have nothing if I just sit.

My family? There really is no relationship cause I don't get along with them. . . . [In the program] I learned that the things they were doing wrong did not necessarily reflect on me. And that just because they were into the drug scene didn't mean I had to follow in their footsteps.

Still another set of markers suggests that the adolescent is acquiring new ways of being. She now seems ready—even eager—to watch and imitate a role model: "Last night I made a salad like you make." She begins to dress more tastefully, "more professionally." She begins to take her child to museums, to eat out with him in nicer restaurants, to seek a better school or day care center for him. As one young mother put it, "I want him to go to the kind of nursery school *your* child would go to." After seeing a movie about a girl who was "out of control," one adolescent mother commented:

It made me think about Vannie and when she gets older. I want men to like her and for her to have lots of dates, but I don't want her to have sex unless she thinks that it is right. I just [want] us to have the relationship that if she ever has any questions she can come to me no matter what it is and I will never yell at her for it. I hope I can do it the right way. . . . I would like it to be like our PGF [parent group facilitator] and her daughter.

Some markers give us clues about the efficacy of specific interventions. For example, if a former Heart-to-Heart participant suspects someone of harming her child, will she do something to prevent or stop the abuse? One young mother was not yet comfortable doing so:

> Maybe it's not happening but I'm so afraid something is going on concerning my baby [Denise] and her dad. She's so afraid of him. She doesn't want to stay home with him. She doesn't even want him to touch her. Things that some people do to her that makes her smile, she doesn't smile when he does it. . . . I love my boyfriend very much. We just had another baby. I would hate to accuse him and be wrong but what if I'm right? . . . Dear Denise, I wish that you could talk and tell me what's going on behind Mom's back. If Buddy is hurting you we can get rid of him but there's no way for me to be sure. What am I to do? Love you, Mom.

Whereas another was able to do so:

> My boyfriend, now, when me and the kids are over there, he got a brother that comes over there and he likes to sleep in the bed with them. I told him "No, that don't go here." He says, "I ain't going to do nothing to these kids. They just like my nieces." I say, "I know you ain't going to do nothing to them, it's just that my girls are getting big and you ain't got no business in the bed with them. . . . It's bunk beds in there, you can put both of them at the top and you can get at the bottom, or you can sleep on the floor, it don't make me no difference. But do not get in the bed with my babies." . . . They're growing up and they ask a lot of questions and when they're outside men look at them. I tell them [the men], "What you looking at? These ain't nothing but some babies. Look at me, I'm grown. I'll tell you where to get off at."

Yet another was proactive, avoiding situations that could lead to abuse and spreading the word about prevention.

I used to just leave them with anybody; a friend, next door neighbor. . . . Now, no more. Now I leave them only with really important people like the baby's grandmother, which I know nothing will happen with her, the baby's father lives with her. I know nothing will happen with him, you know, cause this is his life, his son. Or my mother and my mother-in-law, because my mother-in-law loves him like her own. . . . I advise all my girlfriends the same. . . . I see my girlfriends leave their kids with just anybody, I tell them, "You haven't heard of Heart-to-Heart." They were like, "no." . . . I have one of the girls coming in to [program], signing up for [it] because I think it is a world of good. . . . My mother said [since Heart-to-Heart] I act too protective now . . . cause my aunt wants to keep my little baby but my aunt, she had some men over to play cards and stuff and I said no and she said "why" and then I told her about the men . . . they would be drinking and stuff, so I said no.

These examples also demonstrate how some program effects remain latent. Not until the right moment—when these mothers were faced with a choice—could the results of this preventive program be seen.

Not all indicators used to measure program success are valid markers of change. Why should we assume, for example, that someone who stays in a program longer is necessarily doing better than someone who leaves after a short period of time? A few months and a little help are all some young women need to gain access to work or educational opportunities or to solve immediate problems such as child care, health care, or housing. Over-long dependence on a program can mean that an individual is "stuck." This certainly was the case for some of the participants in the Thresholds Mothers' Project (Musick et al. 1987).

Poor or sporadic program attendance may mean that an adolescent is too disturbed or disorganized to recognize and make use of support. It may mean that her significant others are sabotaging her participation because they are jealous or threatened by her potential unavailability to them. Poor attendance can also signify that a program's offerings are irrelevant to its participants and their needs. In order to decipher the meaning of poor or sporadic attendance, the attributes of the program must be considered in conjunction with those of the adolescents it purports to serve. This holds true for all social and educational interventions, from those with a broad range of components to those confined to a more specific set of goals.

When I got pregnant I came back to get help. Then I left again and I came back, I still wasn't pregnant cause whenever I needed help they were always here. And then I stayed for a while. I left again and when I came back I was pregnant [again]. I came back this summer and I'm still continuously getting help. Whenever I need help they're here. . . . I graduated! They didn't force you to go, but they didn't advise you not to go. They'd say, "Well, you need the education" and show you the opportunities you needed to get your education. Then after they got done talking to me I said, well I don't need to drop out . . . I graduated from high school. . . . I would have probably left my kids on everybody and just hung in the street . . . more than spend time with my kids. . . . [My family and I] never talked, we just walked past each other or yelled at each other. Now we can sit down and laugh . . . and just talk.

This young woman's experience demonstrates the mixed effects of interventions for at-risk teens—how they are differentially effective depending on the domain of the problem. While the program she attended undoubtedly helped her to finish school, become a better mother, and relate to her family in a healthier way, it was not able to prevent her from getting pregnant again.

Is a subsequent pregnancy a sign of program failure? Sometimes it is, but not always. More important, it is a marker and reminder that for disadvantaged girls, fertility is often the arena in which change is played out. For a teenage mother, decisions about having another child are often psychological moments of truth intimately connected to her will and ability to redirect her life, to decide and then stick to the decision to live in a new way. The risks are those of separation from people she cares about and of going from the known to the unknown— without assurance that she will be able to make it in a vast, less familiar world. It may also call for her to be secure enough to deny fatherhood to a new partner, at least for the present.

Another Baby: A Psychological Marker and Moment of Truth

A: Yes, I want more.
Q: What does having kids do for you?
A: I don't know.
Q: Why do you like to have kids?
A: I just want to have them. It makes you feel like your life's about something. It makes you feel good about yourself.

[She has already lost two of her three children to the state; the third lives with relatives because of failure-to-thrive.]

I want to get my school out of the way, then I can think about having another one.

[She has two children but is doing well in terms of school, work, and parenting.]

I sit and cry because I feel I am never going to get out. Now I going to have another baby and I really can't wait but we really can't make it I guess.

This one was an accident because . . . I had April at a young age and I said I'm going to wait until she's old enough so she can actually help. So I feel, well, it happened, so get it over with now, then that's it. [She had her first child at 15. She is 18 now and married to the child's father.]

I was just scared to take the birth control pills cause my momma always told me they give you breast cancer, cervic cancer, something like that. And the doctor was always telling me it wouldn't do that to me, but I'm listening to my momma and I figure she know. . . . They said, "Girl, you pregnant again." It was kinda embarrassing, but come on, don't be embarrassed, you ain't the only one. [She has three children, two born while she was in the program.]

Well the second one, okay they really didn't tell me anything but when I got pregnant with my third one they just couldn't believe it. [She is 16 with three children under 2½.]

I am a 17-year-old mother of two. . . . I might be pregnant again but if I am I'm . . . taking it out [having an abortion]. . . . I already have my girl and boy, I thank God for them, but right now I'm trying to make something [more] out of my life than just being a mother and housewife and student. . . . I want to succeed in the business world. With the kids and my husband [Hispanic girls often refer to their partner as "husband," even when they are not legally married.], then maybe one more but not just yet. God forgive me if this is a sin.

[later] I have gone through the abortion. Man, I was so hurt.

Steffie was supposed to be the last one. . . . The doctor changed me up on my pills and I started getting sick and they didn't explain anything to me so I stopped taking them. Then I went along for about six months and I got caught.

Logically, the adolescent who already has a child has been exposed to at least some information postpartum regarding contraceptive methods. Logically, she should know how to prevent another pregnancy. But by two years postpartum, subsequent pregnancies are in the range of 40 to 50 percent (Polit and White 1988), and subsequent births around 35 percent (Mosena 1986, 1987).[15]

As noted by Polit and Kahn: "Despite their stated goals of postponing further childbearing, and despite the fact that 75 percent of the sample had participated in special teenage-parent programs that discouraged further early births, half of the teenagers went on to become pregnant again in the short two-year study period. . . . They were not motivated *to* have a second pregnancy, but were insufficiently motivated to avoid one" (1986, 170).

15. Approximately 10 percent of the Fund's participants have a subsequent pregnancy within twelve months of program entry, which is generally during pregnancy with a first child or shortly after birth (Ruch-Ross, Jones, and Musick 1992). This figure compares favorably to those reported for some of the national samples (Mott 1986) and for demonstration programs such as Project Redirection (Polit and Kahn 1986), although there are some differences in data-collection methods. The Fund does not systematically collect data on subsequent pregnancies and births at twenty-four months post-baseline mainly because so many of the young mothers have left the programs by this time and because it lacks the funds to reinterview sufficient numbers of former participants.

Although most research on adolescent fertility has centered on first births to teens, the birth of additional children is more likely to exacerbate the negative consequences of adolescent childbearing, with the poorest outcomes associated with having more than two closely spaced children during the teenage years. Women who first give birth at 16 or younger are more likely to bear a second child within the next two years than are women who first give birth at 17 or 18 (Mott 1986).[16] And the younger a woman is when she has her first child, the more children she is likely to have (Furstenberg, Brooks-Gunn, and Morgan 1987) and the more restricted her options will become. Girls who bear several children in their teens curtail their chances for escaping chronic dependency. They generally require more public assistance, and for longer periods of time, and are at higher risk for a variety of adverse outcomes for themselves and their children than are teens who avoid or delay subsequent births (Mott 1986; Polit and Kahn 1986; Furstenberg, Brooks-Gunn, and Morgan 1987; Horwitz et al. 1991a, 1991b). Repeated, closely spaced childbearing may not be the direct cause of all their problems, but it is unquestionably associated with them.

Data on subsequent childbearing are very complex and at times contradictory. Very competent and ambitious teenage mothers typically believe that another child will hold them back, and they make certain not to have one—at least not until they are older and more settled in their careers. Conversely, the least competent, least ambitious young mothers seem to have the largest families. But it is not quite that simple. Pittman (personal communication) makes the point that if a girl plans to have only two children and her chances for marriage are slim, why should her children be four or more years apart? As Furstenberg, Brooks-Gunn, and Morgan (1987) found with their Baltimore sample, many young mothers have several closely spaced births within a few years of the first birth and then curtail further childbearing, commonly through sterilization. Managing two

16. There are important ethnic and racial differences in this regard. According to Mott (1986), this finding is true mainly for black women. For whites, the age at first birth has little effect on having a second birth quickly. Hispanics are more likely than either blacks or whites to have a second birth soon after the first, but the youngest mothers are not significantly more likely than the older mothers to have a second child quickly.

children may not be beyond the capabilities of adolescents who are highly skilled and achievement-oriented and who have ample practical and emotional support. Having two children may slow them down initially, but it does not ultimately hold them back, especially if they have additional support outside the home. For example, Polit, Quint, and Riccio (1988) found that five years after Project Redirection, young mothers in this program had better work and welfare outcomes than young mothers in the comparison group, even though they had somewhat larger families (2.4 versus 2.0 children). When promising, competent girls have additional children while still in their teens, this demonstrates the relative weakness of forces opposing teenage child-bearing in comparison to those promoting it. In communities where teenage childbearing is pervasive, subsequent childbearing per se is not always the most valid marker of who will and who will not ulti-mately succeed. On the other hand, it is a good measure of current inclination and aptitude for change.

A subsequent pregnancy is especially disturbing to a program when a girl is doing well in school or (for older teens) about to make a positive transition, such as going to college, getting a better job, or moving to a nicer neighborhood. The expectations for these girls are higher than for adolescents with lower skills and fewer prospects. Although programs may work diligently with less competent teens, they recognize that the process will be slower and anticipate periodic setbacks.

Certain transitions appear to increase the risk of another pregnancy, particularly for psychologically vulnerable young women: beginning a new love relationship, leaving the family of origin, nearing the comple-tion of a program, getting ready to make a significant change in terms of school or work, and having one's child make the transition from an infant to a toddler. Each of these transitional periods represents a developmental or psychological moment of truth. Each carries a spe-cial symbolic meaning which interacts with a special susceptibility. Each triggers a tendency to avoid psychic pain by resisting change. Objectively, these potential transitions appear positive or neutral, but subjectively the girl may perceive them as negative. If she does, having another baby may serve as her means of fleeing ego-shattering change.

Unless an intervention has increased a girl's psychological resources and repertoire of skills, she will be no better able to cope with the stress of transitions than she was prior to the program. Or she may be able to manage only those transitions that are the least emotionally demanding. Naturally, the more psychologically vulnerable she is, the fewer psychic anchors to steady her, the more predisposed she will be to bending under the pressure of change. Becoming pregnant again is both a reaction to fears of change and a concrete means of gaining a respite from these fears.

Frequently the initiation of a new love relationship leads to a subsequent pregnancy. Either the young mother has never consistently practiced birth control because she has not had a serious relationship since her first pregnancy, or she stops contracepting as soon as she becomes serious about a new partner. Considering the vulnerabilities of girls raised without appropriate father figures, it is not surprising to find them willing to do almost anything to avoid alienating or losing a man. Many girls simply stop using birth control when a relationship begins to look promising. Interestingly, the ensuing pregnancy is not always the result of her partner's pressure to have his child; it may result from pressure within the young woman. She believes (hopes?) that having his baby will bind him to her. It is not unusual for a girl to discuss this issue quite openly. She may remark that her partner threatened—or at least intimated—that if she would not have his baby, he would find some other girl who would. Or she may simply say that she thought he would.

After listening to many of these stories, one suspects that the primary issue may not be the male's insistence or coercion. The young woman rarely puts up much of a fight; she rarely tests her partner's caring or capacity for reciprocity. Rather, she appears to intuit his desire or takes his expressed wish as a necessity. In this situation, the normal adolescent desire for intimacy is entangled with vulnerability to males and generalized longings for caring from others. In such circumstances, men do not need to force psychologically fragile girls to have their babies; they need only to desire it, and it will be done.

There are lessons to be learned by studying teen mothers who do not have subsequent pregnancies with new partners. They are usually

more psychologically robust, self-confident, and somewhat surer of
where they are headed.

> My boyfriend is trying to talk me into having another one for the
> past three years, and it hasn't worked yet. He doesn't have them,
> I do. . . . He's kind of mad at me because I want to wait a few
> years before we get married.

Even they, however, may have difficulty withstanding the stresses of
other transitions. These are of a different order, subtler and possibly
more deeply rooted in the universal human dread of separation and
loss.

Leaving the family home, terminating a meaningful relationship,
and significant educational and vocational transitions strain a need to
stay close to others and thus, under certain conditions, may strain the
capacity for growth. At each step in development there exists the
potential for loss, with (in theory) the attendant potential for equal or
greater gain. On the threshold of opportunity, some girls are compelled to avoid or control their forward movement, to fail at the moment of potential growth. With a limited portfolio of options, how can
they do this except by running away from the opportunity or having
another child? Some young mothers do both.

What makes someone turn back just as she seemed to be moving
ahead? Doesn't she want a nicer apartment, a place of her own? She
kept saying she did. Isn't she pleased to be graduating from the program? Isn't she proud to be accepted to college? It will mean so much
for her future. Not necessarily, if the potential gains of these changes
are outweighed by the potential losses. In assessing the psychological
risks and benefits of any transition, we must first ask how dependent it
is upon the negotiation of developmental tasks concerning independence and interdependence, attachment and separation. If these issues
are not at least partly resolved, a premature transition is likely to result
in a personal crisis. The regression engendered by that crisis may
result in its being resolved through a pregnancy. For example, in one of
the Fund's programs, eleven of fourteen subsequent pregnancies occurred after a teen had moved out of her family's home. Obviously this
type of regressive behavior is more common among less mature girls

from multiproblem families. Well-considered interventions can circumvent such crises by helping girls resolve issues that cannot be worked out in their families. They should not encourage or actively help the girls to move out of their homes unless it is absolutely necessary.

Other transitions precipitate crises that adolescents may attempt to resolve by childbearing. Two of the most striking examples of this are program termination and new challenges around education or work. The very structure of teen-parent programs—even those with an upbeat, nondeficit approach—communicates the message that something has to be wrong with you (for example, pregnancy) in order to be eligible for its benefits. To some degree, this is unavoidable and may not be problematic at first. It becomes so only as teens develop strong attachments to staff members. Here is the abiding, inevitable catch 22 of all supportive or therapeutic interventions: the relationships that are the most healing and health-enhancing elements of a program are what make it the hardest to leave. This effect is stronger yet for highly stressed, emotionally hungry adolescents.

When the Fund was still relatively young, we had a graduation for the Chicago-area teen mothers who had completed a special two-year education and support program. Staff from the programs and the Fund, state government officials, and private funders gathered to celebrate this event. The media were invited to share the pride we felt in these young women's accomplishments; almost all of them were either finishing high school or had graduated, and some were going on to college. Several young mothers had full college scholarships to four-year institutions. We made speeches and so did the girls, skits and songs were performed, certificates were presented to the graduates. We were pleased, and the girls were proud—but most were also sad. They could not fully share our joy because they did not feel ready to leave yet, and they let us know it. Even among this group of "stars," a few were visibly pregnant again.

Similar sentiments are repeatedly expressed by young mothers, but they have also been voiced by paraprofessional staff members (many of whom are former adolescent mothers) completing Heart-to-Heart and other intensive training programs. All were saying to us, "Wait, I'm growing, but I'm not ready to be totally without you yet—give me a little more time." The solution is not very complicated: some form of ongoing program for graduates (staff as well as parents). This can consist of home visits on a more limited basis, education and support groups for mothers of preschoolers and older children, and brush-up workshops (continuing education) for the lay helpers. These continuing but less comprehensive and intensive programs facilitate the consolidation of newly gained psychosocial and educational skills, reinforce positive growth, and catch nascent problems at an early stage. They are another form of preventive intervention.

For a sizable group of adolescent mothers the most challenging, psychologically complex transitions are those involving education and employment. These transitions afford vantage points for observing how adolescent development, individual psychology, and environmental reality interact to block the passage to self-sufficiency. Factors from each domain converge, setting up multiple barriers to gaining, maintaining, and effectively using the competencies vital for productive participation in society. Here, as with other transitions, there are heightened possibilities for failure at moments of potential growth. Leaving a program and having a baby are ways of dropping out of the game when the emotional stakes become too high—and they will be too high whenever an adolescent is faced with the possibility of change without an adequate base of useful skills (social as well as educational), coping strategies, and personal support (family and other social support) to ease the passage to a wider world. As Robert Coles and Maria Piers (1969) point out: "Poverty is often bearable if a familiar and familial environment offers comfort and support. Uprootedness is often made bearable by financial resources and by a people's skills, knowledge and a rich cultural tradition. But uprootedness *compounded* by poverty damages not only the body but the soul" (55). These authors are referring to the immigrant experience, but obviously a number of parallels exist with that of an adolescent mother. Many factors work to make it difficult for the girl to uproot herself from her familiar (and familial) world. These extend far beyond the simple lack of basic skills so frequently cited as holding back disadvantaged young people. Naturally, such limitations play a role in creating major barriers to success in school and job-related situations. Conversely, skill and talent (scholarly as well as artistic or athletic) are essential tools in the struggle to rise up out of poverty. Yet other social and psychological qualities may be of equal or greater significance for making successful school or work-related transitions.

People trying to move from socially isolated worlds to mainstream work worlds often face the dilemmas of: (1) poor technical and basic skills, (2) lack of experience with and knowledge of basic work rules, (3) disparate backgrounds from their supervisors, (4) undeveloped social and psychological coping skills to deal with work stresses, (5) few family members and friends to provide encouragement and advice when work problems arise, and (6) vastly limited material resources and great mental strains that arise from living in poverty (Herr et al. 1987, 7).

These authors suggest that although education and basic skills training are necessary for job retention, they are not by themselves sufficient. In one of their studies, only three out of sixty clients clearly lost their jobs because they lacked the appropriate skills. Rather, they lacked such qualities as working well with others, being a self-starter, showing good judgment, and dedication. Adolescent mothers need precisely these skills to avoid repeating familial patterns of closely spaced childbearing and chronic dependency. Further, they must also want to acquire the requisite educational and work-related skills enough to persist in the face of numerous obstacles. All this before they begin to reap the benefits of all the risks they have taken. The journey from an old life, whatever its pains, to a new one is never an easy one, but without the right skills and resources it is impossible.

I have suggested that adolescent mothers will not shift to more success-engendering modes of behavior unless the psychological benefits substantially outweigh the costs. If not, then why not have another child? The period following a first pregnancy presents an opportunity to shift this cost-benefit balance in favor of benefits and in so doing to prevent or postpone a subsequent birth. To accomplish this, an intervention must come between a young mother and the factors that reinforce her automatic tendency to think, feel, and do as many of the women around her have done. Interventions that are successful in shifting this balance are able to do so principally because they fulfill certain core functions that the girl's family cannot or will not fulfill.

Although an adolescent mother may genuinely want to improve herself and her situation, she is unlikely to be prepared for the challenges she will face—both from the outside and from within herself. The uprooting occasioned by these ambitions can be managed only with a combination of psychosocial competence and a base of critical, age-appropriate skills (or the desire to acquire such skills). She must also have emotionally meaningful guidance and support to make positive life choices and to persist in the effort to reach her goals. Ideally this kind of support and direction derives from the family and immediate social network, but families in socially isolated, poor communities are rarely familiar with the intricacies of the educational and occupational systems. By itself, this should not preclude their supporting their children's striving for achievement, and in some families it does not. But many young mothers have mothers and aunts who are still on welfare and still having babies. Realistically, can these women serve as appropriate role models? Are they likely to provide strong, consistent guidance and direction in regard to school, work, or sexual behavior? How likely are young grandmothers to spend time nurturing their daughters' commitment to do things differently or to actively decide to postpone further childbearing until they are financially independent?

It is optimal to be raised in an actively enabling family, one that respects the adolescent's normal thrust toward competence and independence and encourages her to reach outward to new people and opportunities. Even without such active enabling, an adolescent may still thrive, as long as her efforts are not subverted by her family.[17] If they are, the costs of growth will be too high. Unfortunately, many

17. In a longitudinal study of very high-risk families, Musick et al. (1987) and Stott, Cohler, and Musick (1992) found that some very troubled, low-income mothers encouraged their children to reach out and use other helping adults. At the other end of the spectrum were mothers who consistently thwarted their children's attempts to use outside resources and opportunities and to develop as separate individuals. As these children approached puberty, they were far less competent in terms of school and social relations.

young mothers come from families where their own mothers and other relatives feel threatened or envious. Because adolescents still depend on their families, it is hard to withstand their psychological pressure— spoken or unspoken. Females' strong affiliative needs make it especially hard for them to persevere in educational and vocational pursuits if these are perceived as alienating them from meaningful others. Relatives (and friends) often besiege a new worker with demands for gifts or loans. They tell her that her employment is jeopardizing her family's welfare check or subsidized housing. They phone her at work with their problems, distracting her with worry, and undermining her ability to do her job.

A more subtle form of sabotage occurs when the family simply refuses to discuss or otherwise acknowledge a young woman's efforts to improve her life. Very few family members attended the graduation discussed above, despite encouragement by program staff and offers of transportation. When I asked staff members where the girls' families were, they answered, "Judith, *we* are their families!"

There is one more relationship between subsequent childbearing and developmental or life transitions. The transitions discussed above encompass external changes such as education and work and internal, developmental and psychological transitions around separation and independence, new love relationships, or leaving a program that has come to be emotionally significant. These transitions frequently involve relationships with others, centering on the teen in her role as daughter, girlfriend, student, worker, or program participant. Although they may influence the adolescent's feelings about potential motherhood, none revolves exclusively around her role and functioning as a parent. The last transition to be considered—the shift in the mother-child relationship as infancy gives way to toddlerhood— embodies both internal and external factors and taps into many of the same psychosocial and developmental forces that make the other transitions so challenging.

There are particular points in the early parent-child relationship when some young mothers are more likely to be at risk for a subsequent pregnancy.

Why couldn't they just stay like this—so soft and easy to care for? How she loved them this way. . . . Oh for them to stay like this when they could be fed from her body . . . when she alone could be their substance and their world (Naylor 1983, 111–112).

So speaks Cora Lee in *The Women of Brewster Place*. Her words give us a sense of why she continues to have baby after baby, year after year, and why she feels a sense of melancholy and loss when her babies grow up. Perhaps no period of parenthood until adolescence so strains the parent-child relationship as does the transition from "lap baby" to "floor baby." The hallmarks of this age—greatly increased mobility; curiosity (without attendant self-safety skills); negativism; striving for autonomy; assertiveness; heightened anxieties around strangers and separations; rapid, sometimes inexplicable fluctuations in mood; and progressions rapidly followed by regressions—make this a time of upheaval for mother and infant alike.

It is not the upheavals and difficulties, however, that make this a time of heightened risk for another pregnancy but the mother's over-reaction to the infant's developing need for autonomy. Whenever I hear the mother of a toddler expressing grief over the "loss" of her baby, along with negative projections of how naughty and difficult he or she is going to become, I sense trouble ahead. For some very needy adolescents—those who have a baby to compensate for a sense of inner emptiness and longing for love—the threatened psychological separations brought about by the child's early attempts to individuate are terribly painful. In these instances, a sense of impending loss is magnified by the toddler's tendency to get into everything and by his burgeoning negativism. This duality—vulnerability to loss combined with an overreaction to the more bothersome aspects of toddler behavior—signal danger. Some young mothers are blissful as long as they are symbiotic with their baby, but when the teddy bear starts to develop a will of his own, the psychic scenario shifts.

In other cases it may not be the toddler's thrust to be independent that is so disturbing to his young mother but his equally powerful need for her and her alone. Some young mothers cannot tolerate the demanding quality of their child's need for such exclusive intimacy (Stern 1985). One often hears the complaint, "He wants me to do everything for him!" Finally, if an adolescent has used childbearing as a way to deal with emotional longings, she may be depressed and disappointed if it has not worked. To recapture the expectation of happiness and emotional fullness of pregnancy, she may need to keep having babies.

In one of our programs, four of the fifteen participants fell into this category. These young women reminded me of several of the psychiatrically ill mothers in the Thresholds Project (Musick et al. 1987), who seemed to be virtually addicted to childbearing. As soon as their youngest child got a little older, they would either be pregnant again or in some way harm the child so that he would have to be removed from the home. When this happened, they would get pregnant again.

The four adolescent mothers who stood out as extremely vulnerable during the exit interviews shared a certain cluster of psychological and behavioral characteristics. Each had given birth to at least three children, and several had four. None was over 19 years of age. Each woman had at one point temporarily lost custody of her children for suspected (or founded) abuse or neglect, and each told me (without the slightest self-consciousness) that the first thing she had done when this took place was to try to have another baby as soon as possible. She would do a better job with *this* baby. Rather than trying to change the conditions that had led to the harm of their older children, these young women had shifted their affection and attention to the new (unborn) child.

Not surprisingly, these four young mothers had fewer basic skills, fewer years of high school, and noticeably limited social competencies in comparison to the other group members. All four presented clinically as either depressed or having borderline personality disorders. All four came from extremely troubled, volatile families, and all had personal histories of severe and protracted sexual, as well as physical, abuse.[18] Although the service philosophy of the Fund's programs, like

18. Although such markedly high-risk adolescent mothers may comprise only a relatively small subpopulation of all early child-bearers, they and their children generally account for a substantial proportion of the problems in a community. For

most programs for teenage mothers, emphasizes strengths and coping skills rather than deficits and pathology, insights from developmental psychopathology and adolescent psychiatry are invaluable for this work. Understanding what compels those who are most troubled to have the most children puts us in a better position to recognize when structurally similar but milder forms of the same risk factors (for example, fatalism or poor planning skills) are about to cause problems for healthier, but still vulnerable, young women.

Mechanisms of Change

In our society which in many respects has had its greatest success in mass producing machinery, people are tempted to believe that the same principles which are so eminently successful in the engineering field should also be applicable to human relations and human development.
—Bruno Bettelheim, *A Good Enough Parent*

In this section, concepts presented in earlier chapters reappear in the discussion of mechanisms of change—processes that help adolescent mothers to get and stay on course or to take a new course if the old one was leading them astray. These concepts apply to a range of settings, from programs, to schools, to the wider social context in which young people grow up and go about their lives.

The Role of Relationships

If harmful relationships are the foundation of so many of the problems, they are also the foundation of their solution. Because they are the stepping stones for change, effective intervention strategies— whether their principal aims are mental health improvement, preparation for work, completion of school, preventive health care, parenting,

---

example, in a follow-up study of participants at Our Place, a Family Focus/Ounce of Prevention Fund teen center in Evanston, Illinois, service and research staff were able to trace almost all of the subsequent pregnancies to the same thirty-six families. With further analyses, the data revealed that these actually comprised only six multiproblem, extended-family networks.

child development, or family planning—place relationships at their center.

The best interventions fulfill key family functions for adolescents at risk. Like good families, these interventions have well-articulated expectations that they help teens internalize by consistent support and guidance. They set high standards and reinforce positive values. Like good families, good programs do what more advantaged families do naturally—they link expectations and goals with the tangible means to achieve them, providing real and realistic opportunities to grow. And, like healthy families, they protect, nurture, motivate, structure, mediate, teach, and enable, acting as a psychological safety net so that adolescents can falter without falling.

Competent parents also serve a *scaffolding* function by controlling the elements of a task that are initially beyond the learner's capacity, freeing the child to focus her attention upon the elements that are within range of her competence (Wood, Bruner, and Ross 1976). This unique social process helps the young person to achieve goals and solve problems that would be beyond her unassisted efforts; through scaffolding, her reach can exceed her grasp.[19] Is it possible to learn (or relearn) as an adolescent social and cognitive skills that should have been acquired as a child? Are social strategies that resemble these processes the functional equivalents of support in the natural setting of the family? Surely there are some important differences between naturally occurring family support and constructed social support, differences between families as scaffolds and the transfer of such family functions to outside institutions.

Ideally, those who work with adolescent mothers should also work with their families, but not all families can be reached, especially the most troubled ones. When this is the case, teachers, counselors, home visitors, mentors, and other helping adults step in to fulfill some of the

19. Scaffolding is related to Vygotsky's (1978) notion of the "zone of proximal development"—the distance between a child's actual developmental level as determined by independent problem solving and her potential developmental level as determined through problem solving under guidance. Concepts such as these illustrate the ways in which families either facilitate development and self-righting tendencies or block adaptive routes for children already at risk (Musick et al. 1987). Naturally, these functions take on different forms as the child develops.

family's functions, serving as transitional parents. In this role they may help the adolescent to decouple from a toxic, growth-inhibiting family, rewriting the script it had written for her. "Without this program I think I would have turned out like my mother. She treated me like dirt." Although there are a variety of change mechanisms in effective interventions, all are based on helping and healing relationships.[20]

The Promise

Although each of the Fund's teen-parent programs provides the same core package of basic services, there is substantial variation among them. Despite this diversity, most have a strong, positive impact on school enrollment, employment, and delay of subsequent pregnancy (Ruch-Ross, Jones, and Musick 1992). This suggests that similar processes are at work across program sites. I believe these are based in the relationships participants form with staff members: "You have your sisters, and then you have like a mother, godmother, watching after you." Program staff promote and reinforce change, both through their formalized roles as guides, role models, and teachers and through the personal relationships they build with the young mothers. This helps to explain why some girls delay subsequent pregnancies—even in programs that do not consistently provide family planning services. The combination of curative new relationships and valuable new skills generates options other than additional childbearing.

Many positive effects of teen-parent programs are indirect results of just such combinations. For example, when teens know that a program is empathic to them, this can get translated into a capacity to identify with and be empathic to their children. As they become more aware of how they feel (and how they felt when they were children), they become aware that their children have similar feelings.

I never knew how babies feel. You know you're upset, and I never knew that they feel that way too.

And they begin to self-monitor and to think about who they are as it affects what they do to their children.

20. Especially in family support centers, teens develop a strong, positive transference to the program as a whole, not merely to individual staff members.

I get mad easily and I try my very best to stay calm with him. Now when he does make me mad, I just sit there. I don't do anything. I wait a few minutes before I get ahold of him. . . . I really don't want to hurt him.

I never was respected as a child. I was always a stupid whore or a dumb bitch. It hurt more to hear those words than to be hit. It really hurts when I catch myself calling Lucia stupid.

If an intervention is conceptually valid, it may work even when it is not fully executed. If it has the potential to genuinely fill a void or solve a problem, the adolescent will sense and respond to its promise. For example, girls seemed to benefit from Heart-to-Heart even in those groups that were somewhat disorganized. Sensing the program's promise, girls in these groups asked for extra time with staff (often private time), used their diaries to ask questions or seek help, and pressed group leaders to cover topics in the curriculum that had been passed over. They extracted and used everything the program had to offer; believing its promise, they pushed group leaders to deliver on it. Appreciating whatever they received—even when it was not enough—they sometimes experienced more support than was actually given (Gottlieb 1988). As one participant described it, "It's really like a car's gas tank, you leave home on empty and come back with a full tank for your next day's work."

Telling Your Story

There's a weight off me. I said it all out loud and the world didn't come to an end. I listened to my story, let loose, running around free in the morning air, and it wasn't as bad as I expected.
—Michael Dorris, *A Yellow Raft in Blue Water*

When an adolescent has permission to tell her story—when the forbidden is no longer forbidden—a spell is broken. As secrets (from herself, as well as others) surface, unspoken words lose their power, and her history loosens its grip on her life.

I am happy . . . because I found out things in my life that I have hidden from myself.

My heart feels so clean. (I am not kidding. It feels like I washed it out with soap and water.)

Speaking the unspeakable shifts the sense of control from others to the self; as the past becomes more than what happened to her, it becomes a series of events that she can objectify. When she tells her story, she acts, and in acting she stops protecting (and psychologically collaborating with) those who have done her harm. For many, this process is a first step away from victimhood.

Putting Words to Things

The meta-cognitive process of putting words to things—of making the amorphous concrete and conscious—is applicable to a wide range of intervention issues. When the young woman speaks or writes about things that have hurt her, she puts a cognitive framework on an emotional experience. This helps her to master it. Language, whether spoken or written, also puts a psychological space between feeling and action. It encourages reflection and self-awareness, thinking before automatically doing. Such mechanisms promote personal responsibility. Things do not just happen, we can make them happen—or not.

Putting words to things is not by itself sufficient to encourage change. Sitting around endlessly griping about your boyfriend (or your family or child) inevitably becomes yet another way to avoid doing what needs to be done. Adolescents are not identical to adult therapy patients; they need guided talking and candid, sometimes confrontive conversations. A skilled, sensitive listener leads the teen to connect her past to her present and to see the psychic purposes behind what she does. "You mean I keeping hurting myself in that way because that's how I got along with my father?"[21]

21. Clinicians such as Alice Miller and Selma Fraiberg and researchers such as Mary Main, Byron Egeland, and Martha Erickson believe that unresolved and (often) unconscious issues from the past affect present behavior and act as barriers to using new knowledge for change. Most of this work has been concerned with the behavior of adults; adolescents may need to keep certain issues repressed and unexamined until they are mature enough to cope with the powerful affects these may arouse. Nonetheless, when girls compulsively repeat self-destructive patterns in an effort to work them out psychologically, some examination and interpretation of these psychic ghosts seem warranted.

To be heard is very self-affirming, especially for young females (Fine 1991; Gilligan et al. 1990). Girls tend to be "pleasers" who fear they might offend others—especially males—by saying the wrong thing. A process of transformation is set in motion when girls have a chance to be who they are and say what they have to say—without fear of criticism, retaliation, or estrangement from those to whom they are attached. As one young mother's poem describes this process,

> To converse and share with another
> in light of understanding about me
> is a seed of love and illumination
> that's profoundly healing.

Sharing your experiences with others and having them share theirs with you assuages the sense of being alone with your problems and puts them in a different light.

> I do not worry because I am not the only one who has this experience, and for once in my life I feel normal. . . . A new way has opened. . . . I know how to define my problems.

Younger adolescents especially have questions they need to ask and have answered—directly.

> Is it totally wrong to have sex with your uncle if he's not really a relative?
>
> If you go to a hotel you can make money. But that's selling your body, isn't it?

New Ideas and Experiences

Girls are empowered by accurate knowledge about what is and what is not appropriate sexual behavior.

> If I hadn't been in [Heart-to-Heart] . . . I would be ignorant. If something happens and you don't know, it's just like "O.K. I'm not going to say nothing." It's gonna stay like that . . . and now you know you *have* to do something about it. You know what to do, what to say.

Such knowledge disconfirms negative evidence in regard to themselves.

Now I know that I have a right to my own body.

Adolescent mothers will not be inspired—let alone equipped—to move into the wider world if they have no knowledge of it beyond what they see on television.

We all went to see the ballet, and a play downtown. We had field trips by ourselves and with our kids to the zoo and museums. This summer we're going camping. . . . We raised some of the money for camp ourselves.

Affirming Rituals and Roles

Change, especially during adolescence, requires rituals and affirmation—formalized rites of passage such as award ceremonies, graduations, certificates, and newsletters that recognize and validate accomplishments. For example, Family Focus teen programs have formal graduation ceremonies marking change in status from participant to big sister. Being a big sister, like other volunteer roles, capitalizes on the girl's natural idealism, her wish to be a heroine. Volunteering also acquaints the adolescent with expectations in the domain of work.

Creating the Climate

[This] is a place to open up. To learn more about yourself. . . . The questions that are put to you make you think. It was a place to let out tension that was going on in the family during the day, you could come discuss it with someone. . . . Here is where I got my start. In helping at the office and becoming more sure of myself it caused me to think my problems through and not just act.

We want young mothers to develop the capacity to act wisely on their own behalf and to move beyond their mistakes. For this to happen, the institutions affecting them will have to take on remedial—as well as social, educational, or vocational—functions, although they have never viewed these as part of their role.

Environments that set the stage for positive growth are places where there is structure, stability, and predictability, where there are clear consequences for behavior—probably different from the home and definitely different from the streets. In these settings, girls are made to feel special and protected and worthy of such care.

Program director: I won't send our young mothers to that clinic, and they know why I won't. They treat *people* like *things*!

The best settings have a distinctive feel or atmosphere. This is part of the promise adolescents pick up and respond to. The environment is saturated with positive messages; it is deliberately structured to reinforce new ideas and ways of behaving. This redundancy is grounded in a recognition that developing young people need repeated experiences in order to learn new things and unlearn old ones. All the elements in the intervention support its central goals. The setting communicates a message about how we see these young women and what we believe they deserve for themselves. An aesthetically pleasing setting exposes them to beauty; it says we think they are beautiful. Never underestimate how meaningful this is.

Whenever an adolescent begins to experience the desire for positive change, whenever she musters the will to make it happen, it is because of a shift not only in the external contingencies of her life but in her internal self-concepts as well. For poor adolescents, like all adolescents, positive change comes about only when developmental readiness meshes with realistic opportunities to succeed in personally valued roles and areas of competence. There can be no change if the new (or future) identity required is too discrepant from the present one or if the psychological costs outweigh the benefits to the self. Positive change takes place where adolescents can master new knowledge and skills within the context of strong, repeated, emotionally salient experiences with people they trust and admire, people who care and guide. But caring and guidance are not enough; these people must have high expectations as well. They can and often must bend the rules to reach and help adolescents where they are, but they must also lead and push them beyond themselves.

I know from my own experience that enabling relationships work best when they are nested in a larger caring community or institution, the kind of place that validates and shapes itself to who we are as we enter but expects us to be new and in some ways better people when we leave—expects this from us and holds us responsible for it as well. Such communities widen the world of possibilities for us, transforming our sense of who we are and what we can do. As a nation we have yet to really understand, let alone create, such caring communities and institutions for the increasing numbers of young people who will surely be lost without them. If we expect tomorrow to be better than today, there will be no substitute for certain growth-fostering and healing experiences.

> They helped me with, well I was going through some emotional changes and so the times that I couldn't make it they would visit and talk with me and comfort me in some way. . . . They were a big influence on that, they stayed on me and on me about finishing school. . . . I could have been out on the streets, young girl pregnant you know, just at home on welfare you know, but they showed me I could be more than that, I could be a lot more than that. . . . I see that I can be anything I want to be and still take care of my baby. . . . Life is not that bad and it's not that hard, just give it a chance. . . . Confidence, don't talk about confidence, I didn't have any. My confidence was gone. They picked up my pieces, even put them back together. They showed me I'm a person.

R e f e r e n c e s

Ainsworth, M.; Blehar, M.; Water, E.; and Wall, S. 1978. *Patterns of Attachment: A Psychological Study of the Strange Situation*. Hillsdale, N.J.: Erlbaum.

Anderson, E. 1989. Sex codes and family life among poor inner-city youths. *ANNALS, American Academy of Political and Social Science* 501:59–78.

Anthony, E. J. 1987. Children at risk for psychosis growing up successfully. In *The Invulnerable Child*, ed. E. J. Anthony and B. Cohler, pp. 147–84. New York: Guilford.

Apter, T. 1990. *Altered Loves: Mothers and Daughters during Adolescence*. New York: St. Martin's Press.

Attie, I.; and Brooks-Gunn, J. 1987. Weight-related concerns in women: A response to or a cause of stress? In *Gender and Stress*, ed. R. Barnett, L. Biener, and G. Baruch, pp. 218–54. New York: Free Press.

————. 1989. The development of eating problems in adolescent girls: A longitudinal study. *Developmental Psychology* 25(1): 70–79.

Bachrach, C. 1986. Adoption plans, adopted children and adoptive mothers. *Journal of Marriage and the Family* 48:243.

Beckwith, L. 1990. Adaptive and maladaptive parenting—Implications for intervention. In *Handbook of Early Intervention*, ed. S. Meisels and J. Shonkoff, pp. 53–77. Cambridge: Cambridge University Press.

Belenky, M.; Clinchy, B.; Goldberger, N.; and Tarule, J. 1986. *Women's Ways of Knowing: The Development of Self, Voice, and Mind*. New York: Basic Books.

Belsky, J. 1980. Child maltreatment: An ecological integration. *Amer. Psychologist* 35:320–35.

Belsky, J.; and Vondra, J. 1989. Lessons from child abuse: The determinants of parenting. In *Child Maltreatment: Theory and Research on the Causes and Consequences of Child Abuse and Neglect*, ed. D. Cicchetti and V. Carlson, pp. 153–202. Cambridge: Cambridge University Press.

Benedek, T. 1959. Parenthood as a developmental phase: A contribution to libido theory. *Journal of the Amer. Psychoanalytic Association* 7:389–417.

————. 1970. Motherhood and nurturing. In *Parenthood: Its Psychology and Psychopathology*, ed. E. J. Anthony and T. Benedek, pp. 153–65. Boston: Little, Brown.

————. 1973. *Psychoanalytic Investigations: Selected Papers*. New York: Quadrangle.

Bettelheim, B. 1987. *A Good Enough Parent: A Book on Child-Rearing*. New York: Alfred A. Knopf.

Bibring, G.; Dwyer, T.; Huntington, D.; and Valenstein, A. 1961. A study of the psychological processes in pregnancy and of the earliest mother-child relationship. *Psychoanalytic Study of the Child* 16:9–72. New York: International Universities Press, pp. 9–72.

Billy, J.; and Udry, J. 1984. Adolescent sexual behavior and friendship choice. *Social Forces* 62(3): 653–78.

Bingham, C. R.; Miller, B.; and Adams, G. 1990. Correlates of age at first sexual intercourse in a national sample of young women. *J. of Adolescent Research* 5(1): 18–33.

Blos, P. 1962. On Adolescence: A Psychoanalytic Interpretation. New York: Free Press.

————. 1979. *The Adolescent Passage: Developmental Issues*. New York: International Universities Press.

Blum, R.; and Resnick, M. 1982. Adolescent sexual decision-making: Contraception, pregnancy, abortion and motherhood. *Pediatric Annals* 11:1–9.

Bowlby, J. 1980. *Attachment and Loss*. Vol. 3, *Loss: Sadness and Depression*. New York: Basic Books.

Bowman, P. 1988. Post-industrial displacement and family role strains. In *Families and Economic Distress*, ed. P. Voydanoff and L. Majka. Beverly Hills, Calif.: Sage.

Boyer, D.; and Fine, D. 1992. Sexual abuse as a factor in adolescent pregnancy and child maltreatment. *Family Planning Perspectives* 24(1): 4–11, 19.

Brazelton, T. B.; and Cramer, B. 1990. *The Earliest Relationship: Parents, Infants, and the Drama of Early Attachment*. Reading, Mass.: Addison-Wesley.

Bretherton, I. 1987. New perspectives on attachment relations: Security, communication, and internal working models. In *Handbook on Infant Development*, 2d ed., ed. J. Osofsky, pp. 1061–1100. New York: Wiley.

Brice Heath, S. 1983. *Ways with Words: Language, Life, and Work in Communities and Classrooms*. Cambridge: Cambridge University Press.

Briere, J.; and Runtz, M. 1987. Post sexual abuse trauma: Data and implications for clinical practice. *Journal of Interpersonal Violence* 2(4): 367–379.

Bronfenbrenner, U. 1979. *The Ecology of Human Development: Experiments by Nature and Design*. Cambridge: Harvard University Press.

———. 1986. Ecology of the family as a context for human development research perspectives. *Developmental Psychology* 22:724–742.

Bronfenbrenner, U.; and Crouter, A. 1983. The evolution of environmental models in developmental research. In *Handbook of Child Psychology*. Vol. 1, *History, Theory, and Methods*, ed. P. Mussen, pp. 357–414. New York: Wiley.

Brooks, B. 1982. Familial influence on father-daughter incest. *Journal of Psychiatric Treatment and Evaluation* 4:117–24.

Brooks-Gunn, J.; and Chase-Landsdale, L. 1991. Children having children: Effects on the family system. *Pediatric Annals* 20(9): 467–81.

Brooks-Gunn, J.; and Furstenberg, F. 1986. Antecedents and consequences of parenting: The case of adolescent motherhood. In *Origins of Nurturance*, ed. A. Fogel and G. Melson, pp. 233–58. Hillsdale, N.J.: Erlbaum.

————. 1987. Continuity and change in the context of poverty: Adolescent mothers and their children. In *The Malleability of Children*, ed. J. Gallagher and C. Ramey, pp. 171–88. Baltimore: Brookes Publishing.

————. 1989. Adolescent sexual behavior. *Amer. Psychologist* 44(2): 249–57.

Brooks-Gunn, J.; and Reiter, E. 1990. The role of pubertal processes. In *At the Threshold: The Developing Adolescent*, ed. S. Feldman and G. Elliott, pp. 16–53. Cambridge: Harvard University Press.

Brooks-Gunn, J.; and Warren, M. 1988. The psychological significance of secondary sexual characteristics in 9- to 11-year-old girls. *Child Development* 59:161–69.

Broussard, E.; and Hartner, M. 1971. Further considerations regarding maternal perception of the first born. In *Exceptional Infant: Studies in Abnormalities*, vol. 2, ed. J. Hellmuth, pp. 432–49. New York: Brunner/Mazel.

Bruner, J. 1975. The ontogenesis of speech acts. *J. of Child Language*, 2:1–19.

Bryant, C.; Bailey, D.; Coreil, J.; D'Angelo, S.; and Lazarov, M. 1989. Determinants of breastfeeding in the Southeast Region: Research findings from the BEST START, breastfeeding for healthy mothers and healthy babies campaign. Unpublished.

Bumiller, E. 1990. *May You Be the Mother of a Hundred Sons: A Journey among the Women of India*. New York: Random House.

Burton, L. 1990. Teenage childbearing as an alternative life-course strategy in multigeneration black families. *Human Nature* 1(2): 123–43.

Butler, J.; and Burton, L. 1990. Rethinking teenage childbearing: Is sexual abuse a missing link? *Family Relations* 39 (1): 73-80.

Campbell, B. 1989. *Sweet Summer: Growing Up with and without My Dad*. New York: Putnam.

Card, J.; and Wise, L. 1981. Teenage mothers and teenage fathers: The impact of early childbearing on the parents' personal and professional lives. In *Teenage Sexuality, Pregnancy, and Childbearing*, ed. F. Furstenberg, R. Lincoln, and J. Menken. Philadelphia: University of Pennsylvania Press.

Chase-Landsdale, L.; Brooks-Gunn, J.; and Paikoff, R. 1991. Research and programs for adolescent mothers: Missing links and future promises. *Family Relations* 40:396–403.

Chilman, C. 1983. *Adolescent Sexuality in a Changing American Society: Social and Psychological Perspectives for the Human Services Professions*, 2d ed. New York: Wiley.

Cicchetti, D. 1989. How research on child maltreatment has informed the study of child development: Perspectives from developmental psychopathology. In *Child Maltreatment: Theory and Research on the Causes and Consequences of Child Abuse and Neglect*, ed .D. Cicchetti and V. Carlson, pp. 377–430. Cambridge: University Press.

Cicchetti, D.; and Carlson, V. eds. 1989. *Child Maltreatment: Theory and Research on the Causes and Consequences of Child Abuse and Neglect*. Cambridge: Cambridge University Press.

Clark, R. 1983. *Family Life and School Achievement: Why Poor Black Children Succeed or Fail*. Chicago: University of Chicago Press.

Codega, S.; Pasley, B. K.; and Kreutzer, J. 1990. Coping behaviors of adolescent mothers: An exploratory study and comparison of Mexican-Americans and Anglos. *J. of Adolescent Research* 5(1): 34–53.

Cohen, S.; and Beckwith, L. 1979. Preterm infant interaction with the caregiver in the first year of life and competence at age two. *Child Development* 50:767–776.

Cohler, B.; Gallant, D.; Grunebaum, H.; and Kaufman, C. 1983. Social adjustment among schizophrenic, depressed and well mothers and their school aged children. In *Children of Depressed Parents: Risk, Identification, and Intervention*, ed. H. Morrison. New York: Grune and Stratton, pp. 65–98.

Coles, R.; and Piers, M. 1969. *Wages of Neglect*. Chicago: Quadrangle Press.

Colletta, N. 1981. Social support and the risk of maternal rejection by adolescent mothers. *Journal of Psychology* 109:191–97.

Colletta, N.; and Lee, D. 1983. The impact of support for black adolescent mothers. *Journal of Family Issues* 4:27–43.

Collins, W. 1990. Parent-child relationships in the transition to adolescence: Continuity and change in interaction, affect, and cognition. In *From Childhood to Adolescence: A Transitional Period?*, ed. R. Montemayor, G. Adams, and T. Gullotta, pp. 85–106. Newbury Park, Calif.: Sage.

Collette, L'Etoile Vesper. 1966. In *Earthly Paradise: Collette's Autobiography Drawn from the Writings of Her Lifetime*, ed. R. Phelps, trans.

H. Briffault, pp. 199–206. New York: Farrar, Straus and Giroux. (Orig. pub. Lausanne: Guilde du Livre, 1955.)

Comer, J. 1988. *Maggie's American Dream: The Life and Times of a Black Family*. New York: New American Library.

Conger, J.; and Petersen, A. 1984. *Adolescence and Youth: Psychological Development in a Changing World*, 3d ed.. New York: Harper and Row.

Conte, J.; and Schuermen, J. 1987. The effects of sexual abuse on children: A multidimensional view. *Journal of Interpersonal Violence* 2(4): 380–90.

Cramer, B. 1987. Objective and subjective aspects of parent-infant relations: An attempt at correlation between infant studies and clinical work. In *Handbook of Infant Development*, 2d ed., ed. J. Osofsky, pp. 1037–57. New York: Wiley.

Crittenden, P.; and Ainsworth, M. 1989. Child maltreatment and attachment theory. In *Child Maltreatment: Theory and Research on the Causes and Consequences of Child Abuse and Neglect*, ed. D. Cicchetti and V. Carlson, pp. 432–63. Cambridge: Cambridge University Press.

Crockenburg, S. 1987. Predictors and correlates of anger toward and punitive control of toddlers by adolescent mothers. *Child Development* 58:964–75.

Culp, R.; Culp, A.; Osofsky, J.; and Osofsky, H. 1989. Adolescent and older mothers: Comparison of their interaction with their six-month-old infants. Paper presented at the biennial meeting of the Society for Research in Child Development, Kansas City.

Cvetkovich, G.; and Grote, B. 1980. Psychological development and the social problem of teenage illegitimacy. In *Adolescent Pregnancy and Childbearing: Findings from Research*, ed. C. Chilman, pp. 15–41. Washington, D.C.: U.S. Department of Health and Human Services.

Dalsimer, K. 1986. *Female Adolescence: Psychoanalytic Reflections on Literature*. New Haven: Yale University Press.

Darabi, K.; Dryfoos, J.; and Schwartz, D. 1986. Hispanic adolescent fertility. *Hispanic J. of Behavioral Science* 8(2):157–71.

Dash, L. 1989. *When Children Want Children: The Urban Crisis of Teenage Childbearing*. New York: William Morrow.

De Cubas, M.; and Field, T. 1984. Teaching interactions of black and Cuban teenage mothers and their infants. *Early Child Development and Care* 16:41–56.

DeLissovey, V. 1973. Child care by adolescent parents. *Children Today*, no. 4, 22–25.

Deutsch, H. 1944. *The Psychology of Women*, vol. 1. New York: Grune and Stratton.

DeYoung, M. 1982. *Sexual Victimization of Children*. Jefferson, N.C.: McFarland.

———. 1984. Counterphobic behaviors in multiply molested children. *Child Welfare* 68:333–39.

Diamond, M. 1983. The transition to adolescence in girls: Conscious and unconscious experiences of puberty. Ph.D. diss., University of Michigan.

Dillard, A. 1987. *An American Childhood*. New York: Harper and Row.

Donovan, J.; and Jessor, R. 1985. The structure of problem behavior in adolescence and young adulthood. *Journal of Consulting and Clinical Psychology* 53(6): 890–904.

Dorris, M. 1987. *A Yellow Raft in Blue Water*. New York: Warner Books.

Douvan, E.; and Adelson, J. 1966. *The Adolescent Experience*. New York: Wiley.

Dryfoos, J. 1990. *Adolescents at Risk: Prevalence and Prevention*. New York: Oxford University Press.

Egeland, B.; and Erickson, M. 1990. Rising above the past: Strategies for helping new mothers break the cycle of abuse. *Zero-to-Three* 11(2): 29–35.

Egeland, B.; Jacobvitz, D.; and Papatola, K. 1984. *Intergenerational Continuity of Parental Abuse*. Proceedings from Conference on Biosocial Perspectives on Child Abuse and Neglect. York, Me.: Social Science Research Council.

Egeland, B.; Jacobovitz, D.; and Sroufe, L. A. 1988. Breaking the cycle of abuse. *Child Development* 59:1080–88.

Elder, G. 1974. *Children of the Great Depression*. Chicago: University of Chicago Press.

Elder, G.; Liker, J.; and Cross, C. 1984. Parent-child behavior in the Great Depression: Life course and intergenerational influences. In *Lifespan Development and Behavior*, vol.6, ed. P. Baltes and O. Brim, pp. 109-58. New York: Academic Press.

Elder, G.; Van Nguyen, T.; and Caspi, A. 1985. Linking family hardship to children's lives. *Child Development* 56:361–375.

Ellwood, D. 1987. Understanding dependency: Choices, confidence, or culture? Report prepared for the U.S. Department of Health and Human Services (Executive Summary). Center for Human Resources, Heller Graduate School, Brandeis University.

Ellwood, D. 1988. *Poor Support: Poverty in the American Family.* New York: Basic Books.

Elkind, D. 1967. Egocentrism in adolescence. *Child Development* 38:1025–34.

Elkind, D. 1974. *Children and Adolescents: Interpretive Essays on Jean Piaget.* New York: Oxford University Press.

Elliott, D.; and Ageton, S. 1980. Reconciling race and class differences in self-reported and official estimates of delinquency. *American Sociological Review* 45:95–110.

Emde, R. 1987. Infant mental health: Clinical dilemmas, the expansion of meaning, and opportunities. In *Handbook of Infant Development*, 2d ed., ed. J. Osofsky, pp. 1297–1320. New York: Wiley.

Emslie, G. J.; and Rosenfeld, A. 1983. Incest reported by children and adolescents hospitalized for severe psychiatric problems. *Amer. Journal of Psychiatry* 140:708–711.

Erikson, E. 1959. Identity and the life cycle: Selected papers. *Psychological Issues* 1(1): 18–164. New York: International Universities Press. Rpt. as *Identity and the Life Cycle.* New York: W. W. Norton, 1980.

Erikson, E. 1963. *Childhood and Society*, 2d ed. New York: W. W. Norton.

Erikson, E. 1968. *Identity, Youth and Crisis.* New York: W. W. Norton.

Farber, E.; and Egeland, B. 1987. Invulnerability among abused and neglected children. In *The Invulnerable Child*, ed. E. J. Anthony and B. Cohler, pp. 253–88. New York: Guilford.

Feldman, S.; and Elliott G., eds. 1990. *At the Threshold: The Developing Adolescent.* Cambridge: Harvard University Press.

Field, T. 1980. Interactions of preterm and term infants with their lower- and middle-class teenage and adult mothers. In *High-Risk Infants and Children: Adult and Peer Interactions*, ed. T. Field, S. Goldberg, D. Stern, and A. Sostek, pp. 113–32. New York: Academic Press.

Field, T. 1981. Early development of the preterm offspring of teenage mothers. In *Teenage Parents and Their Offspring*, ed. K. Scott, T. Field, and E. Robertson, pp. 145–75. New York: Grune and Stratton.

Field, T.; Widmayer, S.; Adler, S.; and De Cubas, M. 1990. Teenage parenting in different cultures, family constellations, and caregiving environments: Effects on infant development. *Infant Mental Health Journal* 11(2): 158–73.

Fine, M. 1990. Creating space. *Women and Foundations Newsletter* (Fall/Winter).

Finkelhor, D. 1984. *Child Sexual Abuse: New Theory and Research*. New York: Free Press.

Finkelhor, D. 1987. The trauma of child sexual abuse: Two models. *Journal of Interpersonal Violence* 2(4): 348–366.

Finkelhor, D.; and Associates, eds. 1986. *A Sourcebook on Child Sexual Abuse*. Beverly Hills, Calif.: Sage.

Finkelhor, D.; and Browne, A. 1985. The traumatic impact of child sexual abuse. *Amer. Journal of Orthopsychiatry* 55(4): 530–541.

Fischer, M. 1983. Adolescent adjustment after incest. *School Psychology International* 4:217–22.

Fisher, L.; Kokes, R.; Cole, R.; Perkins, P.; and Wynne, L. 1987. Competent children at risk: A study of well-functioning offspring of disturbed parents. In *The Invulnerable Child*, ed. E. J. Anthony and B. Cohler, pp. 211–28. New York: Guilford.

Forrest, J.; and Singh, S. 1990. The sexual and reproductive behavior of American women, 1982–1988. *Family Planning Perspectives*, 22(5): 206–14.

Fraiberg, S. 1980. *Clinical Studies in Infant Mental Health: The First Year of Life*. New York: Basic Books.

Fraiberg, S.; Adelson, E.; and Shapiro, V. 1975. Ghosts in the nursery: A psychoanalytic approach to the problems of impaired mother-infant relationships. *Journal of the American Academy of Child Psychiatry* 14:387–422.

Freud, A. 1958. Adolescence. In *Psychoanalytic Study of the Child* 13:255–78. New York: International Universities Press.

Freud, A. 1965. *Normality and Pathology in Childhood*. New York: International Universities Press.

Freud, A. 1966. Instinctual anxiety during puberty. In *The Writings of Anna Freud*. Vol. 2, *The Ego and the Mechanisms of Defense*, 2d ed. New York: International Universities Press. (Orig. pub. 1936).

Friedlander, S.; Weiss, B.; and Traylor, J. 1986. Assessing the influence of maternal depression on the validity of the Child Behavior Checklist. *Journal of Abnormal Child Psychology* 14(1): 123–33.

Fromuth, M. 1986. The relationship of childhood sexual abuse with later psychological and sexual adjustment in a sample of college women. *Child Abuse and Neglect* 10:5–15.

Fu, V.; Hinkle, D.; Shoffner, S.; Martin, S.; Carter, E.; Clark, A.; Culley, P.; Disney, G.; Ercanli, G.; Glover, E.; Kenney, M.; Lewis, H.;

Moak, S.; Stalling, S.; and Wakefield, T. 1984. Maternal dependency and child-rearing attitudes among mothers of adolescent females. *Adolescence* 19:795–804.

Furstenberg, F. 1976. The social consequences of teenage parenthood. *Family Planning Perspectives* 8(4): 148–64.

Furstenberg, F.; Brooks-Gunn, J.; and Morgan, P. 1987. *Adolescent Mothers in Later Life*. New York: Cambridge University Press.

Furstenberg, F.; Brooks-Gunn, J.; and Chase-Landsdale, L. 1989. Teenage pregnancy and childbearing. *American Psychologist* 44:313–20.

Furstenberg, F.; Hughes, M.; and Brooks-Gunn, J. 1992. The next generation: Children of teenage mothers grow up. In *Early Parenthood and Coming of Age in the 1990s*, ed. M. Rosenheim and M. Testa, pp. 113–35. New Brunswick, N.J.: Rutgers University Press.

Furstenberg, F.; Levine, J.; and Brooks-Gunn, J. 1990. The children of teenage mothers: Patterns of early childbearing in two generations. *Family Planning Perspectives* 22(2): 54–61.

Furstenberg, F.; Morgan, S.; Moore, K.; and Peterson, J. 1987. Race differences in the timing of adolescent intercourse. *American Sociological Review* 52:511–18.

Furstenberg, F.; Nord, C.; Peterson, J.; and Zill, N. 1983. The life course of children of divorce: Marital disruption and parental contact. *Amer. Sociological Review* 48(5): 656–68.

Gabriel, A.; and McAnarney, E. 1983. Parenthood in two cultures: White, middle-class couples and black, low-income adolescents in Rochester, N.Y. *Adolescence* 18:595–608.

Garbarino, J.; and Associates, 1982. *Children and Families in the Social Environment*. Hawthorne, N.Y.: Aldine.

Garcia Coll, C. 1988. The consequences of teenage childbearing in traditional Puerto Rican culture. In *The Cultural Context of Infancy*, vol. 1. ed. J. Nugent, B. Lester, and T. B. Brazelton, pp. 111–32. Norwood, N.J.: Ablex.

Garcia Coll, C. 1990. Developmental outcome of minority infants: A process-oriented look into our beginnings. *Child Development* 61:270–89.

Garcia Coll, C.; Hoffman, J. Oh, W. 1987. The social ecology and early parenting of caucasian adolescent mothers. *Child Development* 58:955–63.

Garcia Coll, C.; Hoffman, J.; Van Houten, L.; and Oh, W. 1987. The social context of teenage childbearing: effects on the infant's care-giving environment. *J. of Youth and Adolescence* 16(4): 345–360.

Garmezy, N. 1981 Children under stress: Perspectives on antecendents and correlates of vulnerability and resistance to psychopathology. In *Further Explorations in Personality*, ed. A. Rabin, A. Barclay, and R. Zucker, pp. 196–269. New York: Wiley.

———. 1983. Stressors of childhood. In *Stress, Coping and Development in Children*, ed. N. Garmezy and M. Rutter, pp. 43–84. New York: McGraw-Hill.

———. 1985. Stress-resistant children: The search for protective factors. In *Recent Research in Developmental Psychology*, ed. J. Stevenson. *Journal of Child Psychology and Psychiatry*, Book Supplement 4, pp. 213–33. Oxford: Pergamon Press.

———. 1987. Stress, competence, and development: Continuities in the study of schizophrenic adults, children vulnerable to psychopathology, and the search for stress-resistant children. *American J. of Orthopsychiatry* 57(2): 159–74.

Garmezy N.; and Masten, A. 1986. Stress, competence, and resilience: Common frontiers for therapist and psychopathologist. *Behavior Therapy* 17:500–521.

Gershenson, H.; Musick, J.; Ruch-Ross, H.; Magee, V.; Rubino, K.; and Rosenberg, D. 1989. The prevalence of coercive sexual experience among teenage mothers. *Journal of Interpersonal Violence* 4(2): 204–19.

Gerson, M. 1980. The lure of motherhood. *Psychology of Women Quarterly* 5(2): 207–18.

Gibson, J.; and Kempf, J. 1990. Attitudinal predictors of sexual activity in Hispanic females. *J. of Adolescent Research* 5(4): 414–430.

Gilligan, C. 1982. *In a Different Voice: Psychological Theory and Women's Development*. Cambridge: Harvard University Press.

Gilligan, C.; Lyons, N.; and Hanmer, T., eds. 1990. *Making Connections: The Relational Worlds of Adolescent Girls at Emma Willard School*. Cambridge: Harvard University Press.

Goldberg, W. 1989. Introduction: Perspectives on the transition to parenthood. In *The Transition to Parenthood: Current Theory and Research*, ed. G. Michaels and W. Goldberg, pp. 1–20. Cambridge: Cambridge University Press.

Goldfarb, A. 1965. Psychodynamics and the three generational family: Social structure and the family. In *General Relations*, ed. A. Goldfarb. Englewood Cliffs, N.J.: Prentice-Hall.

Gottlieb, B. 1988. *Marshalling Social Support*. Beverly Hills, Calif.: Sage.

Greenspan, S. 1990. Comprehensive clinical approaches to infants and their families: Psychodynamic and developmental perspectives. In *Handbook of Early Intervention*, ed. S. Meisels and J. Shonkoff, pp. 150–72. Cambridge: Cambridge University Press.

Greenspan, S.; Wieder, S.; Lieberman, A.; Nover, R.; Lourie, R.; and Robinson, M., eds. 1987. *Clinical Infant Reports*, no. 3. *Infants in Multi-risk Families: Case Studies in Preventive Intervention*. New York: International Universities Press.

Grotevant, H.; and Cooper, C.; eds. 1983. *Adolescent Development in the Family*. New Directions for Child Development, no. 22. San Francisco: Jossey-Bass.

Grotevant, H.; and Cooper, C. 1985. Patterns of interaction in family relationships and the development of identity exploration in adolescence. *Child Development* 56:415–428.

————. 1986. Individuation in family relationships. *Human Development* 29:82–100.

Gruber, K.; and Jones, R. 1983. Identifying determinants of risk of sexual victimization of youth. *Child Abuse and Neglect* 7:17–24.

Guttmacher Institute. 1991/92. Teenage Sexual and Reproductive Behavior in the U.S. *Facts in Brief*.

Halpern, R. 1990a. Community-based early intervention. In *Handbook of Early Childhood Intervention*, ed. S. Meisels and J. Shonkoff, pp. 469–498. Cambridge: Cambridge University Press.

————. 1990b. Poverty and early childhood parenting: Toward a framework for intervention. *Amer. Journal of Orthopsychiatry* 60(1): 6–18.

Hamburg, B. 1974. Coping in early adolescence. In *American Handbook of Psychiatry*, 2d ed., ed. S. Arieti, pp. 212–36. New York: Basic Books.

————. 1980. Early adolescence as a life stress. In *Coping and Health*, ed. S. Levine and H. Ursin, pp. 121–43. New York: Plenum.

————. 1986. Subsets of adolescent mothers: Developmental, biomedical, and psychosocial issues. In *School-Age Pregnancy and Parenthood: Biosocial Dimensions*, ed. J. Lancaster and B. Hamburg, pp. 115–45. New York: Aldine/De Gruyter.

Hamburg, D. 1986. Preparing for life: The critical transition of adolescence. In annual report of the Carnegie Corporation of New York.

Handler, A. 1987. An evaluation of a school-based adolescent pregnancy prevention program. Ph.D. diss. Chicago: University of Illinois, School of Public Health.

———. 1990. The correlates of the initiation of sexual intercourse among young urban black females. *J. of Youth and Adolescence* 19(2): 159–70.

Handler, A.; and Gersheson, H. 1985. Defining sexuality among female black inner-city young adolescents. Paper presented at the biennial meeting of the Society for Research in Child Development, Toronto.

Hans, S.; Musick, J.; and Jagers, R. n.d. Giving children what they need: Discussions with poor parents who raise competent children. Forthcoming.

Harter, S. 1988. The construction and conservation of the self: James and Cooley revisited. In *Self, Ego, and Identity: Integrative Approaches*, ed. D. Lapsley and F. Power, pp. 43–70. New York: Springer-Verlag.

Harter, S. 1990. Self and identity development. In *At the Threshold: The Developing Adolescent*, ed. S. Feldman and G. Elliott, pp. 352–87. Cambridge: Harvard University Press.

Hartman, C.; and Burgess, A. 1988. Information processing of trauma: Case application of a model. *Journal of Interpersonal Violence* 3(4): 443–57.

Hatcher, S. 1973. The adolescent experience of pregnancy and abortion: A developmental analysis. *Journal of Youth and Adolescence* 2:53–102.

Haugaard, J.; and Reppucci, N. 1988. *The Sexual Abuse of Children*. San Francisco: Jossey-Bass.

Hauser, S.; and Bowlds, M. 1990. Stress, coping and adaptation. In *At the Threshold: The Developing Adolescent*, ed. S. Feldman and G. Elliott, pp. 388–413. Cambridge: Harvard University Press.

Hauser, S.; and Follansbee, D. 1984. Developing identity: Ego growth and change during adolescence. In *Theory and Research in Behavioral Pediatrics*, vol. 2, ed. H. Fitzgerald, B. Lester, and M. Yogman, pp. 207–68. New York: Plenum.

Hauser, S.; Vieyra, M.; Jacobson, A.; and Wertlieb, D. 1985. Vulnerability and resilience in adolescence: Views from the family. *Journal of Early Adolescence* 5:81–100.

Hayes, C.; ed. 1987. *Risking the Future: Adolescent Sexuality, Pregnancy and Childbearing*. Washington, D.C.: National Academy Press.

Herman, J. 1981. *Father-Daughter Incest*. Cambridge: Harvard University Press.

Herr, T.; and Halpern, R. 1991. *Changing What Counts: Re-Thinking the Journey Out of Welfare*. Evanston, Ill.: Northwestern University, The Center for Urban Affairs and Policy Research.

Herr, T.; Olsen, L.; Berg, L, and Westphal, L. 1987. Early job turnover among the urban poor: The Project Match experience. Final Report to the Joyce Foundation. Evanston, Ill.: Northwestern University, The Center for Urban Affairs and Policy Research.

Hetherington, E. M. 1984. Stress and coping in children and families. In *Children in Families Under Stress*, ed. A.-B. Doyle, D. Gold, and D. Moskowitz, pp. 7–33. New Directions for Child Development, no. 24. San Francisco: Jossey-Bass.

Hetherington, E. M. 1989. Coping with family transitions: Winners, losers, and survivors. *Child Development* 60:1–14.

Hetherington, E. M.; Stanley-Hagan, M.; and Anderson, E. 1989. Marital transitions: A child's perspective. *American Psychologist* 44(2): 303–13.

Hill, J.; and Holmbeck, G. 1986. Attachment and autonomy during adolescence. In *Annals of Child Development*, vol. 3, ed. G. Whitehurst, pp. 145–89. Greenwich, Conn.: JAI Press.

Hoffman, L.; and Hoffman, M. 1973. The value of children to parents. In *Psychological Perspectives on Population*, ed. J. Fawcett. pp. 19–76. New York: Basic Books.

Hoffman, L.; Thornton, A.; and Manis, J. 1978. The value of children to parents in the United States. *Journal of Population* 1(2): 91–131.

Hogan, D. 1987. Demographic trends in human fertility and parenting across the life span. In *Parenting Across the Life Span*, J. Lancaster, J. Altman, A. Rossi, and L. Sherrod, pp. 315–349. New York: Aldine/ De Gruyter.

Hogan, D.; and Kitagawa, E. 1985. The impact of social status, family structure, and neighborhood on the fertility of black adolescents. *American J. of Sociology* 90:825–47.

Horwitz, S.; Klerman, L.; Kuo, S.; and Jekel, J. 1991a. School-age mothers: Predictors of long-term educational and economic outcomes. *Pediatrics* 87(6): 862–868.

Horwitz, S.; Klerman, L.; Kuo, S.; and Jekel, J. 1991b. Intergenerational transmission of school-age parenthood. *Family Planning Perspectives* 23(4): 168–72, 177.

Ianni, F. 1989. *The Search for Structure: A Report on American Youth Today*. New York: Free Press.

James, W. 1892. *Psychology: The Briefer Course*. New York: Holt, Rinehart and Winston.

Jessor, R.; and Jessor, S. 1977. *Problem Behavior and Psychosocial Development: A Longitudinal Study of Youth*. New York: Academic Press.

Johnston, M. 1979. The sexually mistreated child: Diagnostic evaluation. *Child Abuse and Neglect* 3:943–51.

Jones, E.; Forrest, J.; Goldman, N.; Henshaw, S.; Lincoln, R.; Rosoff, J.; Westoff, C.; and Wulf, D. 1986. *Teenage Pregnancy in Industrialized Countries*. New Haven: Yale University Press.

Jones, E.; and McCurdy, K. 1992. The links between types of maltreatment and demographic characteristics of children. *Child Abuse and Neglect* 16:201–15.

Jong, E. 1983. *Ordinary Miracles: New Poems by Erica Jong*. New York: New American Library.

Kagan, S.; Powell, D.; Weissbourd, B.; and Zigler, E., eds. 1987. *America's Family Support Programs: Perspectives and Prospects*. New Haven: Yale University Press.

Kalmuss, D.; Namerow, P.; and Cushman, L. 1991. Adoption versus parenting among young pregnant women. *Family Planning Perspectives* 23(1): 17–23.

Kandel, D.; and Lesser, G. 1972. *Youth in Two Worlds*. San Francisco: Jossey-Bass.

Keating, D. 1990. Adolescent thinking. In *At the Threshold: The Developing Adolescent*, ed. S. Feldman and G. Elliott, pp. 54–92. Cambridge: Harvard University Press.

Keizer, G. 1988. *No Place but Here: A Teacher's Vocation in a Rural Community*. New York: Viking.

Kellam, S.; Ensminger, M.; and Turner, R. 1977. Family structure and the mental health of children. *Archives of General Psychiatry* 34:1012–22.

Kelley, M.; Power, T.; and Wimbush, D. 1992. Determinants of disciplinary practices in low-income black mothers. *Child Development* 63(3): 573–82.

Kelly, R.; and Scott, M. 1986. Sociocultural considerations in child sexual abuse. In *Sexual Abuse of Young Children: Evaluation and Treatment*, ed. K. MacFarlane, J. Waterman, and Associates, pp. 151–63. New York: Guilford.

Kett, J. (1977). *Rites of Passage*. New York: Basic Books.

Klaus, M.; and Kennel, J. 1982. *Parent-Infant Bonding*, 2d ed. St. Louis: C. V. Mosby.

Kochanska, G.; Radke-Yarrow, M.; Kuczynski, L.; and Friedman, S. 1987. Normal and affectively ill mothers' beliefs about their children. *Amer. Journal of Orthopscyhiatry* 57(3): 345–50.

Kohut, H. 1971. *The Analysis of the Self*. New York: International Universities Press.

————. 1977. *The Restoration of the Self*. New York: International Universities Press.

————. 1983. Selected problems of self-psychological theory. In *Reflections on Self Psychology*, ed. J. Lichtenberg and S. Kaplan, pp. 387–416. Hillsdale, N.J.: Analytic Press.

Kris, E. 1936. The psychology of caricature. *International Journal of Psychoanalysis* 17:285–303.

Ladner, J. 1977. *Mixed Families*. New York: Anchor Press/Doubleday.

Ladner, J.; and Gourdine, R. 1984. Intergenerational teenage motherhood: Some preliminary findings. *SAGE: A Scholarly Journal on Black Women* 1(2): 22–24.

Lamb. M. 1986. *The Father's Role: Applied Perspectives*. New York: Wiley.

Lamb, M.; Owen, M.; and Chase-Landsdale, L. 1979. The father-daughter relationship: Past, present, and future. In *Becoming Female: Perspectives on Development*, ed. C. Kopp, pp. 89–112. New York: Plenum.

Lefkowitz, B. 1987. *Tough Change: Growing Up on Your Own in America*. New York: Free Press.

LeMasters, E. 1957. Parenthood as crisis. *Marriage and Family Living* 19:352–55.

Lewis, M.; and Brooks-Gunn, J. 1979. *Social Cognition and the Acquisition of Self*. New York: Plenum.

Litowitz, B.; and Gundlach, R. 1987. When adolescents write: Semiotic and social dimensions of adolescents' personal writing. *Adolescent Psychiatry* 14:82–111.

Lusk, R.; and Waterman, J. 1986. Effects of sexual abuse on children. In *Sexual Abuse of Young Children: Evaluation and Treatment*, ed. K. Mac-Farlane, J. Waterman, and Associates, pp. 101–18. New York: Guilford.

Luthar, S.; and Zigler, E. 1991. Vulnerability and competence: A review of research on resilience in childhood. *American J. of Orthopsychiatry* 6(1): 6–22.

Lynn, L. 1990. The rhetoric of welfare reform. *Social Science Review* 64(2): 175–88.

Maccoby, E. 1984. Socialization and developmental change. *Child Development* 55:317–28.

Maccoby, E.; and Martin, J. 1983. Socialization in the context of the family: Parent-child interaction. In *Handbook of Child Psychology, Vol. 4. Socialization, Personality, and Social Development*, ed. E. M. Hetherington, pp. 1–101. New York: Wiley.

Main, M.; and Goldwyn, R. 1984. Predicting the rejection of her own infant from mother's representation of her own experiences: Implications for the abused-abusing intergenerational cycle. *Child Abuse and Neglect* 8:203–17.

Main, M.; and Hesse, E. 1990. Parents' unresolved traumatic experiences are related to infant disorganized attachment status: Is frightened and/or frightening parental behavior the linking mechanism. In *Attachment in the Preschool Years*, ed. M. Greenberg, D. Cicchetti, and M. Cummings, pp. 161–82. Chicago: University of Chicago Press.

Main, M.; Kaplan, N.; and Cassidy, J. 1985. Security in infancy, childhood, and adulthood: A move to the level of representation. In *Growing Points of Attachment Theory and Research*, ed. I. Bretherton, and E. Waters. Monographs of the Society for Research in Child Development 50(1–2): 66–104.

Maine, M. 1985. Engaging the disengaged father in the treatment of eating disordered adolescents. Newington, Conn.: Newington Children's Hospital. Unpublished. (Cited in Sarigiani and Petersen 1988, reference below.)

Maracek, J. 1985. The effects of adolescent childbearing on children's cognitive and psychosocial development. Unpublished.

Marcia, J. 1966. Development and validation of ego-identity status. *Journal of Personality and Social Psychology* 3:551–58.

————. 1980. Identity in adolescence. In *Handbook of Adolescent Psychology*, ed. J. Adelson, pp. 159–77. New York: Wiley.

————. 1988. Common processes underlying ego identity, cognitive/ normal development, and individuation. In *Self, Ego, and Identity: Integrative Approaches*, ed. D. Lapsley and F. Power, pp. 211–25. New York: Springer-Verlag.

Marcia, J.; and Friedman, M. 1970. Ego identity status in college women. *Journal of Personality* 38:249–63.

Martin, E.; and Martin, J. 1978. *The Black Extended Family*. Chicago: University of Chicago Press.

Masnick, G. 1986. The nation's children: A demographic profile. Paper prepared for the Conference on Children in a Changing Health Care System.

Mayfield-Brown, L. 1989. Family status of low-income adolescent mothers. *J. of Adolescent Research* 4(2): 202–13.

McAdoo, H. 1989. *Black Families*. New York: Sage.

McCool, W. 1991. Developing levels of reactivity and anxiety in pregnant adolescents: Relation to maternal and infant labor and delivery outcomes. Paper presented at the biennial meeting of the Society for Research in Child Development, Seattle.

McCord, J. 1990. Problem behaviors. In *At the Threshold: The Developing Adolescent*, ed. S. Feldman and G. Elliott, pp. 414–30. Cambridge: Harvard University Press,

McLanahan, S. 1988. Family structure and dependency: Early transitions to female household headship. *Demography* 25:210–34.

Mead, M. 1953. *Growing Up in New Guinea*. New York: New American Library.

————. 1958. Adolescence in primitive and modern society. In *Readings in Social Psychology*, ed. G. Swanson, T. Newcomb, and E. Hartley. New York: Holt.

Meares, R.; Penman, J.; Milgom-Friedman, J.; and Buker, K. 1982. Some origins of the difficult child: The Brazelton Scale and the mother's view of her newborn's character. *British Journal of Medical Psychology* 55:77–89.

Meisels, S.; and Shonkoff, J., eds. *Handbook of Early Intervention*. Cambridge: Cambridge University Press.

Michaels, G. 1988. Motivational factors in the decision and timing of pregnancy. In *The Transitions to Parenthood: Current Theory and Research*, ed. G. Michaels and W. Goldberg, pp. 23–61. Cambridge: Cambridge University Press,

Michaels, G.; and Brown, R. 1987. Values of children in adolescent mothers. Unpublished.

Miller, A. 1983. *For Your Own Good*. New York: Farrar, Strauss and Giroux.

————. 1986. *Thou Shalt Not Be Aware*. New York: Penguin.

Miller, P. and Sperry, L. 1987. The socialization of anger and aggression. *Merrill-Palmer Quarterly* 33(1): 1–31.

Mills, M.; Puckering, C.; Pound, A.; and Cox, A. 1985. What is it about depressed mothers that influences their children's functioning? In *Recent Research in Developmental Psychopathology*, ed. J. Stevenson. *Journal of the American Academy of Child Psychiatry*, Monograph Supplement, no. 4. Oxford: Pergamon Press.

Montemayor, R.; and Eisen, M. 1977. The development of self-conceptions from childhood to adolescence. *Developmental Psychology* 13:314–319.

Montemayor, R.; and Flannery, D. 1990. Making the transition from childhood to early adolescence. In *From Childhood to Adolescence: A Transitional Period?*, ed. R. Montemayor, G. Adams, and T. Gullotta, pp. 291–301. Newbury Park, Calif.: Sage.

Moore, K. 1991. *Facts at a Glance*. Washington, D.C.: Child Trends, Inc.

Moore, K.; and Caldwell, S. 1977. The effect of government policies on out-of-wedlock sex and pregnancy. *Family Planning Perspectives* 9(4):164–69.

Moore, K.; Nord, C.; and Peterson, J. 1989. Nonvoluntary sexual activity among adolescents. *Family Planning Perspectives* 21(3): 110–14.

Mosena, P. 1987. Repeated pregnancy and childbearing among adolescent mothers. Report prepared for Parents Too Soon and the Illinois Department of Public Health, Chicago.

Mott, F. 1986. The pace of repeated childbearing among young American mothers. *Family Planning Perspectives* 18(1): 5–12.

Mott, F.; and Marsiglio, W. 1985. Early childbearing and completion of high school. *Family Planning Perspectives* 17(3): 118–24.

Musick, J. 1987. The psychological and developmental dimensions of adolescent pregnancy and parenting: An interventionist's perspective. Paper prepared for the Rockefeller Foundation.

————. n.d. Dear Diary: Journals of adolescent mothers. Forthcoming.

Musick, J.; and Halpern, R. 1989. Giving children a chance: What role early parenting interventions? In *Giving Children a Chance: The Case for More Effective National Policies*, ed. G. Miller, pp. 177–94. Washington, D.C.: Center for National Policy Press.

Musick, J.; Handler, A.; and Wadill, K. 1984. Teens and adoption: A pregnancy resolution alternative? *Children Today* 13(6): 24–29.

Musick, J.; Hans, S.; and Jagers, R. 1992. A change of heart: Conversations with teachers of inner-city children. Unpub. report.

Musick, J.; Stott, F.; Spencer, K.; Goldman, J.; and Cohler, B. 1987. Maternal factors related to vulnerability and resiliency in young children at risk. In *The Invulnerable Child*, ed. E. J. Anthony and B. Cohler, pp. 229–52. New York: Guilford.

Musick, J.; and Stott, F. 1990. Paraprofessionals, parenting and child development: Understanding the problems and seeking solutions. In *Handbook of Early Intervention*, ed. S. Meisels and J. Shonkoff, pp. 651–67. Cambridge: Cambridge University Press.

Muus, R. 1988. *Theories of Adolescence*, 5th ed. New York: Random House.

Naylor, G. 1983. *The Women of Brewster Place*. New York: Penguin Books.

Norton, D. 1990. Understanding the early experience of black children in high risk environments: Culturally and ecologically relevant research as a guide to support for families. *Zero-to-Three* 10(4): 1–7.

Offer, D. 1969. *The Psychological World of the Teenager: A Study of Normal Adolescent Boys*. New York: Basic Books.

Offer, D.; Ostrow, E.; and Howard, K. 1981. *The Adolescent: A Psychological Self-Portrait*. New York: Basic Books.

O'Leary, K.; Shore, M.; and Weider, S. 1984. Contacting pregnant adolescents: Are we missing cues? *Social Casework*, 65(5): 297–306.

Osofsky, J.; and Eberhart-Wright, A. 1988. Affective exchanges between high risk mothers and infants. *International Journal of Psycho-Analysis* 69:221–31.

————. 1989. Risk and protective factors for parents and children. Paper presented at the Cornell Symposium on Human Development.

Osofsky, J.; Osofsky, H.; and Diamond, M. 1988. The transition to parenthood: Special tasks and risk factors for adolescent parents. In *The*

Transitions to Parenthood: Current Theory and Research, ed. G. Michaels and W. Goldberg, pp. 209–32. Cambridge: Cambridge University Press.

Osofsky, J.; and Ware, L. 1984. Developmental and clinical perspectives on adolescent mothers and their infants. Paper presented for the American Academy of Child Psychiatry, Toronto.

Panaccione, V.; and Wahler, R. 1986. Child behavior, maternal depression, and social coercion as factors in the quality of childcare. *Journal of Abnormal Child Psychology* 14(2): 263–78.

Parke, R. 1981. *Fathers.* Cambridge: Harvard University Press.

Pavenstedt, E., ed. 1967. *The Drifters: Children of Disorganized Lower-Class Families.* Boston: Little, Brown.

Pavenstedt, E. 1971. The meanings of motherhood in a deprived environment. In *Crises of Family Disorganization: Programs to Soften Their Impact on Children*, ed. E. Pavenstedt and V. Bernard, pp. 59–69. New York: Behavioral Publications.

Pavenstedt, E.; and Bernard, V., eds. 1971. *Crises of Family Disorganization: Programs to Soften Their Impact on Children.* New York: Behavioral Publications.

Peters, S.; Wyatt, G.; and Finkelhor, D. 1986. The prevalence of child sexual abuse: Reviewing the evidence. In *A Sourcebook on Child Sexual Abuse*, ed. D. Finkelhor, and Associates, pp. 15–59. Beverly Hills, Calif.: Sage.

Petersen, A. 1988. Adolescent development. In *Annual Review of Psychology*, ed. M. Rosenzweig, 39:583–607. Palo Alto: Annual Reviews.

Petersen, A.; and Crockett, L. 1985. Pubertal timing and grade effects on adjustment. *J. of Youth and Adolescence* 14(3): 191–206.

———. 1992 Adolescent sexuality, pregnancy, and child rearing: Developmental perspectives. In *Early Parenthood and Coming of Age in the 1990s*, ed. M. Rosenheim and M. Testa, pp. 34–45. New Brunswick, N.J.: Rutgers University Press.

Petersen, A.; and Ebata, A. 1987. Developmental transitions and adolescent problem behavior: Implications for prevention and intervention. In *Social Intervention: Potential and Constraints*, ed. K. Hurrelmann, and F. X. Kaufmann, pp. 167–84. New York: de Gruyter.

Petersen, A.; and Hamburg, B. 1986. Adolescence: A developmental approach to problems and psychopatholgy. *Behavior Therapy* 17:480–99.

Petersen, A.; and Taylor, B. 1980. The biological approach to adolescence: biological change and psychological adaptation. In *Handbook of the Psychology of Adolescence*, ed. J. Adelson, pp. 117–55. New York: Wiley.

Pianta, R.; Egeland, B.; and Erickson, M. 1989. The antecedents of maltreatment: Results of the Mother-Child Interaction Research Project. In *Child Maltreatment: Theory and Research on the Causes and Consequences of Child Abuse and Neglect*, ed. D. Cicchetti and V. Carlson, pp. 203–53. Cambridge: Cambridge University Press.

Pittman, K.; and Govan, C. 1986. *Model Programs: Preventing Adolescent Pregnancy and Building Youth Self-Sufficiency*. Washington, D.C.: Children's Defense Fund.

Polit, D. 1986. *Comprehensive Programs for Pregnant and Parenting Teenagers*. Saratoga Springs, N.Y.: Humanalysis.

Polit, D.; and Kahn, J. 1986. Early subsequent pregnancy among economically disadvantaged teenage mothers. *Amer. Journal of Public Health* 76(2): 167–71.

Polit, D.; with White, C. 1988. *The Lives of Young Disadvantaged Mothers: The Five-Year Follow-Up of the Project Redirection Sample*. Saratoga Springs, N.Y.: Humanalysis.

Polit, D.; White, C.; and Morton, T. 1990. Child sexual abuse and premarital intercourse among high-risk adolescents. *Journal of Adol. Health Care* 11(3): 231–34.

Polit, D.; Quint, J.; and Riccio, J. 1988. *The Challenge of Serving Teenage Mothers: Lessons from Project Redirection*. New York: Manpower Demonstration Research Corporation.

Polit, D.; Kisker, E.; and Cohen, R. 1989. *Barriers to Self-sufficiency among Welfare-Dependent Teenage Mothers: Evidence from the Teenage Parent Demonstration*. Princeton, N.J.: Mathematica Policy Research.

Pound, A.; Cox, A.; Puckering, C.; and Mills, M. 1985. The impact of maternal depression on young children. In *Recent Research in Developmental Psychopathology*, ed. J. Stevenson. *Journal of the American Academy of Child Psychiatry*, Monograph Supplement, no. 4. Oxford: Pergamon Press.

Powers, S.; Hauser, S.; Schwartz, J.; Noam, G.; and Jacobson, A. 1983.

Adolescent ego development and family interaction: A structural-developmental perspective. In *Adolescent Development in the Family*, ed. H. Grotevant and C. Cooper. New Directions for Child Development, no. 22, pp. 5–24. San Francisco: Jossey-Bass.

Provence, S.; and Naylor, A. 1983. *Working with Disadvantaged Parents and Their Children: Scientific and Practice Issues*. New Haven: Yale University Press.

Rachman, S. 1979. The concept of required helpfulness. *Behavior Research and Therapy* 17:1–6.

Radin, N. 1981. The role of the father in cognitive, academic, and intellectual development. In *The Role of the Father in Child Development*, 2d ed., ed. M. Lamb, pp. 379–427. New York: Wiley.

Rickard, K.; Forehand, R.; Wells, K.; Griest, D.; and McMahon, R. 1981. Factors in the referral of children for behavioral treatment: A comparison of mothers of clinical-referred deviant, clinical-referred non-deviant and non-clinic children. *Behavioral Research and Therapy* 19:201–5.

Ricks, M. 1985. The social transmission of parental behavior: Attachment across generations. In *Growing Points of Attachment Theory and Research*, ed. I. Bretherton and E. Waters. *Monographs of the Society for Research in Child Development* 50 (1–2): 211–27.

Rogers, C.; and Terry, T. 1984. Clinical intervention with boy victims of sexual abuse. In *Victims of Sexual Agression: Treatment of Children, Women, and Men*, ed. I. Stuart and J. Greer, pp. 91–104. New York: Van Nostrand Reinhold.

Rosenberg, M. 1979. *Conceiving the Self*. New York: Basic Books.

———. 1986. Self-concept from middle childhood through adolescence. In *Psychological Perspective on the Self*, ed. J. Suls and A. Greenwald, pp. 182–205. Hillsdale, N.J.: Erlbaum.

Ruble, D.; and Brooks-Gunn, J. 1982 The experience of menarche. *Child Development* 53:1557–66.

Ruch-Ross, H.; Jones, E.; and Musick, J. 1992. Comparing outcomes in a statewide program for adolescent mothers with outcomes in a national sample. *Family Planning Perspectives* 24(2): 66–71, 96.

Ruch-Ross.; H. Stucki, B.; and Musick, J. 1990. Coercive sexual experiences of African American and white American teenage mothers during childhood. Paper presented at the annual meeting of the American Public Health Association, New York, October 1990.

Ruch-Ross, H.; and Mosena, P. 1991. Inner-city Perspectives on Rapid Repeat Childbearing. Paper presented at the annual meeting of the American Public Health Association, Atlanta, November 1991.

Russell, D. 1986. *The Secret Trauma: Incest in the Lives of Girls and Women.* New York: Basic Books.

Rutter, M. 1979. Protective factors in children's responses to stress and disadvantage. In *Primary Prevention of Psychopathology*, ed. M. Kent and J. Rolf. Vol. 3, *Social Competence in Children*, pp. 49–74. Hanover, N.H.: University Press of New England.

————. 1985. Resilience in the face of adversity: Protective factors and resistance to psychiatric disorder. *British J. of Psychiatry* 147:598–611.

————. 1986. The developmental psychopathology of depression: Issues and perspectives. In *Depression in Young People: Developmental and Clinical Perspectives*, ed. M. Rutter, C. Izzard, and P. Read, pp. 3–30. New York: Guilford.

————. 1987a. Continuities and discontinuities from infancy. In *Handbook of Infant Development*, 2d ed., ed. J. Osofsky, pp. 1256–96. New York: Wiley.

————. 1987b. Psychosocial resilience and protective mechanisms. *American J. of Orthopsychiatry* 57:316–31.

————. 1987c. Parental mental disorder as a psychiatric risk factor. In *Amer. Psychiatric Association's Annual Review*, vol. 6, ed. R. Hales and A. Frances. Washington, D.C.: American Psychiatric Association.

————. 1989. Intergenerational continuities and discontinuities in serious parenting difficulties. In *Child Maltreatment: Theory and Research on the Causes and Consequences of Child Abuse and Neglect*, ed. D. Cicchetti and V. Carlson, pp. 317–448. Cambridge: Cambridge University Press.

Rutter, M.; and Cox, A. 1985. Other family influences. In *Child and Adolescent Psychiatry: Modern Approaches*, 2d ed., ed. M. Rutter and L. Hersov, pp. 58–81. Oxford: Blackwell Scientific.

Sameroff, A. 1987. The social context of development. In *Contemporary Topics in Developmental Psychology*, ed. N. Eisenberg, pp. 273–91. New York: Wiley.

Sameroff, A.; and Chandler, M. 1975. Reproductive risk and the continuum of caretaking casualty. In *Review of Child Development Research*, vol. 4, ed. F. D. Horowitz, M. Hetherington, S. Scarr-Salapatek, and G. Seigel, pp. 187–244. Chicago: University of Chicago Press.

Sameroff, A.; and Emde, R., eds. 1989. *Relationship Disturbances in Early Childhood.* New York: Basic Books.

Sameroff, A.; and Fiese, B. 1990. Transactional regulation and early intervention. In *Handbook of Early Intervention,* ed. S. Meisels and J. Shonkoff, pp. 119–49. Cambridge: Cambridge University Press.

Sandler, H.; Vietze, P.; and O'Connor, S. 1981. Obstetric and neonatal outcomes following intervention with pregnant teenagers. In *Teenage Parents and Their Offspring,* ed. K. Scott, T. Field, and E. Robertson, pp. 249–63. New York: Grune and Stratton,

Sandven, K.; and Resnick, M. 1990. Informal adoption among black adolescent mothers. *Amer. J. Orthopsychiatry* 60(2): 210–24.

Sarigiani, P.; and Petersen, A. 1988. Perceived closeness with parents and adjustment in early adolescence. Unpublished paper, Pennsylvania State University.

Schellenbach, C.; Whitman, T.; and Borkowski, J. 1991. Adolescent parenting: Toward an integrative model. Paper presented at the biennial meeting of the Society for Research in Child Development, Seattle.

Schorr, L.; and Schorr, D. 1988. *Within Our Reach: Breaking the Cycle of Disadvantage.* New York: Anchor Press.

Seitz, V.; and Provence, S. 1990. Caregiver-focused models of early intervention. In *Handbook of Early Intervention,* ed. S. Meisels and J. Shonkoff, pp. 400–427. Cambridge: Cambridge University Press.

Seligman, M. 1975. *Helplessness.* San Francisco: W. H. Freedman.

Sexton, A. 1988. *Selected Poems of Anne Sexton,* ed. D. Middlebrook and D. George. Boston: Houghton Mifflin.

Shanok, R. 1990. Parenthood: A process marking identity and intimacy capacities. *Zero-to-Three* 11(2): 1–9.

———. 1989. Parenthood and personhood. Paper presented at the National Center for Clinical Infant Programs 6th Biennial National Training Institute, Washington, D.C.

Shaw, V.; and Meier, J. 1983. The effect of type of abuse and neglect on children's psychosocial development. Unpublished, Children's Village U.S.A.

Shonkoff, J.; and Meisels, S. 1990. Early childhood intervention: The evolution of a concept. In *Handbook of Early Intervention,* ed. S. Meisels and J. Shonkoff, pp. 3–31. Cambridge: Cambridge University Press.

Silbert, M.; and Pines, A. 1981. Sexual child abuse as an antecedent to prostitution. *Child Abuse and Neglect* 5:407–11.

Simmons, R.; Blyth, D.; Van Cleave, E.; and Bush, D. 1979. Entry into early adolescence: The impact of school structure, puberty, and early dating on self-esteem. *American Sociological Review* 44:948–67.

Simmons, R.; Blyth, D.; and McKinney, K. 1983. The social and psychological effects of puberty on white females. In *Girls at Puberty: Biological and Psychosocial Perspectives*, ed. J. Brooks-Gunn and A. Petersen, pp. 229–72. New York: Plenum.

Simmons, R.; Burgeson, R.; and Reef, M. 1988. Cumulative change at entry to adolescence. In *Development during Transition to Adolescence: Minnesota Symposium on Child Psychology*, vol. 21, ed. M. Gunnar and W. Collins, pp. 123–47. Hillsdale, N.J.: Erlbaum.

Simon, K. 1986. *A Wider World: Portraits in an Adolescence*. New York: Harper and Row.

Smith, E.; and Udry, J. R. 1985. Coital and non-coital sexual behaviors of white and black adolescents. *Amer. Journal of Public Health* 75:1200–1203.

Smith, P. 1986. Sociologic aspects of adolescent fertility and childbearing among hispanics. *Developmental and Behavioral Pediatrics* 7(6): 346–49.

Spencer, J. 1978. Father-daughter incest: A clinical view from the corrections field. *Child Welfare* 57:581–590.

Sroufe, L. A. 1988. The role of infant-caregiver attachment in development. In *Clinical Implications of Attachment*, ed. J. Belsky and T. Nezworski, pp. 18–38. Hillsdale, N.J.: Erlbaum.

Steele, B.; and Alexander, H. 1981. Long-term effects of sexual abuse in childhood. In *Sexually Abused Children and Their Families*, ed. P. Mrazek, and C. H. Kempe, pp. 223–34. New York: Pergamon.

Stein, M. 1967. Sociocultural perspectives on the neighborhood and the families. In *The Drifters: Children of Disorganized Lower-Class Families*, ed. E. Pavenstedt, pp. 299–320. Boston: Little, Brown.

Steinberg, L. 1988. Reciprocal relation between parent-child distance and pubertal maturation. *Developmental Psychology* 24:122–28.

———. 1989. Pubertal maturation and parent-adolescent distance: An evolutionary perpective. In *Biology of Adolescent Behavior and Development*, ed. G. Adams, R. Montemayor, and T. Gullotta, pp. 71–97. Newbury Park, Calif.: Sage.

———. 1991. The logic of adolescence. In *Adolescence and Poverty: Challenge for the 1990s*, ed. P. Edelman and J. Ladner, pp. 19–36. Washington, D.C.: Center for National Policy Piess.

Stern, D. 1985. *The Interpersonal World of the Infant: A View from Psychoanalysis and Developmental Psychology*. New York: Basic Books.

———. 1989. The representation of relational patterns: Developmental considerations. In *Relationship Disturbances in Early Childhood*, ed. A. Sameroff and R. Emde, pp. 52–69. New York: Basic Books.

Stern-Bruschweiler, N.; and Stern, D. 1989. A model for conceptualizing the role of the mother's representational world in various mother-infant therapies. *Infant Mental Health Journal* 10(3): 142–56. Special issue, *Internal Representations and Parent-Infant Relationships*, ed. C. Zeanah and M. Barton.

Stott, F.; Cohler, B.; and Musick, J. n.d. Psychiatric disorder and mothering.

Stott, F.; Musick, J.; Cohler, B.; Spencer, K.; Goldman, J.; Clark, R.; and Dincin, J. 1984. Intervention for the severely disturbed mother. In *Intervention with Psychiatrically Disturbed Parents and Their Young Children*, ed. B. Cohler and J. Musick, pp. 7–32. *New Directions for Mental Health Services*, 24. San Francisco: Jossey-Bass.

Sullivan, H. 1947. *Conceptions of Modern Psychiatry*. New York: W. W. Norton.

———. 1953. *The Interpersonal Theory of Psychiatry*. New York: W. W. Norton.

Sum, A.; and Fogg, W. 1991. The adolescent poor and the transition to early adulthood. In *Adolescence and Poverty: Challenge for the 1990s*, ed. P. Edelman and J. Ladner, pp. 37–109. Washington, D.C.: Center for National Policy Press.

Summit, R. 1983. The child sexual abuse accommodation syndrome. *Child Abuse and Neglect* 7:177–93.

Teachman, J. 1983. Early marriage, premarital fertility, and marital dissolution: Results for blacks and whites. *J. of Family Issues* 4:105–26.

Tobin-Richard, M.; Boxer, A.; and Petersen, A. 1983. The psychological significance of pubertal change: sex differences in perceptions of self during early adolescence. In *Girls at Puberty: Biological and Psychosocial Perspectives*, ed. J. Brooks-Gunn and A. Petersen, pp. 127–52. New York: Plenum.

Tufts New England Medical Center, Division of Child Psychiatry. 1984. *Sexually Exploited Children: Service and Research Project*. Washington, D.C.: U.S. Dept. of Justice.

Unger, D.; and Wandersman, L. 1988. The relation of family and partner support to the adjustment of adolescent mothers. *Child Development* 59:1056–60.

Vander Mey, B.; and Neff, R. 1982. Adult-child incest: A review of research and treatment. *Adolescence* 17:717–735.

Vygotsky, L. 1978. *Mind in Society*. Cambridge: Harvard University Press.

Walker, A. 1982. *The Color Purple*. New York: Pocket Books.

Wallerstein, J.; Corbin, S.; and Lewis, J. 1988. Children of divorce: A ten-year study. In *Impact of Divorce, Single-Parenting, and Step-Parenting on Children*, ed. E. M. Hetherington, and J. Arasteh, pp. 198–214. Hillsdale, N.J.: Erlbaum.

Wasserman, G.; Brunelli, S.; and Rauh, V. 1990. Social supports and living arrangements of adolescent and adult mothers. *J. of Adolescent Research* 5(1): 54–66.

Wasserman, G.; Rauh, V.; Brunelli, S.; Garcia-Castro, M.; and Necos, B. 1990. Psychosocial attributes and life experiences of disadvantaged minority mothers: Age and ethnic variations. *Child Development* 61:566–80.

Waterman, A.; ed. 1985. *Identity in Adolescence: Processes and Contents*. San Francisco: Jossey-Bass.

Weiss, H.; and Halpern, R. 1988. *Community-Based Family Support and Education Programs: Something Old or Something New?* New York: National Resource Program for Children in Poverty, Columbia University.

Weissbourd, B. 1987. A brief history of family support programs. In *America's Family Support Programs: Perspectives and Prospects*, ed. S. Kagan, D. Powell, B. Weissbourd, and E. Zigler, pp. 38–56. New Haven: Yale University Press.

Weissman, M. and Klerman, G. 1977. Sex differences and the epidemiology of depression. *Archives of General Psychiatry* 34:98–111.

Werner, E. 1989. High risk children in young adulthood: A longitudinal study from birth to 32 years. *American J. of Orthopsychiatry* 59(1): 72–81.

——. 1990. Protective factors and individual resilience. In *Handbook of*

Early Intervention, ed. S. Meisels and J. Shonkoff, pp. 97–116. Cambridge: Cambridge University Press.

Werner, E.; and Smith, R. 1977. *Kauai's Children Come of Age*. Honolulu: University of Hawaii Press.

———. 1982 *Vulnerable but Invincible: A Longitudinal Study of Resilient Children and Youth*. New York: McGraw-Hill.

Whiting, B., ed. 1963. *Six Cultures: Studies of Child Rearing*. New York: Wiley.

Williams, T.; and Kornblum, W. 1985. *Growing Up Poor*. Lexington, Mass.: Lexington Books.

Wilson, W. 1987. *The Truly Disadvantaged: The Inner City, The Underclass and Public Policy*. Chicago: University of Chicago Press.

Wilson, W. 1989. The underclass: issues, perspectives and public policy. *ANNALS, AAPSS* 501:182–92.

Wyatt, G. 1985. The sexual abuse of Afro-American and White American women in childhood. *Child Abuse and Neglect* 9:507–519.

Yates, A. 1982. Children eroticized by incest. *Amer. Journal of Psychiatry* 139:482–485.

Youniss, J.; and Smollar, J. 1985. *Adolescents' Relations with Mothers, Fathers, and Friends*. Chicago: University of Chicago Press.

Zeanah, C.; and Barton, M. 1989. Internal representations and parent-infant relationships. In *Infant Mental Health Journal* 10(3): 135–41. Special issue, *Internal Representations and Parent-Infant Relationships*, ed. C. Zeanah and M. Barton.

Zelnick, M.; and Kantner, J. 1980. Sexual activity, contraceptive use, and pregnancy among metropolitan area teenagers, 1971–1979. *Family Planning Perspectives* 12(5): 230–37.

Zelnick, M.; Kantner, J.; and Ford, K. 1981. *Sex and Pregnancy in Adolescence*. Beverly Hills, Calif.: Sage.

Zelnick, M.; and Shah, F. 1983. First intercourse among young Americans. *Family Planning Perspectives* 15(2): 64–70.

Zigler, E.; and Hall, N. 1989. Physical child abuse in America: Past, present, and future. In *Child Maltreatment: Theory and Research on the Causes and Consequences of Child Abuse and Neglect*, ed. D. Cicchetti and V. Carlson, pp. 38–75. Cambridge: Cambridge University Press.